Patricia Beer was born and brou[ght up in Devon. She taught] for seven years in Italy, and the[n at the University of London,] Goldsmith's College, Universit[y ... . She has for some] time now been a full-time writer and occasional Writer in Residence.

Among her collections of poetry are *Loss of the Magyar*, *The Survivors*, *Just Like the Resurrection* and *Driving West*. More recently her *Selected Poems* were published.

She has also published *Introduction to the Metaphysical Poets* and a much praised study of the 19th-century fictional heroines, *Reader, I Married Him*. In 1968 her first novel, *Moon's Ottery*, a story set in Elizabethan Devon, came out.

As *Mrs. Beer's House* leaves in no doubt Patricia Beer was raised among the Plymouth Brethren, an experience she shares with another Devon-born writer and critic, Edmund Gosse. Mrs. Beer will be introducing Gosse's classic *Father and Son* for the forthcoming *Devon Library* edition.

THE DEVON LIBRARY
NUMBER FOUR

Mrs Beer's House
PATRICIA BEER

ANTHONY
MOTT
LTD

LONDON

Published by Anthony Mott Limited 1983
50 Stile Hall Gardens, London W4 3BU

First published by Macmillan and Company Ltd 1968

This edition published by Hutchinson 1978

Copyright © Patricia Beer 1968

ISBN 0 907746 23 3

Printed in Great Britain by
Richard Clay (The Chaucer Press) Ltd

This book is sold subject to the condition that it shall not, by way of trade or otherwise, be lent, re-sold, hired out or otherwise circulated without the publisher's prior consent in any form of binding or cover other than that in which it is published and without a similar condition being imposed on the subsequent purchaser.

For Dickie and Bister

Contents

1	The Loss of the *Magyar*	1
2	Exmouth and Torquay	16
3	Plan of Salvation	34
4	Playtime, Break, Recess	58
5	Doctors and Nurses	79
6	First Love	95
7	Thou Shalt Not	119
8	Worldly Pleasure	146
9	Arising from Vicissitude	170
10	Three Against One	188
11	A Wonderful Result	209
12	Death	229

CHAPTER ONE

The Loss of the *Magyar*

No member of my family lives in Exmouth now, and probably never will unless I go there myself. What removed them was not so much death as the stronger claims of Torquay. I was brought up by my mother to think of Torquay as the home of both goodness and civilisation. She herself was born there, in the parish of St Marychurch on the east side of the town, about the only one of its districts to have any character at all. Her parents' house was the second of a small Victorian terrace on the road that led down to Petitor, a beautiful but fiercely stony beach that I connect chiefly with bleeding feet. She went to college in Exeter to train to become a teacher, and then took her first post in Exmouth, where she met my father and soon married him.

She often told us how, as a lonely young teacher, she used to stand on Exmouth sea-front, looking across the estuary and down the coast towards Torquay, crying. After her marriage she never stood looking tearfully at Torquay; she went there. At the beginning of every school holiday, half-terms and all, she set off with me and my sister Sheila, leaving my father to fend for himself, and there we stayed, away from our friends and our books and our bicycles, till term began again and we had to come back to Exmouth. The tearfulness of her single days changed into the acrimony with which she met my father at Exeter station, and which lasted in its outspoken form for the whole of the first evening.

They are both buried in Torquay, in the municipal

cemetery. With its clean angels and its sharp stone-chippings, the cemetery is nothing like a churchyard, nothing like St John's-in-the-Wilderness, where the tombstones of my father's family can hardly be picked out from the overgrown illegible blur. As children we visited the graves of the Jefferys more than those of the Beers, or at any rate took more flowers to them, and I associate the cemetery with one of the most exciting smells of childhood, that of water being poured out of vases after the flowers had been in them for a week, a superb stench that was also socially admissible. The cemetery is in two parts and lies on opposing sides of a road, and so do my parents. My father is buried in a grave chosen for him by his third wife, a native of Torquay. My mother is buried with her family.

My father was born in Exmouth of Devon forebears. From the middle of the nineteenth century the glamorous ancestor to whom everyone looked back was his grandfather, Andrew Alexander Beer, Master and part-owner of a brig called the *Magyar*, which was sunk off Hartlepool on a calm clear evening. An account of the disaster was published in the *Exmouth Chronicle* on the occasion of the death of William Beer, Andrew Alexander's son, who lived to be old. There was perhaps nothing much to say about William, and the loss of the *Magyar* was an excellent story, so the column commemorating the son speaks almost entirely of the father.

'About half-past seven, the master and mate who were on deck, saw a steamer bearing down on them; when she arrived within hailing distance they hailed her repeatedly to keep away, but no notice was taken by those aboard the steamer. Mr Beer, seeing a collision was inevitable, called to his crew to stand by and jump for their lives. Scarcely had he done so, when the steamer struck the ill-fated brig on her port-bow with so much force as to cut her completely through. She went down instantly.' The one survivor, Henry Winsor, had 'seized hold of a life-buoy, and taking a hasty glance at the scene on deck jumped overboard. In that glance he saw that Mr Beer had given up all hope, for he had his arms around his son; the others were standing near him.'

The *Exmouth Chronicle* allocates the blame unhesitatingly: 'There can be no doubt this terrible calamity was the result of great carelessness on the part of those on board the steamer'; and indeed the master of the steamer 'wept bitterly on learning that six of the crew had perished'.

Andrew Alexander had three children as well as the one who died with him, and for two generations the descendants he left were less daring and less colourful than himself. There is a family story that someone swindled them out of their rightful inheritance after the *Magyar* went down, so that they had to live frugally and do humble work, but this insistence on the part of the Beers that they had fallen from high estate is embodied in so many tales and rumours – it only needed one of the Beer wives to be called Wilmot for distant kinship with the seventeenth-century Earl of Rochester to be suggested – that I think of it as part of their character rather than as fact.

I certainly cannot entertain their romantic account of the family's origins. It was invented and told, I suspect, not only out of simple snobbery, but also from a wish to justify the comic name of Beer, from which my ancestors presumably suffered at school as much as I did. In 1745 a Scottish chieftain, involved in the Jacobite rising, had to fly to France after its failure. His vessel was shipwrecked, and he was washed up on the south coast of Devon. His Christian names – Andrew Alexander, of course – he was able to keep, but for the sake of anonymity he took as surname the name of the town where he was washed up, that is, Beer, and in Devon he stayed, married and procreated. I cannot remember his original aristocratic name. I am sure there is not one word of truth in this story from first to last. It seems to me a very natural fabrication, however; I am only surprised that a Spanish grandee was not picked on, alternatively or as well, for a great many such really did land up in Ladram Bay after the Armada. In point of fact, most authorities on names say that people were called Beer because they lived near a wood. There are hundreds of woods in Devon and certainly hundreds of Beers.

If I had to define an essential difference between the Beers and the Jefferys, two families of similar means, class and environment at the time when my parents married, it could be that, whereas my mother's family thought in terms of what they would have been had they lived later, my father's family rested on what they would have been had they lived earlier.

William Beer became a carpenter specialising in coffins, and towards the end of his life he took on some of an undertaker's work such as putting the corpses in them. My father had a much-told story of how he once helped his father to lift a dead body into a coffin and how cold its heels felt. This should have been a good anecdote, but somehow it always sounded like a set-piece, not at all perceptive and not even true.

I do not know who is responsible for the tale that when one of William's young relatives asked him why, when robbed of his dues, he had chosen to be a carpenter, he replied that a better man than he had been proud to be one, but I hope this is not true either. However, if William Beer did not say it, the relative must have invented it, so the point of view is there in the family background.

My father and my uncle became railway clerks. Uncle Harry did well; he was promoted to Waterloo and finally came back to the West Country as stationmaster of Seaton Junction. I once saw him standing masterfully on top of the footbridge that linked the platforms, making sure his station was running properly. My father stayed at Exeter Goods all his life. His great ambition, his one ambition for himself, was to become Chief Clerk. Time after time he was passed over; other men were promoted over his head or brought in from outside. At first we used to plan as a family how we would celebrate his promotion when it came – one idea was to go up to London to see Maskelyne's Mysteries – but eventually we stopped speaking about it. At last, during the Second World War, when he was over sixty, he received the appointment, and it brought him true satisfaction. At his farewell speech the fourteen-year-old office-boy burst into tears.

My father was the eldest child and had been given the famous name, Andrew. My mother, who did not like it, called him John and made all her relatives do the same.

There were relics of the Master. The most important was a portrait. The *Exmouth Chronicle* describes its origin: 'That Captain Andrew Alexander Beer was a brave and intrepid mariner, as so many of the old Exmouth sea-going captains were, is proved by the fact, if such were wanting, that when the Spaniards blockaded Holland he succeeded in running a vessel with provisions through to a Dutch port. As a mark of appreciation and gratitude, the inhabitants presented him with his portrait in oils by a Dutch artist.' He does look intrepid, and very handsome, but surprisingly young and innocent, and rather gentlemanly, too, with his hands lying idle and a red velvet curtain draped behind him. It is a fine picture, though the restorers have said that the city fathers of the Dutch town in question were mean about the quality of the paint.

There are two pictures of the brig. One is a painting done in Naples, to which the brig often took coal, obviously a standard composition with the particular vessel fitted in. Everything is very bright blue, the smoke of Vesuvius and the pennants of the brig are blowing in opposite directions, and Exeter is spelt with a small *e*. In this the *Magyar* is unnaturally static, almost in a trance, but she can be seen in action, billowing and listing, sailing down the side of a bowl which was presented to the Master for some feat. There are also an inkstand that he used on board and an inlaid table that he brought back from Sorrento on his last voyage.

All these things have now come into my possession by various means, from legacy to open cadging, and I prize them so much that it is hard to believe that I had only occasional glimpses of them while I was a child and that the knowledge that they existed was not allowed to be important. My mother would not give them house-room, and they were kept by relatives of my father's to whom she would not give house-room either.

This refusal of my mother's to have anything to do with her husband's family, except, marginally and disagreeably, with his mother, led to some puzzling situations. One day we were coming out of school and a friend said 'That was your aunt' about an unknown woman we had just passed. I never heard any explanation of my mother's attitude; I can only guess. If there had been some definite offence or quarrel, we would certainly have been told.

Her devotion to her own family was absolute. They were Devonians, too. Her father made tombstones. I remember him first of all working in a yard with an outbuilding at the bottom of St Marychurch High Street, and later in a workshop that he had built in the back garden of his house in Petitor Road. His eldest son, Uncle David, worked with him, and afterwards took over the business, making such a success of it that before he himself retired he was employing a man. For the first five or six years of my life they did mostly headstones for war graves, standard in shape and almost uniform in inscription; the same battle and the same age seemed to keep coming up in these brief biographies. When all the soldiers had been labelled, my grandfather and uncle turned to fancier effects for civilians, with luxurious varieties of stone, sensuous outlines and indulgent epitaphs, including texts and nicknames.

Before her marriage, my maternal grandmother had been in service as a housemaid. It was always described emphatically as good service, though no details were given, and I often wondered what was good about it. At the time I knew her she did not look in the least like a housemaid, more like a bitter duchess, with aquiline features.

My mother in becoming a teacher took a step away from all her siblings, which caused lasting discomfort to herself and to them; she felt she was appreciated neither by those above her nor by those beneath her, and her relatives both feared and despised her pretensions. I suppose her parents were proud of her; they must at least have consented to her higher education and have paid what was necessary, but I used to hear many jibes. I was greatly shocked when my grandfather said that the first thing a teacher had to do was to learn to pee into a bottle, an allusion to the medical examination my mother had undergone when applying for the Training College. He also said, less coarsely and more seriously, on another occasion, that he would never have let his other daughters become teachers, as it had ruined the temper of the one who had. His refusal had not been necessary, however, for my mother's sisters, both younger than herself, neither stayed at school for longer than they had to, nor, according to their own accounts, liked it while they were there.

My mother, though so emotionally tied to her own family, could find no challenging company inside it, none of the mental equality which would have made her happy and less assertive. She seemed not to find it in her marriage nor in her Exmouth neighbours and friends. She fell back on indoctrinating her children with the idea that they were to be teachers. It was a fixed and sacred plan which it would have been unthinkable not to fit in with. My father either really did share her ambitions for us or soon became indoctrinated too. In point of fact, I think his high hopes came naturally to him. In their schemes for our advancement my parents agreed. It was perhaps their one true point of unity. When my mother was dying, her last injunction to my father was to see the children through college and then marry again, which he faithfully did.

My mother was pretty, and my father was handsome. They did not seem so to me, but they said it of themselves and of each other, and it was probably true. I later discovered a photograph of my father with his first bride – he had been a widower when my mother came to Exmouth and was ten years older than herself – and in this he was certainly good-looking in an upstanding whiskery way. When I was about ten I used to think he looked like the picture of Rudyard Kipling in the *Children's Encyclopaedia*, which pleased him, as he had a great respect for literature.

My mother had been very popular with the young men at her Training College. She once showed us some copies of the students' magazine – it came out of the same drawer as my father's first wedding group – and under the introductory heading 'On Dit', which we had to have explained to us, there were many references to her such as ' . . . that the Queen has heard but refuses to be Frank' and 'that Royalty is fond of Mutton'. Her real name was Harriet; Queen was the name Uncle David had given her when she was a baby, and she was always called this. In fact Queen is the name carved on her tombstone, where it looks rather odd. She was small and flat-chested. Her hair was thick and had been brown; she went grey very early. It must have been beautiful. She often used to say with pride that, of course, she had neglected it since her marriage.

My father's family was God-fearing, and he had been brought up as a member of the Church of England. As he had a taste for singing and a powerful untrained tenor voice he sang in the choir of All Saints in the Exeter Road until his marriage to my mother. He was a loyal churchman, even during the years of his banishment, and seemed to feel at home with the Anglican way of doing things. Once we were passing Withycombe Church on our way back from Exmouth in the twilight just as the congregation launched into the *Magnificat*. 'There they go,' said my mother scornfully, but my father paused, rather daringly, and repeated: 'and hath exalted the humble and meek,' turning wistfully to the lights and music like an exile. In his third marriage he relapsed and sang happily in the choir of All Saints, Torquay, till the Sunday before his death.

My mother's family were Plymouth Brethren and despised all churches and choirs. At that time the movement was still strong in Devon, and its Gospel Halls, which later had to be closed at about the same rate as the cinemas its members so much hated and feared, were many and well attended.

The two cardinal points of Plymouth Brethren belief were, firstly, that the saving blood of Jesus was the only means of access to Heaven; good works, charity, humility and cheerfulness got no one anywhere without it, so that it followed automatically that these virtues were thought little of by those who *were* saved; and, secondly, that the Scriptures should be followed implicitly and exclusively; the Holy Ghost could interpret the Bible directly to seekers after guidance, and no ignorance on their part could impede the process. As a logical consequence to this second tenet there was no minister and no set form of service, that is, from the point of view of liturgy; the actual programme never varied. No sophisticated brain was present to tamper with whatever slippery underwater ideas might evolve and prosper in the Brethren's minds, no trained intelligence to inform their confident piety.

My mother seemed never to have wavered in her adherence, though normally even the breath of higher education made young people lose hold of their faith; it was that kind of faith. I never noticed that during her lifetime it brought her any peace or help at all, but on her deathbed it clearly did.

Up till then it provided the material and setting of some of her bitterest jibes. I remember that as we were going home one Palm Sunday morning from the Gospel Hall, where the fact that it was a feast was naturally ignored, except for a few sideswipes at Popish mummery in some of the prayers, the congregation of All Saints was coming out, carrying palm crosses and relaxing in the road outside. She told everybody for weeks that really she wondered which was their passport to Heaven, the cross in one hand or the pipe in the other. She made a point of saying it to her mother-in-law, normally a woman of spirit, but who on this occasion only replied: 'Aw, well, Queen, 'tis a custom.'

These remarks must have hurt my father throughout his years of allegiance to the Plymouth Brethren Persuasion, as my mother grandly called it when people came to the door collecting for other sects. He did not officially join the Brethren for some time after his marriage. I know nothing of the stages by which he came to do so and prefer not to think about them. (It was bad enough to watch him being cajoled and blackmailed and bullied into giving up smoking.) It must have been a drawn-out process, as I can remember his setting off to the ceremony. Admission to the Assembly was by total immersion;

that was how it had been done in the Bible, and no considerations of climate, custom or other relevant circumstances were ever taken into account by the Brethren. It was a summer evening, and he was carrying a change of clothes rolled up in a towel, an unpleasantly fraught version of someone going bathing. My mother did not accompany him, on the pretext of having to stay and mind us, but she stood looking out of the front bedroom window, as I so often saw her do, and watched him bicycling down the lane. She said: 'There's Daddy, going to be baptised,' and I felt embarrassed and ashamed.

My parents were married during the First World War. There was no question of my father's being called up, as he was extremely short-sighted. My sister and I were born after the War, and it hardly seemed part of our background at all, except for Father's anecdotes about how he had given up sugar in the post-war rationing period so that we could have it, and the photographs of my uncles in uniform, looking young and smooth and doomed, though in fact they came back safely, and, later, the sad faces of some of our schoolteachers during the two minutes' silence while the dogs barked dementedly at the warning gun. We were brought up in isolation from the history of the time. This was partly a rural isolation; Devon was really remote in those days, and London almost inaccessible except to the rich, though as a family we did quite well in this respect, having four free passes a year on the railway and any number of privilege tickets. National happenings were far away. But in our case it was also religious. Politics was for the children of this world. Plymouth Brethren did not vote, though if they had it would have been Conservative.

> The rich man in his castle,
> The poor man at his gate,

> God made them, high or lowly,
> And ordered their estate

was not in the Brethren hymn-books because of its Anglican associations, but the sentiment lay, however resentfully, in our hearts.

One of the few events that impinged on us was the General Strike. My father had never joined the Railway Clerks' Association, believing unions to be wicked, and on the first day of the strike, when the trains were not running, he bicycled to his work at Exeter or at least set out; he never got there, as the devil sent him a puncture just outside Lympstone. I heard him describe this, but I do not remember it. I clearly remember, however, the reaction of the Brethren and Sisters at the Gospel Hall a decade later to the flight into exile of King Alfonso of Spain; they wept, and prayed for the dethroned, victimised king, who, though he was a Roman Catholic, represented the aristocratic authority they loved in secular rulers. As at the time of the strike, they felt that the forces of evil were taking over.

Throughout the fourteen years of my childhood we lived in the village of Withycombe Raleigh, which was two miles inland and even in those days practically joined to Exmouth. There was not much village life left in Withycombe, except perhaps in the Holly Tree Inn and the parish church, which were both forbidden to Brethren on what sounded like much the same grounds, but had there been more, we, as a family, would not have taken part in it, any more than we did in the life of Exmouth. Unnecessary contact with unbelievers was harmful, and, in any case, though my father was of a decidedly sociable disposition, my mother was not.

My father was proud of being a citizen of Exmouth, though here again my mother was not. He spoke with feeling of the town as he had known it in boyhood,

with its one-man bands, its German bands, its sellers of
hokey-pokey and its brutal, primitive dentists. He
always made it sound like a dark town, perhaps because
he described the lamp-lighters so well. In our childhood
it must have been an interesting place with many forceful
personalities and a great deal going on. The publicans
and the tradespeople, especially those who kept the big
shops that were household names to us, were obviously
clever, lively men; my father used to tell endless anecdotes
either about them or about their fathers, who had kept
the pubs or the stores before them. Sheila and I occasion-
ally met their daughters. One of the Stockers of Holly
Tree Inn was a friend of ours at the Grammar School and
so was Barbara Morey, whose father was the rival
bookseller and stationer to Eland's, and once I had Poppy
Chown pointed out to me in a Carnival Procession.
(Chown's was the big outfitters in Rolle Street.) But that
was all. My father had other stories, too: about the
members of the Urban District Council, which appeared
to consist of the usual range of personalities, from mad,
through eccentric, to fairly normal. Here again, when any
of them came into our lives it was only marginally. It
seemed marginal even in the case of Councillor George
Beavis, our landlord, to whom Father paid a weekly rent
of just over a pound. He always gave Father back sixpence
of it for Sheila and me, because he paid so promptly.

At that time Exmouth had already changed socially
from what it had been before the War. My mother often
lamented the passing of the old families and the big
houses, which every year were being turned into schools
and institutions. My father regretted it too, but more
because of the loss of glamour than the loss of tone.
Bystock and Marley were two stately homes about a
mile from us, set on the rising wooded ground that led
up to Blackhill. They had both been owned within
living memory by a family called Bryce, who, according

to a large body of local rumour and scandal, had been
mad and bad, but not dangerous to know, as they were
so far above everyone's sphere that in fact nobody did
know them. There were stories of coaches-and-six and of
wild young men shooting themselves, in Paris, of course.
But that was all over, and the two houses, one due for
demolition and the other for partial occupation, were
peacefully sleeping away what was left of their lives,
surrounded by trees and a few ghosts in full evening dress.

The road from Exmouth to Withycombe, which I
must have taken thousands of times, left the town through
a district of rigid parallel terraces, and went under the
railway bridge that carried the branch line from Sidmouth
Junction. (The railway cut right across Phear Park; its
coming had caused the Phears great inconvenience, my
father used to tell us, torn between his loyalty to the
Southern and his conviction that the gentry should not be
inconvenienced. It must in fact have annoyed the
citizens as much as it had the Phears, for several houses
were left leaning right up against it as though listening
to the trains.) It skirted Phear Park, a pleasant undulating
piece of land, with rough edges and no flower-beds and
a great many people always playing games, and passed
the Grange, as everybody still called Exmouth Grammar
School, either from habit or from feelings like my mother's,
though I must say that, with her, education was as good
as a squire. At the parish church the village began.
The church was a squat, stocky building made of grey
stones arranged in a random-looking way. Opposite was
the huge Vicarage in its enormous grounds and beyond
it a group of thatched cottages mixed with red-brick
terrace houses. Some of the cottages were white and
humble and had seats coming out on to the pavement;
others were grander, set back behind lush, clumpy
gardens and tending to be painted pink. Farther on were
half a dozen handsome houses glimpsed up leafy drives.

Then came the village shops, Withycombe Infants, a bad-tempered dog called Pincher, the Holly Tree Inn and a very narrow street between tight little terraces, one of them called Jubilee, with another pub at the far end. The road then widened again, sloughed off buildings and approached the open country, passing the brickworks and the forge, both still working and not yet curious relics.

Here Bradham Lane went off to the right, uphill. It was still very much a lane, though with scattered hints of the built-up road it later became. On the first bend of the hill was a cornfield, where every year two large red horses, Prince and Farmer, came to cut the corn, dragging their flailing, rattling machine in diminishing squares. Opposite the field there was a short terrace, and here we lived, in a small red-brick house called Petitor, on the front door of which my sister Sheila chalked, almost as soon as she could write: MRS BEERS HOUSE.

CHAPTER TWO

Exmouth and Torquay

I SOMETIMES try to enter into my mother's feelings as she approached Exmouth for the first time. She must have come across the estuary on the Starcross ferry, which was the recognised route from Torquay, as it saved going up to Exeter and down again on the Exmouth line. (Later, because my father could get us privilege tickets, it paid us, as a family, to do the whole journey by train.) It is impossible for me to recreate her impression of coming into exile or to think of Exmouth as a hated, hostile town; I feel too differently. But I admit that the estuary could look cheerless on its worst days, and this may have been one of them. Wet sand is a very depressing sight, and the ferry-boat would have got a long, uninterrupted view of Dawlish Warren, which stretched half-way across the mouth of the river as well as the two-mile line of beach from Exmouth Harbour to Orcombe Point.

The estuary was hardly ever blue. It varied only from silver at its brightest to pewter at its dullest, and was always tarnished with currents, which seized the ferry-boat with some violence as it left the shelter of Dawlish Warren at the last stage of the crossing.

As the boat entered the harbour, swinging awkwardly in the current and hardly ever head-on, the passengers, I suppose, would have been as conscious of the residents' shoes as they waited on the jetty above as the residents were of the passengers' hats. My mother may have looked into the inner harbour, where the boats tended to huddle up in corners like sheep and where a few swans and a great many rotten apples were usually swilling about. She would have been too far away and perhaps in no mood to enjoy the smell of cut wood from the saw-mill just beyond. The boards and planks of the landing-stage and the steps were slimy and green, with every corner worn off. It may have been raining, and she certainly suffered from seasickness. Perhaps it was one of those terrible first impressions from which people never wholly recover.

The Beers, whom my mother was very soon to meet, lived in Albion Street, in the centre of the town, a hilly Victorian row of humble brick houses, not yet dominated by the big gasometer which later closed the view and filled the sky at the top. I do not remember my grandfather. He died suddenly when I was too young to recall any of the pother it must have caused, though apparently I noticed it at the time. In later years my father was very fond of telling an anecdote on the subject. The undertaker's name was Ted Long, and as my poor father went plunging down the back lane on his bicycle to fetch him it seems I remarked appreciatively, 'Daddy's going headlong for Ted Long.'

Although I do not remember my grandfather personally I remember him through his grave, and in fact I have far pleasanter and more vivid impressions of visiting it, though this happened seldom, than of going to see any living relative. St John's-in-the-Wilderness had a wonderful churchyard. It was not so much peaceful as silent, very, very silent. Though the church was on high ground, the fields were even higher and sloped down to it all the way round. As I recall them, they were perpetually lying fallow, with no animals in them and no crops. The red paths that crossed them were rough with plants that no one seemed to have trodden down for years. In the churchyard itself there was ivy everywhere, prising up the slabs on top of the tombs, upholstering the urns and dangling from the angels' shoulders. There was every type of monument, each made more interesting by something nature had done to it: a column that was cut off half-way to indicate a premature death had tilted sideways, too, which made life look a particularly uncertain thing, and a dignified baby angel was spattered with lichen as though someone had flicked gold paint at him.

I knew my grandmother for many years but have no very accurate impression of her. In appearance she tended to merge with my maternal grandmother. They were much the same size and were both handsome and strong-featured, with white hair and black clothes. It is even more difficult to define her character. My mother enjoyed the sort of running battle with her that left a child feeling that both parties were tartars, and in fact I would have put Grandma Beer down as quite a termagant, had not other members of my father's family described her as the dearest, sweetest soul alive; saintly, one of them said. However, as they all, especially the one who said 'saintly', hated my mother, I hardly know how to value their testimonials.

We did not see her very often, but when we did she complained constantly in a quavering, querulous voice, which Sheila could imitate beautifully. With well-judged boldness she once did this imitation in front of my mother, who laughed with a minimal pretence of reluctance and reproach. Whenever we were taken to see my grandmother, on rare but regular duty visits, her first remark nearly always was 'You don't know how bad your Gran bin.' She suffered from delusions, which, as she got older, left probability farther and farther behind. To begin with, she was being annoyed by the people opposite, who used to come out on their roof to see the sunset. In point of fact their roof was so steeply pitched they could not possibly have come out on to it, and in any case Devonians are not given to admiring sunsets, but the story sounded reasonable. Later, however, they became angels who kept looking in at her bedroom window. We used to hope she would go into details about them, but she never did in my mother's presence; we heard about them at second hand from my father. The angels were not beckoning, sympathetic harbingers, apparently; they used to scoff and peer.

She lived to be over ninety. As she became older and weaker there was an increasing problem as to what was to be done with her. No one seemed willing to have her; it was not only my mother. Once she went on a visit to my Uncle Harry and his wife, who were then living in New Malden, fell sick there and stayed for five months. This was awkward. My mother felt that for very shame she ought to go up and see her, as she had no intention of sharing the burden in any other way. So we went up to London one day on one of the four free passes. The problem was what to wear. We never put on our best clothes for train journeys for fear of getting them dirty, and yet we wanted to impress my father's relatives. In the end the solution seemed to be to wear old clothes with a haughty manner.

Eventually my grandmother came back to Devon, and my father found lodgings for her in Bradham Lane. Here she died. She had seemed to be dying, or not exactly living, for some weeks, and there was no perceptible change on the day when she actually did. Sheila and I did not see her at all during this time, and my mother very seldom, so we depended on my father's accounts. He told us children that she must have known she was going as she crossed her hands on her breast. He knew better than to tell my mother this as she would certainly have pronounced it to be both Popish and sloppy.

My father's brother Harry and his sister Marianne were both married and both lived away from Exmouth, Marianne, however, no farther than Exeter. Uncle Harry had a son, Andrew, about our age, of whom we caught interesting glimpses from time to time, usually on Exeter station. He was tall and foreign-looking. Aunt Marianne had no children. Her husband was an Irishman, a Roman Catholic though lapsed, who did everything that Plymouth Brethren do not do, such as go to the races.

But there is no doubt that the Beers were shadowy compared with the Jefferys. This was not surprising. Because of Mother's habit of taking Sheila and me to Torquay for the entire length of every school holiday, we spent about a third of each year there, and as we left all our friends and pursuits behind us in Exmouth and were given no opportunity to find new ones in Torquay, we were nothing but adjuncts of my mother's family. We trailed around the shops behind Mother and my aunts, while they interminably discussed and bought reels of cotton and skeins of wool; it was extremely boring. We were dragged down to the beach and hauled up again – at first physically, later on psychologically – always by the Jefferys and always in the sound of the assertive, happy, chattering voice of Mother, who had in fact run away from home and involved us in the desertion.

This feeling was clearly ungrateful, apart from being priggish and censorious, and it must have been more intermittent than it seems in memory. I must have enjoyed the picnics and the bathing. Petitor was a small, quiet, grey beach, surrounded by large, flamboyant, red cliffs. The state of the tide made so much difference to it that we were perpetually conscious of the movement of the sea and always took it into account. When the tide was in, the sea looked fuller and deeper than on other beaches, and, when it was out, the shore looked exaggeratedly decayed and gaping, and we cut our feet and left trails of blood on the boulders. I know I enjoyed the attentions of my young aunts, Olly and Da, too. They were very kind to us, and indeed one of my earliest memories is of coming into the hall of the house in Petitor Road and of Da, who worked in a cake-shop, hurrying forward with a magnificent birthday cake she had brought home for me. She had to kneel right down to get it within my field of vision.

I remember my mother's parents well, even Grandpa Jeffery who died when I was nine. I saw him mostly in profile at the kitchen table in the St Marychurch house. He sat at the head of the table, slewed round with his left elbow resting on it. Even from this position he had full command of what was going on. If I was not concentrating on eating and was playing about with my food, he would sometimes pretend to put a laden spoon into his ear rather than into his mouth with a fine assumption of absent-mindedness.

One of my earliest memories of him is an embarrassing one. For some reason, while we were staying in Torquay, I came down to the kitchen one morning with not much on. A great fuss was made and was still continuing when he came in. 'Did she come down stark naked?' he asked coarsely. I was greatly put out. I did not like being called 'she' and having an enquiry about my motives and behaviour addressed to my mother, who was only too eager to answer for them. I would not have dreamed of coming down with nothing on, and I resented the expression 'stark naked', which I was meeting on this occasion for the first time and which sounded crude.

I do not know whether he or my grandmother was the stronger. It is significant that he was not a born member of the Plymouth Brethren, although when I knew him he seemed so long-established in the faith, but had joined the Meetings as a result of her representations. He had

once been a bellringer at his parish church, much as my
father had been a choirman at his. He seemed very much
the head of the house, but she would reprove him almost
automatically. One day I was in the back garden picking
a snail out of its shell. My grandfather came down the
path and rebuked me in solemn words. My grandmother,
who was in the outside privy at the time, heard the tone
of his voice but not what he was saying and, slightly
opening the door with her black-booted foot, snapped:
'Don't be such a killjoy, Dad.' Not that she had any
brief for me. The kindest thing she ever said about me
when I was a child was that my back view made her laugh.
She thought I was odd and too clever by half and that my
forehead was too high.

I looked up to my grandfather as a craftsman. I spent
many absorbed hours in his workshop and learnt from
him how to do the lettering on the tombstones. This
seemed cheerful work, not in the least connected with
death. I was not skilled enough, of course, actually to
carve the letters, but I could drill the holes in them, bang
in the lead with the rubber hammer and make quite a
fair attempt at scooping off the surplus afterwards.
Though this talent turned out not to be my real line, I
still feel pleasure at having learnt from my grandfather
in this way. He helped me with my reading, too. Tombstones have difficult words, especially war graves, and
it was he who taught me at a very early age not to pronounce 'corps' as 'corpse'.

From him and from Uncle David, from my father and
my aunts' husbands, too, I learnt what skilled and
conscientious work was. They all worked so hard and so
well that I was quite old before I met laziness and
inefficiency. Not one of them grumbled, not even Jack,
who, as a baker employed by a popular café near the seafront, during the twenties and thirties had to work
dreadfully long hours in the busy season, leaving the

house well before dawn and not getting back till late at night. The bakehouse, which we loved to visit, was primitive and rat-ridden, but the speed and elegance with which he did everything – getting the bread out of the oven on the long peel, rolling pastry, putting mixtures into tins – made it all seem very glamorous to us. I never felt quite the same about the sort of work done by my father and my other aunt's husband, who was employed by the Gas Company and whose chief duty was to empty gas-meters. I realised that they, too, were capable and trusted, but I never saw them making anything, as I saw Jack and Uncle David and my grandfather doing. They did not wear special working clothes, either; a uniform did not count.

We were not very lucky with cousins. Just as Andrew Beer was lost to us in childhood, so were the four children of my mother's second brother, Uncle Ted. He was a clever, interesting, aggressive man, who eventually worked his way up to be a lecturer in the local Technical College and a Justice of the Peace, but unfortunately he was not a Plymouth Brother. He had never been saved either, so he had not even the status of a backslider. This made him seem less than a blood relation. The Assembly was the real family, and he not only did not belong but openly abused it. Unfortunately the remarks he made were not of the reasoned sort which could have opened our eyes. The things he called the Brethren, such as sodding hypocrites, were just what you would expect the unregenerate and heathen to say and showed a hardness of heart rather than any superiority of mind. His observations were, in substance, if not in language, the very ones that any obdurate sinner in the Bible might have made and therefore tended to show how right we were.

If his wife had said only a tenth of what she was rumoured to have said, she must have felt even more strongly than he did. My mother and my aunts were unanimous in their comeback; they had compiled over the years a body of critical remarks about their sister-in-law and on this they drew whenever they were provoked. I knew it off by heart. It had two main categories: her indolence, exemplified by her habit of doing the ironing sitting down, and her loose morals, proved by the fact that she and Uncle Ted had had to get married in a hurry and by the quite unsubstantiated legend that her friends had frequently been seen down on the Strand with their handbags, as the local euphemism went. Every Christmas without fail these two characteristics of hers seemed to my mother and my aunts to be united in and expressed by the fact that she always gave them highly scented soap and pink frilly garters, which of course they never used.

Because of his unsaved condition, I tended to ascribe to Uncle Ted all the misdeeds which I had been taught to believe were characteristic of this state. Smoking was an example; when we were doing leatherwork at the Council School I confidently made him a tobacco-pouch and was amazed to discover that he did not smoke, though fortunately I found this out in time to remodel the pouch into a Bible-cover for Uncle David. And to my mind, conditioned as I was not only by Plymouth Brethren doctrines but by my mother's snobbery, the fact that during the years of my childhood he and his family lived in a council house fitted in perfectly.

All this meant that we saw little of these Jeffery cousins, though their ages spanned ours. It would be artificial to regret this, as we would have had little in common. The ambition of the three eldest, all girls, was to leave school as early as possible and never to open a book again. I cannot pretend either that their home was a haven of independent thought and relaxed affection which it was a pleasure to visit. They were as limited as the Brethren and not noticeably happier.

At one point in our lives it looked as though Reen, the eldest, was going effectively to cross our paths. One Sunday evening, when we were staying at St Marychurch, my grandmother came back from the Gospel Meeting with red face and trembling hat, strode into the middle of the kitchen and cried: 'Reen's saved.' Everyone exclaimed. I cannot imagine how Reen came to be at the Gospel Meeting, but saved she certainly had been; my grandmother went on to give us convincing details. There was great rejoicing, with a certain waspish undercurrent. It was agreed that Sheila, Reen and I would now go forward together in the way of salvation and perhaps even be baptised at the same time. And indeed this is what did happen a couple of years later, though we never felt any closer or more similar to Reen than we had before.

This uneasy sense that the three of us ought now to have a great deal in common persisted for a few years, but was finally dissipated by another announcement of my grandmother's. Coming back from the Gospel Meeting once again, and in much the same state of excitement, she burst in with 'Reen's courting.' Though she had no more to go on than that Reen had attended the meeting with a young man and had walked off with him afterwards, her information now proved to be just as accurate as it had been before. Reen was indeed courting. This did it. We still had most of the Grammar School and our teachers' training to get through before we could think of courting. Reen moved away from us into the adult world, eventually married the young man she had been seen with that evening, gradually and peacefully left the Brethren, and was looking matronly before we had even become engaged.

My mother's sisters, being younger than herself, did not have any children till we were over ten, so in fact the only cousin we grew up with was Wilfred, Uncle David's son. He was a defective. How he would be categorised nowadays I do not know; no one ever applied a name to his particular type of deficiency (not 'mongol' or 'cretin' or 'spastic', for example), and it would have seemed rather odd to me if anyone had, as I accepted him completely as an individual. I noticed he could not walk or move his hands very accurately, or talk in anything but single words and then not clearly, but I did not pity him or feel superior to him or suffer embarrassment when walking beside his push-chair, even when he was gibbering at the top of his voice and rocking backwards and forwards. If he had been my brother I might have felt differently, of course, or if I had been seen with him anywhere but in Torquay, an alien town where I, personally, knew nobody.

He was a few years older than Sheila and me. The story we were told was that Uncle David's wife had developed severe kidney trouble when pregnant with Wilfred, and the doctor had tried to bring on an abortion. This had failed, and Wilfred had been born as he was, and his mother had died in childbed. This last fact was certainly true, but I have sometimes wondered if the rest of the tale were not a fiction. My mother seldom faced the truth where illness was concerned, and this story neatly did away with the idea of there being deficiency in the family.

I was never kind to him as we were often told to be. One day when the three of us had been given a bunch of grapes to share as a great treat, I deliberately took the last two, though I knew my mother was watching and that I was renouncing a splendid opportunity of being seen to be unselfish. I did not like grapes much, either.

I thoroughly enjoyed his company. He was always cheerful or quite prepared to be, with his mad bray of laughter rising to an even madder shriek. He was always affectionate. He either did not realise that my sister and I were two people or, which is more likely, refused for some reason of his own to recognise the duality, but he would greet each of us very enthusiastically as Sheilapat. He was fond of singing and had a good ear for a tune, though his voice was terrible, unbelievably piercing and strident. He had a sense of malice, and if people were trying to listen to a quiet passage on a gramophone record he would join in the air with tremendous volume and an appearance of simple enjoyment, breaking off into wild giggles when he sensed how annoyed they were getting. Of course, they dared not show their annoyance, and he knew perfectly well that 'being unkind to Wilfred' was an unthinkable sin.

He once played what seemed to be a deliberate trick on a Mrs Sturtridge, who had come to see my aunt one day when Wilfred, now a large fifteen-year-old, was there on a visit. She was a friend of the family, but not so close as to know precisely what Wilfred could or could not do. My aunt very naturally did not think to mention specifically that he could neither stand nor walk and went out to the kitchen to get the tea, leaving Mrs Sturtridge, Wilfred and me in the room together. Wilfred immediately slid to the edge of his chair and started rocking backwards and forwards with an increasing momentum as though he would rock on to his feet and lurch across the room at any minute, his eyes fixed on Mrs Sturtridge and a frightening leer on his face. Mrs Sturtridge sat there looking more and more apprehensive; I suppose she did not like to rush out or call, especially as I was so calm and matter-of-fact. It never occurred to me to intervene or explain.

In his early years various cures were suggested for him. One was sea-water to strengthen his legs, and every day Uncle David, who was a devoted father, struggled up from Petitor, a really stiff climb, with full buckets for Wilfred's bath. By the time I knew him, however, all hope had been given up.

We saw a great deal of him, but the darker aspects of his condition were kept from us, such as the recurrent fits he underwent. We were necessarily present at the first stage in which his head turned abruptly sideways and seemed to lock. We were then sent out of the room, but we could hear them clearly through the door getting on with the only treatment they knew, that of speaking firmly to him. When he went in again he was all right, except that he looked at us sheepishly and said 'Aw' in a tone of self-reproach.

He seemed always to be dressed in the same clothes, a dark sweater with knee-breeches and woollen stockings. The breeches had a leather patch on the seat, as he could slide on the floor from place to place with considerable speed, and indeed this was his usual way of getting about. If someone held him under the armpits, taking all his weight, he could move his legs as though walking, but it meant practically carrying him, and only a man could do it.

By the adults of the family he was treated with unswerving kindness. He responded immediately and fully to cheerfulness, and everyone, including those who married into the family, treated him with the consistent heartiness he so much liked. I cannot know what sacrifices were made, what wishes suppressed, by those who made him feel the centre of loving attention: perhaps not many, for he was, it seemed to me, truly lovable. But there was almost a conspiracy among the grown-ups to accept his shortcomings in a way which emphasised them. If we were acting a word at a Christmas party, for example, and had put on other people's hats and coats to achieve the effect, we were loudly told on entering the room to 'speak to Wilfred', who was in fact showing no signs whatever of bewilderment or fear, but was more likely yelling with laughter. His speech was another case in point. It is true he could not talk clearly, but his mispronunciations were seized on and turned into a holy canon; no one was allowed to depart from them.

Many of his nicknames for people, therefore, were hardly of his own choosing, but one of them must have been. He used to call Brother Johnson of the Exmouth Assembly 'Heave-ho'. The reason was that Brother Johnson resembled in disposition the man who ran the Oddicombe Belle, the pleasure-boat which Wilfred had often watched when he was taken down to Oddicombe Beach for an outing. The expression 'Heave-ho' must have come from some story or song about mariners; the captain of the Oddicombe Belle had obviously never said 'Heave-ho' in his life. But to pick out the bossy officiousness which characterised both the captain and Brother Johnson by linking them in this way still strikes me as highly perceptive.

I enjoyed Wilfred's company all through childhood. If remembered sensation is a true guide, I can say that I loved him more peacefully than I loved anybody. Far from being a weakling he seemed a support. He was, I suppose, one of the few people I knew who was not neurotic, the only person who had gone as far as he could. It was after I went away to college that his dark days began. I heard all about it later. He was over twenty now, and it was becoming increasingly difficult for Uncle David, who was no longer young, and his wife (he had married again when Wilfred was about five) to keep him at home. His fits got worse and more frequent. He masturbated continuously. Uncle David was often up all night with him.

They kept postponing the decision, they struggled on, but eventually the step was taken. He was driven away to Newton Abbot workhouse, as it used to be, on the way to the asylum at Exminster. He was at Newton Abbot for one night, during which, as a nurse told my aunt afterwards, he called out two words repeatedly: 'Daddy. Home.'

I never saw him again, but Sheila did. Soon after this she was visiting me in Exeter hospital, where I had just had my appendix out, and she went on to the asylum afterwards. When I was better she told me, in great distress, how she had been shown into the presence of a shrunken, middle-aged man, who had obviously had all his teeth taken out; he had looked up and said, in not even a familiar voice and with no sign of pleasure, 'Hello, Sheilapat.' A few months later we heard he was dead.

My grandparents could hardly have borne these events. Wilfred was the first grandchild, the son of the eldest son, which was important even in a family where the heir had nothing to inherit and even when the first of his generation to be called Jeffery did not need a surname at all, as he never mixed with the world in any way which required one, except in the last few months. But they had been dead themselves for many years.

Grandpa Jeffery had died in his sleep of a heart-attack, without any previous ill-health. My grandmother told us all later that, from her side of the bed, she had half heard what she took to be particularly irritating snoring for some time before a certain strangeness in the note dragged her up out of sleep into what had become complete silence. Uncle David was roused by neighbours and went through the darkness to knock at the doors of her daughters. Olly afterwards described how she heard Jack with his head out of the bedroom window saying, 'Whatever shall I tell Olly?' at which she jumped out of bed, pushed him aside and called down, 'Tell me the truth. Oh, 'tis Dave. Tell me the truth, Dave.'

My mother did not hear the news till the next morning. By coincidence she was taking me to Torquay that very day. I had just had my tonsils out, and I was going there to convalesce. There was not much point, as the air would be exactly the same, but Torquay was the panacea for everything. My father met us in Exeter, Queen St, as he would have done in any case, in order to see us on our way to Exeter St David's, where we caught the Torquay train. They had telephoned him the news at his office. I noticed nothing unusual in his manner, nor heard what he said to my mother, but I was not particularly startled when she burst out wailing, with words that conveyed the news, and nothing like as distressed as when she cried in the course of quarrels with her sisters.

At last, after cups of Bovril, which my father agitatedly got us from the station buffet, she and I went on to Torquay, my father being commissioned to go back to Exmouth as usual, look after Sheila and break the news gently to her. I asked her later how he had done this. Apparently he had been very quiet all through tea, and they were in the middle of washing-up, when he suddenly said, 'How nice to know that Grandpa's safe with the Lord.' Sheila had naturally had no fears for Grandpa's welfare nor doubts about his eternal salvation, but she was impressed, and so was I, by this *tour de force* of diplomacy, especially coming from someone who had often been called the most tactless man in Withycombe.

When my mother and I got to Petitor Terrace, we walked down the passage without anyone hearing us or greeting us and opened the kitchen door. My grandmother was huddled up by the stove crying and moaning. My mother started towards her calling out with great feeling and in a trembling voice, 'Oh, I know. I know.' My grandmother rose to her feet and faced her. 'No, you don't,' she shouted. 'You don't, Queen. You don't know.' I made little of this at the time, though it was clearly momentous, but I think I see now that the housemaid was telling the schoolteacher, the wife was telling the favourite daughter, the uneducated woman was telling the know-all that to be a widow was outside her experience.

I had stayed by the door. At this point Olly came up

to me and suggested in a whisper that I might like to run down the hill and play with Wilfred for a while. I found him sitting up to the table on which someone had placed for his entertainment two dead flatfish on a plate. He was gazing down at them very intently, giving an appreciative 'Aw' from time to time. He greeted me cheerfully with his usual 'Hello, Sheilapat,' and I sat down beside him and stared at the fish, too, until they were taken away to be cooked for dinner. It was a pleasant morning.

As Grandpa had died without warning, there had been some talk of an inquest earlier in the day, and when I got back to Petitor Terrace everyone was waiting with horror for a message to come about it. I gathered that an inquest would be an overwhelming disgrace. There was a knock at the door, and, as one of my aunts tensely opened it, I could see a policeman on the steps. I had never been in a house that a policeman was calling at. After a short mumbled conversation my aunt came rushing back into the kitchen. ''Tis all right. 'Tis all right. No inquest,' she said, and everyone started crying.

That evening my mother asked me if I would like to see my grandfather. I said, 'No, thank you,' but apparently it had been a rhetorical question, as she insisted. 'Grandpa would never have done anything to hurt you, would he?' she cajoled as I hung back. That was simply not the point, but it was the Brethren illogic and I was conditioned to it.

He was lying on a trestle-table in the front room. I must have been taller than the table, but I seemed to have to look up at him, as it might have been at a range of hills. He looked harder and much cleaner than in life, I noticed, but I felt nothing at all. I remember my childhood as a series of incidents where some reaction seemed to be called for and yet I did not know how to react. This incident, death, was one of the most important, but I had no idea what to think or how to feel. My grandfather was a fact to be observed, as he had always been, a rather different fact this time.

Grandma Jeffery did not die till I was over ten years old, and her death was not very exciting – I cannot remember the details at all – partly because the idea was no novelty any more and partly because she became so very cantankerous in her last years that everyone was relieved when the end came. Not that anyone admitted it, but it was so obvious that a neighbour actually spoke in these terms to my mother, almost congratulating her. My mother and aunts, who, quite naturally, did not welcome honesty on this point, seemed to fear that our moral training might have been undermined by Mrs Bright's remarks, for they staged a little dialogue, to be overheard by Sheila and me, one day when we were walking in Phear Park, to the effect that though they had appeared to dance attendance on their mother, they had done it voluntarily and gladly because she was so precious.

I had seen my grandmother in the full force of her perpetual bad temper for many years. Olly and Jack had given up their home and their independence to look after her, and yet she had repeatedly and unreasonably taken offence at Jack's gardening and Olly's housekeeping, always in my grandfather's name. Jack would be accused of digging up a plant Grandpa Jeffery had been particularly fond of, and Olly of violating domestic associations such as the exact position of his favourite chair. I had seen her make her grown-up children weep and quarrel and mutter to each other in the scullery and could hardly bear the word 'precious', spoken by my mother in a theatrical tone, especially as I felt it was their own fault for not standing up to her.

CHAPTER THREE

Plan of Salvation

THE Morning Meeting, or the Breaking of Bread as it was called on the board outside the Gospel Hall, was the central point of Plymouth Brethren belief and practice. Those who expounded the Scriptures or led in prayer relied solely on the direct guidance of the Holy Spirit, with regard both to when to stand up and to what to say. Even the central part of the Meeting, the administering of the bread and wine, was done extempore by someone who felt called on. In all this waiting on God everything happened to time. The Holy Ghost, who, we were taught, dwelt in Eternity, seemed to have his eye as firmly on the clock as I did, for it was always within seconds of quarter to twelve – the meeting started at eleven – that some Brother walked out to the table to officiate, and always within seconds of half-past twelve that the last speaker of the morning approached his peroration. Once a visiting Brother who went on too long received glares from the Sisters which suggested that he was inspired by some hostile force rather than the true Spirit.

The service was well called the Breaking of Bread, as the round loaf was big and tough-looking and had to be torn apart with great effort by the ministering Brother before he passed it round on a plate, at which stage it was quite easy to pick bits off. Most of the Brethren had strong hands and were confident from long experience, but it must have seemed an ordeal to young Brethren just starting out in the Lord's ministry, a test which

might find them impotent. Indeed according to my
father, the older men sometimes discussed this practical
difficulty, and once a wily Brother had come forward
with the idea that when it seemed likely that young Brother
Palk was going to be moved by the Holy Ghost — all
these old Brethren had true prescience in these matters —
they might cut the loaf up a bit, surreptitiously, before-
hand. The idea was treated respectfully, but had to be
dropped in the end as they felt they could not actually
tell young Brother Palk that this was what they had done.

The administering of the wine was easier, as it was just
poured into a goblet and passed from hand to hand.
Before I was old enough to take part myself, I used to
enjoy the strange smell that wafted nearer and nearer
as the cup came round and the wine was tipped up and
fell back into it again, though it seemed bizarre on the
lips and breath of my parents and quite out of keeping
with the rest of the service. It was later that the wet
marks on the rim, where the mouths had been, struck
me as unhygienic.

The others sometimes had this thought, too. One
Sunday, when Sister Christmas was in the Fever Hospital
with diphtheria, Brother Christmas, as the wine came
round, stalked importantly to the back of the hall to be
the last to get it, so as not to spread infection. It did
occur to me that he would have done better not to be
there at all, and I took care not to breathe deeply any-
where near him, but most people were impressed by his
action.

I found the whole concept of the Lord's Will confusing,
as embodied in this incident and many others. The Lord's
Will, on which we were taught utterly to depend, was, it
seemed, so irrational, so unpredictable, so likely to lead
to something unpleasant, that if we had all gone down
with diphtheria the following week, no one would have
batted an eyelid at hearing it described as the Lord's

Will, and some farrago of fantasy might have been produced in which a wardful of Saints could be expected to lead to a mass conversion of the Fever Hospital staff. On the other hand, God could have spared us without the heroic intervention of Brother Christmas.

Perhaps I should explain why I call the Brethren the Saints, as it seems to me entirely natural to do. Saints in the usual sense of the word were quite unacceptable, being not only Popish but entirely out of line with God's plan of salvation. Saints existed to be prayed to, and this was dreadfully wrong; only Christ could intercede with God. 'There is one mediator between God and man, the man Christ Jesus' was one of the most prominent texts in our own Gospel Hall, which was fairly papered with them. All were equal through the blood of Christ, that is, if they had consciously availed themselves of it. So we were all Saints and openly referred to ourselves as such, with a vainglory which it would have been heretical to think of as vainglory, seeing we were all Saints.

The Morning Meeting was exclusively for believers, that is, for those who had been baptised by total immersion, and for believers' children, though they could not actually break bread until they too had undergone the ceremony. The tone of the meeting was therefore not evangelical. It was one of complacency. We meditated on the details of our redemption, guided by whatever passages of scripture might be brought to our attention by the speakers. These expositions, dictated we believed by the Holy Ghost, and certainly uttered by sincere and devout men, were conceived in a spirit of the most extravagant and deliberate ignorance.

At that time, and in Devon, the Brethren as a social group were remarkably homogeneous; they were all of lower-middle-class or upper-working-class backgrounds, and they were not ambitious, though sometimes resentful. The only professional man I ever met among them was a doctor in the Exeter Assembly, and, instead of being regarded as a natural leader, he was treated with suspicion. Usually, when he had spoken a few well-constructed sentences in his cultured voice, some outstandingly rough Brother would get up and virtually contradict him, and indeed "Tis all very well for he' was the prevalent attitude, if not 'What do he know about it?' I think high birth would have given him more status in the Assembly than learning.

The display of any knowledge of history, geography, philosophy, theology or foreign languages, which in any case no one possessed, would have been regarded as conceited interference with the Spirit's guidance. One uppish young man who alluded to the fact that Tiglath-Pileser was on the throne at the time of the birth of Jesus Christ, was rebuked, though he had not even specified which throne, and the River Jordan might have run all the way uphill to the cedars of Lebanon for all we knew or were allowed to care. Edifying points were wrenched out of the syntax and vocabulary of the Authorised Version, as though God had spoken in early seventeenth-century English, and words were regarded as being significantly connected which had no relationship at all in the original. Linked with this disposition to play on words were the slogans with which we were stimulated, all of them expecting the worst: 'Disappointments are His appointments' and 'The hardest field is the harvest field.'

Although there was no minister, there had to be some sort of organisation, and each Assembly was run by a small group of Brethren called the Oversight. Once selected – I cannot say elected, as there was no question of anything so worldly as a democratic vote – they were in power for a lifetime. I cannot remember any of them dying, but had it happened the survivors would have chosen his successor.

The principal duties of the Oversight were to book speakers for the Gospel Meeting on Sunday evening and to run the finances of the Assembly. The second task could sometimes be heavy. At one time the lease of the hall at St Marychurch was about to expire, and they were deeply worried. Prayers mentioning a freehold were offered every Sunday morning. I had no precise idea what a freehold was, but, being painfully impressed by the Brethren's need, I pointed out to my mother a large board in the neighbourhood saying FREEHOLD FOR SALE, convinced that they could buy what they wanted there.

The first duty was easier, though it consisted of finding fifty-two Brethren every year, usually from other Assemblies in the district, who were able and willing to preach the Gospel. It meant a lot of letter-writing, but otherwise it was not difficult. Nobody who was not dying to hear the sound of his own voice would have joined the Plymouth Brethren in the first place, and in fact they were men of considerable natural eloquence. There must have been charm, too, in having a diary full of Sunday entries, and in cycling through the lanes to remote village Assemblies where there would be a cordial, even a deferential, welcome.

Trouble only arose if someone was ill, not that the word 'ill' was used; 'laid aside' or even 'laid on one side' was the proper way of referring to it. There was always great rancour if a Brother was asked to fill in. Any idea of the Lord's Will went overboard, and the substitute would allude to himself bitterly as a stopgap, often from the pulpit itself.

From time to time there was controversy as to how the Oversight should be addressed on an envelope. (In the letter itself there was no problem; you just started 'Dear Brethren in Christ Jesus'.) It was the nearest approach to an intellectual argument the Brethren engaged in. The accepted version was 'The Oversight Brethren, The

Gospel Hall etc.', but a sophisticated member of the Exeter Meeting once pointed out that this was not correct; it should be the Overseeing Brethren. Strangely enough, this was received appreciatively, but, although when the letters arrived everyone looked curiously at 'The Overseeing Brethren' and said, 'Well, 'tis right really, you know,' no one ever followed suit.

The lines of the Gospel Meeting were rigidly defined – hymn, prayer, hymn, Bible Reading, hymn, Gospel Address, hymn, prayer – and I never knew this procedure departed from. The aim of the Meeting was, of course, to save souls. The Saints all had to be present, to form a happy, confident nucleus for the sinners to join.

We lived with the fiction that sinners would attend. There were always a few hymns before the meeting, sung seated, 'while our friends are coming in'. 'Our friends' was a euphemism for the unsaved. In all my experience no sinner ever did come in, and I now wonder how the Saints would have reacted if one had. Plymouth Brethren were essentially born not made. They proselytised all their lives, distributing tracts and buttonholing strangers, but nearly always unsuccessfully. Perhaps they really preferred it so.

I myself had only a faint wish to convert sinners. My youth did not debar me from this activity; according to the books we read, children had a special aptitude for it. It was just that my zeal was always less than thorough. One Sunday morning a Brother who was getting us to look into our hearts on this matter asked us if we would be more diligent about leading the ungodly to Christ if we got a hundred pounds for every soul that was saved. I felt my face lighting up. I knew *I* would, and I could not help taking the idea as a wonderful suggestion instead of a hypothesis that should have brought me to shame.

But proselytising was not the only reason for the presence of the Saints at the Gospel Meeting. When I protested early in life that I had *been* saved and that there was no need for me to attend, I had it explained to me that it did people good to hear the message of salvation again and again; it built them up spiritually. Later on I heard one Brother use the expression 'the feeding gospel', which summed it up very well.

At one point in my life, when I was about six, I think, I went through a period of being terrified at the Gospel Meeting, as the accounts of Hell were very vivid, not so much the descriptions of the flames, which in any case could not hold the horror they were meant to for a child with chilblains and a poor circulation brought up in an icy little house in the country, as the notion of being left on my own, cut off from God and the Saints. The Meeting started at six-thirty, but it always seemed very late at night with the darkness pressing against the windows – I do not remember the summer evenings – and in a panic I got saved every Sunday, trying frantically to go through the process thoroughly and in a way which would leave no loophole, though the mechanics of 'believing on the Lord Jesus Christ' and accepting his offer of salvation were like catching a train in a nightmare.

Gradually I became more secure and more complacent, and on the whole I really enjoyed the Gospel Meetings. I liked the harmonium, which was played with agility and dash by a rota of Sisters. No musical instrument was used in the more rarefied Morning Meeting; some Brother with a good ear gave us the pitch and started us off. I liked the singing, too, preferring the hymns themselves to those used at the Breaking of Bread. The morning hymns were doctrinal and crammed with obscure references to Old Testament ritual, and, though the book was called *Hymns of Light and Love*, they seemed very dry and full of notions. One which started 'Through thy precious body broken' had alternating refrains of 'Inside the Veil' and 'Outside the Camp'.

In the evening we used Sankey's *Sacred Songs and Solos*, which I loved. This resourceful collection included hymns for every occasion, but most of the sections were denied to us, for one reason or another: 'God the Son: His Birth', because any celebration of Christmas was Popish; the last two parts of 'God the Son: His Humiliation, Resurrection and Glory', because any celebration of Easter was Popish; 'Public Worship: Songs of Praise', because the tone was too inclusive and too social; 'Public Worship: The Lord's Day', because the Brethren's idea of how to spend Sunday could not be admitted to correspond with any other sect's, and 'Public Worship: The Lord's Supper', because we had the special book for that.

Many individual hymns were also out of the question, as being too obviously Anglican: 'Praise, my soul, the King of Heaven', 'O worship the King'. Others, though acceptable in tone and general subject-matter, contained heresies, for example, 'My Jesus, I love Thee, I know Thou art mine', the third verse of which ran:

I will love Thee in life, I will love Thee in death,
And praise Thee as long as Thou lendest me breath;
And say when the death-dew lies cold on my brow,
'If ever I loved Thee, my Jesus, 'tis now.'

This was quite unorthodox, as no one could be sure he would die: the Second Coming might take place first. As another and right-minded hymn put it:

> I know not when my Lord may come;
> I know not how or where:
> If I shall pass the vale of death,
> Or 'meet him in the air'.

So we were left with a very small proportion of Sankey's thousand-odd hymns, but this was rather suitable; as a clique we accepted only the choice and the hand-picked from what was offered to us. And Sankey's, when weeded, was aggressively orthodox; its version of 'Onward Christian Soldiers', for example, was the very one we were allowed to sing ourselves:

> Onward, Christian soldiers, marching as to war,
> Looking unto Jesus, who has gone before.

It would have been an extremity of Popish error to have the cross of Jesus going on before.

In the hymns that we *were* allowed to sing there was much that was rich and splendid. 'Heaven Anticipated' was a very popular section. A dazzling light shone on the far side of the river, and in it swam incoherently a number of recognisable glittering objects: golden streets, jasper gates, shining hosts, a white throne and a crystal sea. On this side of the valley there was darkness, with mists, shadows and gloomy valleys. But there was no doubt at all that we could and would pass from one to the other. The time would probably be sunset. The Lord would not only welcome but congratulate us, and the eyes of our loved ones, radiant like everything else, would beam a greeting, and we should be more delighted to see them than we had ever been in life. The whole conception was authenticated by more swimming, glittering, recognisable objects: phrases from the Old and New Testaments, often incomprehensible in their original context but significant and evocative here.

> Some day the silver cord will break
> And I no more as now shall sing;
> But oh, the joy when I shall wake
> Within the palace of the King.

> *And I shall see ... Him face to face ...*
> *And tell the story – Saved by grace.*
> *And I shall see ... Him face to face*
> *And tell the story – Saved by grace.*

Another much-used section was 'The Gospel: Invitation', and through these hymns straggled a procession of weary, footsore men and women, laden with burdens, hungry, broken-hearted and branded with shame. These were the sinners. They wandered everywhere, on lonely seas, through mazes and especially over the mountains. The call that went out to them echoed across barren tracks and shot through the roar of tempests.

> 'Whosoever will! Whosoever will!'
> Send the proclamation over vale and hill.
> 'Tis a loving Father calls the wanderer home.
> 'Whosoever will may come!'

They were enticed with ideas of homecoming, with open doors, harbour bells and banquets. Some hymns became too specific, saying, for example, that the invitations to the feast were in red as they were written with the blood of the Lamb, but the majority depended on the diffused symbolism of hearth and home and rest, and induced the most potent nostalgia in the saved if not in the sinners.

The next section 'Warning and Entreaty' began to get frightening as there was more spirit in the warning than in the entreaty:

> Time is gliding swiftly by,
> Death and judgement draweth nigh,
> To the arms of Jesus fly:
>   Be in time!
> Oh, I pray you count the cost,
> Ere the fatal line be crossed,
> And your soul in hell be lost:
>   Be in time!

My deep fear that it was later than anyone realised was brought to the surface by hymns like this one, and reinforced by the assertion of all of them that there was nothing to be done except . . . nothing. This was sometimes illustrated from Old Testament history:

> 'Twas vain for Israel bitten
> By serpents on their way
> To look to their own doing
> That awful plague to stay;
> The only means for healing,
> When humbled in the dust
> Was of the Lord's revealing –
> It was not Try, but Trust!

and so one was left with the weird and desperate gymnastics of trusting.

Action was sometimes permissible, however: when fighting the forces of evil, for example. The section 'Conflict and Victory' was very heartening and extrovert. The military imagery was comfortingly familiar, too, as we both saw and heard it frequently elsewhere: in visits to churches with war-stained banners; in loyal exhortations about King and Country. So it was invigorating and releasing to sing:

> Only an armour-bearer, yet may I share
> Glory immortal, and a bright crown wear.
> If in the battle to my trust I'm true
> Mine shall be the honours of the Grand Review.
>
> *Hear ye the battle-cry! 'Forward' the call.*
> *See, see the faltering ones, backward they fall.*
> *Surely my Captain may depend on me*
> *Though but an armour-bearer I may be.*

And while we were standing by our Captain he was standing by us; though the metaphor changed, the meaning was clear. 'Divine Protection and Guidance' supplied us with soothing images of shelter and enclosure: God was a man who surrounded us with his arms, a rock in whose cleft we could hide, a bird that covered us with his wings, a shepherd who tucked us up into a fold, a shadow that covered us in the heat.

I did not listen to the sermons if I felt like daydreaming, but when I did listen I enjoyed them too. The Brethren certainly were eloquent. Their style was rather windy, and they fell back on tricks like calling the ageing Peter 'this grand old man', plumping out 'now' into 'this present moment of time' and 'us all' into 'each and every one of us' and shamelessly repeating the text in what would otherwise have been a pause; one Brother popped in 'And God saw that it was good, very, very good' at the end of every third or fourth sentence. But they never dried up or lost the inspiration, and I saw nothing wrong or irritating in their mannerisms; I welcomed them.

Both the Morning Meeting and the Gospel Meeting were attended principally by adults. I cannot remember any other children there at all, but there must have been some, though it was a fact that the Brethren were not very fruitful. But we felt much more at home in these meetings than at the Sunday School which every Assembly held in the afternoon. As children of the elect we did not fit in very well with the unsaved, which is what most of the scholars were assumed to be, and our rather genteel manners marked us out from the rumbustious youth of Exmouth, especially the boys. They seemed very wild and unregenerate to me, though I enjoyed the jokes from afar.

There was a hymn, the chorus of which ran:

> Throw out the lifeline
> Throw out the lifeline
> Someone is drifting away-hay.
> Throw out the lifeline
> Throw out the lifeline
> Someone is drifting today.

It was greatly in demand, not so much because it was a good tune or because we lived by the sea and many of our ancestors had drowned without a lifeline, but so that the boys could bellow their version of it: 'Joe Pine is drifting away-hay' and 'Joe Pine is drifting today'. Joe Pine was a member of the Sunday School, but I never knew whether he was a drifter or a natural butt, or whether it was just that his name fitted the rhythm. I did not aspire to be teased like that.

The School was divided into classes, but there was usually an address to which everybody was supposed to listen. I remember with amazement the stories which speakers seemed to think were suitable for children. Once a Brother was reminding us that though we were young we might die at any minute. This did not startle me, as I was used to the theme and in any case was something of a hypochondriac, but his illustrative story did. A little boy developed a lump on top of his head, and, as the days went by, it grew and grew until it was as big as the head itself. At last it burst, and the contents of it ran down over his face and he died. The boys shouted with laughter at the dénouement of this story and were told off.

All the talks to the Sunday School were evangelical, but occasionally the effort was intensified, as when a visiting Brother of known persuasive powers was enlisted. One afternoon Mr Sellers of Tunbridge Wells, a grey-haired glamorous man, spoke enchantingly about salvation. Afterwards he and Mr Jones, the head of the Sunday School, stood waiting to advise anyone who felt like being saved, and in fact a great many scholars went up to them. One was Cynthia Boswell, who for some time shared a desk with me at the Council School, and she gave me her account of it next day when we were supposed to be reading *Uncle Tom's Cabin*. She had sensibly made a beeline for Mr Sellers; Mr Jones was too well-known, too humdrum. Another girl had got there simultaneously, but Mr Sellers, according to Cynthia, had said firmly to this rival, 'You go over to Mr Jones. He'll save you. *I'm* going to save *this* little girl.' The nature of Cynthia's interest in God's plan of salvation was so clear, even to me, that I can have had no good motive in repeating the story verbatim to my mother, as I did that evening. My mother was furiously angry, because, she said, it was wicked of Cynthia to speak as though humans could save other humans. Only God could save.

Every summer there was a School Treat. The Exmouth Assembly usually chose Bicton Park. This was not very far away, just the other side of Budleigh Salterton in fact, but older Saints pointed to the ambitiousness of the outing as a sign of the times: *they* only got as far as Orcombe for theirs *and* thoroughly enjoyed it. Now that Bicton Park is open to the public I know the grounds to be magnificent, but I had a limited vision then, and they seemed to consist of an ordinary field with stalls set up for tea – plates of food with a tall urn at each end looking like a windbreak – and Sisters fussing.

There were organised games, some rather difficult to follow as the Brethren made them up. One my father invented was a puzzling mixture of riddles and horseplay, which ended up with the girls guessing and the boys thumping each other. One feature of the Treats that was always a success was when a Brother came on to the field dressed in an old coat on which were sewn about fifty bags of sweets. When he was spotted he started running, immediately pursued by a yelling pack who soon got near enough to grab and tear. In the end he fell down, not always voluntarily, and they gathered above him, plucking savagely and finally. The memory of this writhing figure having pieces torn off it troubles me now, but I took it for granted then, though I always held back.

There were two regular weeknight services, the Prayer Meeting and the Bible Reading, but we hardly ever went to these, at first because of bedtime and later because of homework. Logically I suppose that study of the Lord's Word should have come before study of French and Geography, but fortunately my mother's wish for us to get on, by means of education, was stronger than her religious principles. Of course, we occasionally went to Prayer Meeting, in the holidays, for example, and it was here I observed the extempore method breaking down sometimes, owing to people having their eyes shut most of the time, either in prayer or sleep. Most of the Brethren worked very hard indeed all day, and when they sat down in the evening drifted from prayer to sleep and back again in a very natural way. This meant that quite often two Brethren would find themselves on their feet praying aloud simultaneously, especially as most of them started with a subdued 'O God, Our Heavenly Father' and rose to full pitch only after a sentence or two.

The Plymouth Brethren sent out missionaries, though perhaps 'sent out' is hardly accurate, as they were not financially responsible for them, nor did they in any way influence the working of the Call.

The Call was what Brethren, and Sisters too, kept back though they were in other respects, received when God wished them to become missionaries, and the correct response, uttered aloud by many, according to their later reminiscences, was 'Lord, here am I. Send me.' For many years I lived in intermittent dread of hearing the Call (a groundless fear, as Mother would certainly have shouted it down), but I never did, though I actually saw others doing so. Often at the end of a Fellowship Meeting, a missionary home on furlough (a word which I confused with 'furlong', which made it rather mystifying) would take the floor and ask us to meditate not on the subject of our suitability for the Mission Field — this would have been an alien, academic notion — but of our receptivity to the Call should it come. Worldly pleasure, for example, would effectively get in its way. We then sang a hymn. It was curious that the one which got the best results was nothing to do with missionary work at all. It spoke of the miseries and fatigues of this world and the return of the Lord Jesus Christ to release us.

> 'Mid danger and fear, Lord,
> I'm oft weary here, Lord.
> O hasten the day
> Of thy coming again.
> Thou art gone over there, Lord,
> A place to prepare, Lord.
> Thy joy I will share
> At thy coming again.

It was a very moving hymn, one of my favourites, and even its well-known ability to bring on the Call did not stop me enjoying it. And once I saw the lightning strike. I was sitting opposite Nellie Melhuish, a pleasant young woman in her early twenties who worked in a shoe-shop, and suddenly, in the middle of the verse I have quoted, her face, under her cloche hat, began to glow until it became so luminous that most of the Assembly noticed. Afterwards at tea I heard one Sister remarking, rather sourly, 'Well, Nellie Melhuish got the Call all right,' and everyone agreed. She never in fact did go to the Mission Field; I have no idea what went wrong.

The part of the Field which most Brethren missionaries chose, or rather were guided to, was some Roman Catholic country. The tradition of Protestantism was very strong indeed in the Assemblies and showed itself in many interesting ways. One Brother, for example, maintained that all believers should wear beards as it was the custom of Popish priests to be clean-shaven, but this did not catch on. Then there was the occasion when a Roman Catholic service was to be broadcast on a Sunday evening. At that time the wireless was on the whole considered a tool of the Devil. Several Brethren were in fact weakening, but they usually hid the apparatus when stricter Brethren called. Who, therefore, was brave enough or artful enough to convey the news that a transmission was to take place is a puzzle, but conveyed it was and badly received. Brother Jelfs went so far as to suggest getting up a Prayer Meeting to ask God that the wireless should break down, but, to do them justice, most of the Saints would not support him. One Brother even laughed.

Anti-Catholicism almost certainly affected our vocabulary too. The popular word among us for 'to fart' was 'to pope', which probably was not solely onomatopoeic. So it is not surprising that the heathen in his blindness selected for the missionaries by the Holy Ghost was a Roman Catholic heathen, who bowed down to wood and stone not in the shape of totem-poles and fetishes, but of images of the Virgin Mary and the so-called Saints.

The missionaries worked on what were known as Faith Lines, that is, they had no assured sum of money coming from anywhere. When funds were running low they prayed, and help arrived, usually by the next post. It really did seem to work; I never heard of a missionary having to come home. The Assembly which the missionary left was, of course, concerned for his welfare, or at least survival, and collections were taken up from time to time, but spasmodically. The Sisters supported him with sewing; they had a weekly meeting for that purpose called the Dorcas Meeting, named after a member of the Early Church, mentioned in the New Testament for her helpful needlework. They worked hard and turned out a complete range of garments from rompers for the Roman Catholic babies to over-practical aprons for the missionary's daughters.

In summer a regular activity of most Assemblies was the Open Air, a kind of Gospel Meeting which took place out of doors at some strategic point on Lord's Day evenings after the six-thirty service. The proceedings were an etiolated version of what the Salvation Army did so well; we had no band, no uniforms, no bravura, and no record of social work or heroism in tough spots to make us popular. We must have put up a very ragged and unalluring show, though there was more organisation than in the Morning Meeting and more variety than in the Evening Meeting; there were several speakers, who had been specially asked to join in, and any famous visiting Brother would certainly be invited beforehand to take part. Even so the extempore element encouraged at most Meetings kept breaking in. There was, for example a middle-aged tough-looking ex-seaman called Cooky, who could never resist any mention of China; he had been saved there, and, whenever the country was alluded to, which with visiting Brethren happened surprisingly often — the local Brethren kept off the subject — he pressed forward as soon as the speaker had finished, to tell in a joyful bellow the ever-marvellous story of how one desperate evening long ago in China, 'HEEE found MEEE.' I liked Cooky and his contributions.

It may sound rather an ordeal, this attempt on the part of about thirty people, with no props or costumes, to impose themselves on the inattentive, scornful or even hostile population of a town, but no one seemed embarrassed or nervous. The Brethren were as confidently voluble as when in their safe Gospel Halls. The Sisters who swelled the group and helped on the singing with their loud, scooping voices, looked quite matter-of-fact. I felt no embarrassment myself. It was mostly in Torquay that we attended the Open Air, therefore no school friends were likely to go past, and they were the only people I knew who thought differently from my parents and the Brethren. It was thought desirable for believers' children to go to the Open Air, so that they could testify by their presence. I suppose what they were really testifying to was the might of parental authority; having made this act of submission myself I had no other feelings that I can recall. No doubt passers-by jeered, but it was not their approval that I wanted; it was the approval of the group of which I was already securely a member.

Torquay was more zealous in the Open Air than Exmouth. It had more holiday-makers to be converted and also more suitable places to convert them in. Babbacombe Downs, the grassy cliff-top above Oddicombe Beach, was a favourite spot, though the lustiest singing and preaching tended to get blown away from time to time. Worldly, watery noises came echoing up attractively from the beach, suggesting the last bathe or the last boat-trip of a fine summer evening. The seagulls, high above the cove though on a level with us, screamed distractingly throughout, especially, it seemed, in pauses between the verses of a hymn.

Wall's Hill was another regular setting, an impressive tract of downland above a promontory called Hope's Nose, much wilder than Babbacombe Downs, which had a bandstand, seats and flower-beds. The Fair came to Wall's Hill every year at Regatta time. Its arrival was the source of a typical and perennial piece of Brethren illogic. We were allowed to visit the Fair and buy the excellent bright-pink nougat they sold – 'nugget' we called it – but not to patronise it in any other way. When I complained at not being allowed to go on the roundabouts, my mother told me I could hardly do so if I was going to attend the Open Air which was being held on the fairground the following Sunday. I could not see this;

it seemed to me that as my presence at the Open Air would not aim at persuading the Fair people not to go on their own roundabouts, it would not be inconsistent to go on them myself. I lacked the courage to say this, but it was clear in my mind and remained for years a point of conscious, though secret, rebellion against the Brethren, the very thin end of what was to be a very large wedge.

The Brethren's point of view was based on the assumption that what went on at Fairs was enticingly and luridly immoral; going on the roundabouts, therefore, would identify one with evil courses, even though eating their nougat apparently would not. Most of the Open Air, when it took place, consisted of the Brethren's making rude remarks about the Fair people's way of life. One Brother used to single out the mascots they sold for special ridicule, abusing their superstition for quarter of an hour at a time. The Fair people either did not listen at all or listened with indifference. There was never any reaction. Once a woman tipped a bucket of unbelievably smelly urine out of her caravan door on to the grass just as Brother Hocking was going on about lucky charms, but I got the impression it was a coincidence.

Each Gospel Hall had a slightly different way of doing things; one Assembly in Torquay, Warren Road, believed in moving from place to place in the course of the Open Air, with one speaker at each of the four or five vantage-points, the shapeless procession singing as it moved. There were several obvious drawbacks to this, which I imagine most people felt, such as getting tired and looking silly — this *was* embarrassing — but there was no difficulty about the choice of hymn for the procession. The great majority of Sankey's were conceived in terms of journeying. They saw the movements of the believer not as restless but as a progress, and his life as a steady though arduous advance from place to place, by land:

> Then let our songs abound
> And every tear be dry;
> We're marching through Immanuel's ground
> To fairer worlds on high.

by sea:

> Must I be carried to the skies
> On flowery beds of ease,
> While others fought to win the prize
> And sailed through bloody seas?

and, *in extremis*, by air:

> Till, from Mount Pisgah's lofty height
> I view my home and take my flight...
> And shout, while passing through the air,
> 'Farewell, farewell, sweet hour of prayer.'

Paignton did things in the greatest style. Their Open Airs were held on the Green, a fine expanse of grass just inland from the promenade, and they had a collapsible rostrum which two Brethren used to lug down from a hotel owned by a member of the Paignton Assembly bitterly envied for his wealth.

The social life of the Brethren took place mostly in the Gospel Halls, hardly ever in the private houses of the Saints, who were not much given to entertaining, and the highlight of the social year was the series of Fellowship Meetings which began with the better weather every spring. (The Fellowship Meetings at Exeter, the big city, could, of course, be held at any time, but for country districts comparatively good weather was essential.) Each Assembly in turn would act as host to all the neighbouring ones, and it was a great occasion for the personalities of the district to make an appearance and go through their paces. There would always be Brother Norcombe, the grocer, whose son was a backslider and living with a married woman to prove it, Brother Muggeridge, retired, who wore a ginger wig and was said to be much richer than he let on, and Brother Slee, the schoolmaster, who worshipped with the Barton Brethren at the prefabricated hut called Hebron, with his dashing suntan and incisive London voice, so different from our slovenly drawling, in everything showing the gifts of leadership which in the Second World War, when a stray plane was machine-gunning the gasometer near Hebron, enabled him to guide the Assembly to safety with vigorous cries of 'Under the seats, Brethren and Sisters. Under the seats.'

It was exciting to watch the Saints gathering from railway station and bus-stop, to see the cycling Brethren wobbling or wheeling round the corner with their neat caps and clips, to see the glowing, gasping Brethren who had come on foot.

I remember the Fellowship Meetings by a composite picture made up of invariable factors: the goodwill and sociability, the warmth inside, usually with bluebottles droning, and the bright day outside, the smelly privies labelled 'Sisters' across a back yard, and the tea. Before what was obviously going to be the last prayer — anyone brought up on extempore worship has an infallible instinct about such things — the Sisters of the Assembly acting as host tiptoed out, and discreet sounds could be heard coming from behind a closed door where all the arcane activities of the Saints went on, the counting up of the collection, the unpacking of the non-alcoholic wine for the Morning Meeting, the rubbing down of those who had undergone total immersion and the preparing of the Fellowship teas. Sometimes there would be a cackle of laughter followed by shushing. When the last prayer was over, they reappeared in flowered aprons, still with their hats on, of course, carrying plates of the local buns, called chudleighs, and seed-cake.

It was at this moment that two Brethren took up their places at the back of the room, holding the largest white jugs I have ever seen, filled with hot tea. As grace was said they bowed their heads reverently into the steam, but lifted them quickly at the closing words '. . . in the name of Jesus Christ our Lord. Amen' in order to utter hospitable shouts of 'Tea with sugar' and 'Tea without sugar' respectively. They were so ready that often 'Tea with sugar' overlapped ' . . . our Lord. Amen.'

What was said at the Fellowship Meetings – hours and hours of discourse, as there was another session after tea – I cannot really say, as I seldom listened. These were opportunities for prolonged daydreaming, invaluable practice in shutting out sounds. But I suppose it was Morning Meeting material, tempered to a holiday mood. One of the addresses that I do remember, by Brother Shaw, had as its theme: 'the Bath, the Basin, the Bosom [pronounced booosom] and the Badge.' Though the format was more playful than would have been seemly at the Breaking of Bread, it was not as skittish as it may sound. The booosom was Jesus Christ's, and the basin the one in which he washed the disciples' feet. I cannot now identify the bath and the badge, but they would have been spiritual emblems of some sort.

There was pleasure and security in these gatherings for many years, gratification at being with the grown-ups, at feeling approved of and seeing so much good temper. There was real human interest and opportunity for hero-worship. And often there were incidental treats, as when the Meeting was at Stoke Fleming, which involved a ferry-ride from Kingswear to Dartmouth and a cliff-top walk. But later there must have been the most terrible boredom. What makes me think so is that one day, when Sheila and I were both at Exmouth Grammar School, my mother told us with a furious assumption of incredulity that the mother of some of our friends had asked if we could spend the Saturday with her girls, as otherwise, Mrs Tucker had gathered from us, we would have to go with our parents to a Fellowship Meeting in Exeter, and she wanted to spare us this dreadful ordeal. We must have spoken in these terms, though, of course, we weakly denied it to our mother. She brushed aside the denial, demanding something much more in the way of an avowal. 'Don't you *want* to hear more about the Lord Jesus?' she asked, and neither of us could say 'No', not only through fear, but also because at that stage it would not have been quite true.

Throughout my childhood I took the Plymouth Brethren completely for granted. I was in my teens before anything external happened to shake my acceptance of them and my assumption that either the whole world was like them or that it ought to be. I can remember two incidents particularly which began to rouse me from this attitude. The first was when a schoolmistress teaching Scripture said very kindly, apropos of a certain point of theology, 'Now the Plymouth Brethren believe that . . .', gave an accurate summary of Brethren doctrine, and then went on to give some perfectly sensible views of quite a different nature, held by other sects. The second was when, after great screwing up of courage, I asked a schoolfriend if she was saved. I expected a dramatic reaction of some kind – offence, hardness of heart, scorn, shy acknowledgement – but she only said, again very kindly, 'Oh, do you have that at your church?'

CHAPTER FOUR

Playtime, Break, Recess

WITH regard to education we were marked out from the start. We did not go to school at the age of five, but were taught at home by my mother. Withycombe Infants was thought to be too tough, and the walk into Exmouth was out of the question until we were old enough for the Council School in Exeter Road.

I remember nothing of the lessons at home except the regular visits of an attendance officer who came to check that we really were being taught. He never questioned us, so I hardly know how he satisfied himself about our progress. I suppose it was a routine call, and obviously he knew that Mother was a teacher. He had one black hand. I imagine he had had an artificial arm fitted after a war injury, and had covered the part of it that came out of the sleeve in a perpetual glove, but it seems odd that he should have chosen a brilliantly black one. You could see it from a long way off. I know because I once met him in the lanes and was frightened, though he was only going for a stroll with his family.

Even after a year or so of home education we were still considered too tender for Withycombe Infants, and the next alternative to it was Mrs Brooker's. This was a kindergarten organised in a private house in Lyndhurst Road, half-way between Withycombe and Exmouth. The only memorable thing about it was that Mrs Brooker was a Roman Catholic. As always, when there was a clash between my mother's religious principles and her plans for our education, the latter won. But I think that in this case the conflict must have been painful, for at this period she used frequently to remark, with impressive daring, that, when the time came, we might well find several Roman Catholics in Heaven.

Certainly we were safe enough from any proselytising at Mrs Brooker's. The only piece of Popish mummery she ever imposed on us was, in morning prayers, to get us to leave out 'for Thine is the kingdom, the power and the glory' at the end of the Lord's Prayer. But this did not really distress my mother, not on the grounds that in fact Jesus Christ himself stopped at 'Deliver us from evil' just like Mrs Brooker, instead of adding 'for Thine is the kingdom', but because no Plymouth Brother would defend or put much weight on any set form of words, even Our Lord's.

At last, when our legs were considered strong enough, our traffic sense sufficiently developed and our training not to speak to strangers thoroughly established – years later than in the case of most children from the village – we went to the Council School. It was just along the Exeter Road from the Gospel Hall, a single-storey, red-brick building, with the emphasis entirely on the roof, which was large, gabled and intricately decorated with fancy tiles. There was a small yard in front, used for nothing except for the teachers to come in by, and a big playground at the back with lavatories at the far end. 'The Council School' was regarded as an up-to-date name for it. In the old days it would have been called the Board School, as I gathered from a joke my mother used to tell: 'I go to the Board School.' 'Oh, really? Ours is made of brick.'

It was now that the long, continuous and successful run of my free education began, with its ambition, its top-of-the-class, its scholarships and its examples to the other children. With my rigidity, my respect for authority, my bookishness and my anxieties, I was admirably fitted to be a teacher's pet, a swot, a conformer, and to profit as no rebel could have done from the educational methods of those days.

What went on in Exmouth Council School was probably similar to the procedure in comparable schools all over the country in that decade. We were quiet and well-disciplined; we kept to our desks, put up our hands and answered questions. We were given little opportunity to think and no encouragement to do so. The timetable was divided strictly into subjects, and in no subject was there any sense of discovery. The more quickly we mastered a few accepted ideas the better we did. I mastered them all with outstanding speed and did very well.

In Arithmetic we worked sums so unreal that even when the average age of an imaginary class came out to be 107 no one noticed it was odd, and to the teacher it was not odd, merely wrong. We did measurement, sitting in our desks. Why feet and inches were so called and why anyone had ever felt the need for standard measurements had nothing to do with it. There were twelve inches in a foot and three feet in a yard; you were praised for knowing it, and that was that. We learnt the multiplication tables by means of a sort of drill in the yard. Each item of the tables had a different physical routine which we went through as we chanted. 'Seven sevens are forty-nine', for example, had three skips and a clap.

In History, by some reorganisation of the curriculum, we did the Tudors two years running, from tatty books which illustrated everything and explained nothing, so that as a companion piece to the pictures of the Court of Star Chamber and Lambert Simnel which were really there, I still see Cardinal Morton in my mind's eye wielding a two-pronged pitchfork. My knowledge of the basic dates of the period, however, is wonderfully sound and in fact has stood me in very good stead in further studies. I remember absolutely nothing of Geography except the pretty chant 'Sheep, goats and esparto grass', which moved about isolated in my head, unconnected with any country, but which either by rhythm or content appealed to my imagination.

English, as far as I can remember, consisted of learning poetry by heart and writing compositions. I did both with exceptional ease. I can hear myself now reciting *Abou Ben Adhem*, a vivid memory because of the theological conflict it had caused. My mother, who heard me learning it, regarded it as a wicked poem. The hero's modest claim that, though he did not love God, yet he could be written down as one who loved his fellow men, had resulted in a revised catalogue in which 'lo! Ben Adhem's name led all the rest', and this was the most heinous heresy, as only the saving blood of Jesus could get anyone's name on any list that really counted. To the Plymouth Brethren love of one's fellow men was in itself suspect. She did not forbid me to learn or recite the poem, but I felt terribly torn while doing so.

The chief point of Composition was not to express oneself but to write neatly and to spell and punctuate correctly. The material was a blackboardful of further received ideas. The only criterion governing the choice of subject – naturally it was prescribed – seemed to be that it should have nothing whatever to do with our experience or interest. 'A Trip in an Aeroplane' was an excellent example, as no one in the school, teacher or pupil, had ever flown. (One summer a biplane came and did five-shilling hops from one field to another off the Salterton Road, but, although most of us watched, no one went on it, and it did not seem particularly real.) So was 'The Beach in Winter'; nobody went near the sea except in the summer months. And as for 'An Autumn Walk', this was a topic on which country children of our day and class were quite inarticulate and unobservant;

we did buds in Nature, but few of us knew an oak from an ash in real life. However no direct perception was required. A list of appropriate words and phrases was written on the blackboard after a perfunctory pretence at class discussion: 'terra firma', 'mournful billows' and 'russet hues' would see you through. Indeed you would not get very far without them and their kind. It was a warning to me when Cynthia Boswell was openly ridiculed for putting in a composition on 'A Fire' 'The firemen looked lovely in their helmets.'

Possibly the most revealing incident of all with regard to the true nature of our education occurred after we had taken the Scholarship and heard the results. Miss Webster got together the girls who had passed and said that as we would be starting French at the Grammar School she thought it would be a good idea if a Mrs Read, who lived nearby, came in to give us a smattering of the language before we left the Council School, so that when the moment came we would know what the teacher was talking about.

These methods suited me so well that I sometimes wonder what I should have done had they been more progressive and modern. I should have been quite at a loss and certainly not top of the class. I feel now that I might even have had a sort of breakdown.

But after all we were in the late twenties and early thirties, and theories of education were beginning to change, if not yet in Devon, at least elsewhere. From time to time we had hints of approaching reforms, and some of the things we did were quite in the new mode. Reading round the class was out, for example; we had group reading instead. There was a great deal of dramatisation. In a scripture lesson I was one of the attendants of the Queen of Sheba, and we walked colourlessly across the room behind her, waited aimlessly while she mumbled, 'The half hath not been told me', turned round and walked back again. This may not have brought anything much home to anybody, but I suppose it was better than just sitting at one's desk or repeating the story. And although we had the sort of drill lesson that started with 'Toe the line' – I always heard it as 'Toll the line' which was more interesting – there was the livelier swing of Morris Dancing and Sword Dancing as well.

We sang frequently, with complete lack both of comprehension and of wish to comprehend. I did not marvel that someone in a cauld blast, which sounded like a cross between a cauldron and a blast furnace, could be sheltered by a plaidie, for who knew what that might be? Many of the songs were loyal and patriotic – 'God bless the Prince of Wales' was a great favourite – as we were carefully trained in notions of King and Empire, and a surprising number were Irish.

The two teachers whose classes I was in, from eight to nine, and from nine to ten, were Miss England and Miss Britain. Their names were regarded mildly as an example of pleasant coincidence, not with the hilarity they would certainly have inspired had those been the days of Beauty Queen contests. (We had a Carnival Queen every year, a schoolgirl, but she was not Miss Exmouth, merely Beryl Matthews from the Council, or whatever it was.) They were dedicated teachers, and I was very fond of both of them and very happy in their classes. I suppose they were young women. They both came from small towns on the Exeter–Exmouth line, Miss Britain from Topsham and Miss England from Lympstone. While I was at the Council School Miss England bought a motorbike and a leather coat to go with it, which was genuinely dashing in those days.

Miss Britain was the prettier of the two and the more capable of throwing you into delightful confusion. It was exciting to know that her name was Sophie – I never knew Miss England's – and, when I had gone up into her form I chose seasonal presents for her with greater care than I had for Miss England. I remember an Easter egg in the selection of which I was deeply involved. I half imagined that she would eat a piece of it while sitting on the lavatory, which was always a great treat of my own, but was old enough to dismiss the idea as absurd. She had a fine set of brilliant white teeth, which she brushed after every meal, not just at night.

Her great interest was Country Dancing. She competed at County Festivals and nearly always got a good criticism even when she did not win. One adjudicator said she moved her arms rather stiffly and not in co-ordination with the rest of her body, but we could not see it and did not much like hearing it. She naturally introduced a great deal of Country Dancing into her own class timetable. I loved it; with prescribed figures and steps I felt safe and could really let myself go within the discipline. Sellenger's Round, Gathering Peascods, Black Nag and Brighton Camp are still stirring names and tunes to me, and I can hear the long exciting note of the tinny wind-up gramophone which warned us to be ready to start into the pattern of setting, turning singles, arming, siding and leading down the middle.

Dancing was, of course, strictly forbidden by the Plymouth Brethren, but Country Dancing did not count. In the first place it did not happen in a Dance Hall; not even a Saint could have imagined anything heady about the village halls, schoolrooms and playgrounds which were its customary setting. Secondly, it did not involve tempting décolleté clothes; if anything, Country Dancers looked dowdier than usual when engaged in their hobby. And thirdly, hobby was the operative concept; it was not done for sexual reasons. The symbolism of the Sword Dance escaped us all.

Often there were huge Country Dancing rallies. I remember an enormous one which filled the whole field down by the Plantation. The grass was covered with sets, the music blared, and I had to dance with half-shut eyes and great concentration, as the vistas and avenues of siding, arming dancers gave me a sort of lateral giddiness. One Saturday we went to Powderham Castle on the other side of the river. I had always admired their park from the train because of the deer.

The Headmistress of the Council School was Miss Webster, who was respectfully said to be mad. She was certainly irrational and eccentric, but such qualities have been found in the greatest Heads, and the school seemed well organised and harmonious; the staff stayed for years and the pupils did well. Her wild, plunging personality made a particular impression in Morning Assembly, which went on a long time, often until Mary Jones fainted, and which always had something new, some act, some weird piece of information, some bizarre advice. It was a one-woman performance, often including snatches of singing and dancing. In everything that was said or done there was something strange to arrest the attention.

One morning the Scholarship results had arrived, and Miss Webster announced that those who had passed would come on in a procession in front of the assembled school while we sang a hymn for them, one which might have been written with them in mind. They walked in simpering, and we sang 'Who are these like stars appearing?' So far, quite fitting. But the hymn went on to describe the mental and physical agonies of the early Christian martyrs,

> Sore with woe and anguish tried
> Who in prayer full oft have striven
> With the God they glorified,

and concluded by showing their final triumph:

> Now in God's most holy place
> Blest they stand before his face.

Such words applied to a bunch of ten- and eleven-year-olds who had done a few sums right and written a nice little composition on 'The Woods in Spring' should, I suppose, have seemed a heartless exaggeration, but in her own way Miss Webster had hit on the truth. The Scholarship meant so much in those days that it involved at least something of the striving, the heartburning and the dedication of Early Christians. It was the chance to be better than our parents, a fact which our parents were the first to realise and impress on us, it was the chance to be better than our friends, an opportunity to escape from the country, from provincialism, from serving in shops or houses, from the airs and patronage of the local gentry. It was the way out, the way to middle-class jobs and middle-class friends.

I think nearly all the fathers and mothers of our schoolfellows felt like this, but my own parents felt it most acutely. For my father it was not only the way out, but the way back, to the status the Beers had had in the middle of the previous century, when to become Master and part-owner of a brig was a natural step for an eldest son to take. Even girls, by means of higher education, could restore the family fortunes. For a long time, until it was very plain it was not going to happen, his ambition was that I might become a headmistress. Perhaps he felt it was the female equivalent of being a ship's captain.

For my mother it was the second and more important half of the way she had started out on herself. She had not gone far enough to be satisfied, merely to be made discontented, and at this stage of her life she gave up and handed it all over to us. Though she successfully gave the impression that her life was irremediably barren, I imagine, looking back on it now, that there were several things she could have done, such as attend evening classes or go in for some serious reading on her own, instead of paying resentful lip-service to the Masters, as one who had been robbed of their company for ever, while in fact reading nothing but trash. But she had a real grievance all the same. We were the first generation to whom state-provided higher education was fully available in the sense that public opinion now made it easy. It had been disastrously hard for my mother to do what it would have been difficult for us not to. We had to work for it, of course, but it was the expected thing, and we were praised for doing it.

But to return to Miss Webster's harangues at Assembly: a typical one was a blackboard demonstration of how a drink of water before breakfast would ward off constipation. She never stood still at Assembly – indeed I remember her as positively running up and down – and a blackboard perfectly suited her darting style. On this occasion she drew a piece of intestine and then with quick chalk strokes indicated more and more food falling down into it while it swelled and swelled. When it was packed solid, and constipation was before our very eyes, she sent down a round pill. This seemed to do it. She rubbed out the food, but unfortunately the intestine was left baggily distended; it could not spring back. But now came the picture of a new intestine and of a glass of water, which every morning before breakfast washed the food along, smoothly and cleanly, so that it never piled up.

Sometimes Miss Webster would give us a few thoughts on the use of vocabulary. At the Council School, for example, we said 'playtime' didn't we? Those of us who won the Scholarship and went on to the Grammar School would learn to say 'break'. But at Southlands they always said 'recess'. Southlands was the local public school for girls, a source of much envy and bitterness. They would not take the daughters of tradesmen. My mother must have thought there was something in this criterion, for she frequently said to us that we could have gone to Southlands if she had had the money, for at least our father wasn't a tradesman. Miss Webster now made us chant 'playtime, break, recess', I have no idea with what purpose.

Miss Webster's concern for our bowels was matched by the care taken of every aspect of our health and well-being by the local authorities. There were few cases of under-nourishment or neglect in the school, no wizened, depraved slum-dwellers. We looked what we were, reasonably well-fed, reasonably clean and rather lethargic children, living in the good, extremely relaxing air of a small seaside town surrounded by open country.

But there was always the danger of dirty heads apparently, as Nurse Frailing was constantly on the watch. What seemed like every few weeks she would arrive and set up her apparatus in the cloakroom, bowl, combs and rubber gloves, and in twos and threes all the girls in the school were sent out to her. There she stood among the sour-smelling coats in her nurse's uniform, with an outdoor hat on and the rubber gloves, gravely and ritually lifting locks and peering. She said little, but she had a pleasant personality and seemed to rouse no resentment.

I imagine that these regular visits did not reveal anything much; nothing was said, and no one was pointed at afterwards, though this may have been from delicacy on the part of Nurse Frailing and the staff, as to have nits was regarded as a slur and a disgrace. Once, however, there was such a plague of these creatures that discretion and concealment were useless, as everyone was affected, girls from both good homes and bad. They were mysterious criminals, as none of us knew the look of them; we could not see our own heads even with mirrors, we were not confidential enough to search one another's, and some grown-up did the combing and inspecting. I had the same mental picture for them that I had for germs, except that germs were obviously better at flying. We could feel the nits crawling heavily about. This surprised me at first, as I would have expected them to scuttle. It was a most painful time for Sheila and me, as Mother, affronted, bought a sandcomb and gave us a vicious going-over every evening, making our scalps bleed. We plunged and protested, but she raked on and on.

Routine medical inspections caused little comment or reaction, as the doctor did nothing painful. The chill of the stethoscope on your chest was the worst of it. Eye-testing was quite uneventful, too, unless you had to have drops. But the visits of the school dentist roused a slaughter-house panic. Children trembled and rolled their eyes, all except those, that is, whose parents had filled in a form saying they would be consulting their own dentist privately. Sheila and I were among these fortunate few, and, although we knew it would be coming to us some time, it would be later and not in this atmosphere of blood and hysteria.

The dentist in those days did not come to school to inspect, he came to act. The chair was carried in through the side door of the playground across to the building where Domestic was taught to classes from all the neighbouring schools. The bowl and the chair were set up in an empty room, the dentist and the nurse arrived, and the guillotine started to rise and fall. Girls were called out of class and disappeared. They came back with bloody handkerchiefs which they plied for hours. Some had blood on their lips.

There was a fearful compulsiveness about it. I knew only one girl do what now seems the obvious thing. She did not cry or wet herself in the classroom. She answered the summons with calm, set off across the playground, nipped out of the side door and went home. She did not show up for two days, and, though she was then formally abused in Assembly for cowardice, by this time the dentist had gone. She was called Péronne, as her father, a war hero, had distinguished himself in that battle years before her birth.

The school had a high reputation in the town, and people took an interest in it. The age of the benefactor was not quite over, and, although we were a state school, we had two benefactors who took a very particular interest in us. They were retired gentlemen called Mr Barrow and Mr Farleigh, and they lived in large houses in the prosperous residential district up behind the Beacon. Mr Farleigh was the less personally conspicuous of the two; he was hardly more than a name, though I did once see his back as he bent over a cash-box. Whenever anything was organised which required the handling of money – fêtes, concerts, sales of work, plays – he was thanked so profusely and so repeatedly afterwards that he must have done wonders in his invisible way.

Mr Barrow was the opposite of self-effacing. He was always in and out of the classrooms, beaming, joking with the teachers and talking to the clever children. He liked us to call him Puck. He had published several boys' school stories and often presented girls who had done something outstanding with a copy of one of them, signed 'From Puck'. He came to school parties and was made a great fuss of, usually being presented with something himself. We sent him Christmas cards which we drew and painted in class; I sometimes composed verses for mine, full of sycophantic gush. One year he wrote a pageant for us, which we enjoyed doing, though it was so dense with local tradition and vocabulary – he was not a Devonian – that we had to have it explained to us first. One of the characters, a sort of sprite dressed in grey, was called Dimpsy Glim; 'dimpsy' was supposed to be a beautiful dialect word for twilight, though I never heard anyone actually use it. There were all kinds of allusions which needed long glosses. One chorus ran:

> Little Miss Maer
> Was buxom and fair
> As sweet as a Devon maid can be,
> But now she's not grand
> For she's lost all her sand
> And she pines for the tree she calls Danby.

The brook down by the Plantation, which, if we thought about it, we remembered was called the Maer, had apparently once been quite a river. Danby was a painter who had specialised in local scenery and been inspired by a tree which had since gone rotten and collapsed.

In my last year at the Council School I found myself being pushed into an extrovert role – bright girl, clown and showman all in one – which I ought not to have accepted, but it seemed irresistible at the time. It had started two years earlier with my being able to read aloud with such exceptional fluency that not only was I shown off as an example to my own form, but on one occasion I was led with my open book into a higher form to put them to shame by demonstrating how it could be done. Great weight was attached to the ability to read; it was taken as a symbol and certain indication of every other potentiality. So in Miss Britain's class, when the English lesson had taken the rather progressive form of lecturettes, it was I who had to give the lead by speaking on the topic 'Eat more Fruit', which I did with great rhetorical spirit, though having no real views on the subject except that oranges at Christmas were bitter and messy and a poor alternative to chocolates.

At this period I showed acting ability for the only time in my life. For a twelvemonth I was such a success that it took me years to realise that I had lost the knack or, rather, had never had it except by the suggestion of others. But one winter evening, while I was at the height of my powers in this respect, all the Exmouth schools collaborated in a concert given at the Town Hall. This was a great occasion. Our school contributed a short play. It was a dramatic version of the events leading up to the scene in the picture 'When did you last see your Father?' and I was the Roundhead who asked the crucial question. We got the grouping absolutely right, but our costumes were so eccentrically inaccurate that when we paused and formed a tableau at the pay-off line, as we had been told, in order to receive claps of delighted recognition, none came. It was not surprising. I, for example, was wearing a tall fur hat and a sort of dressing-gown, more like a Cossack than a Parliamentarian captain. However, we spoke up well, remembered our words and were heartily applauded at the end.

It was in the course of this evening that I received one of the roughest shocks of my life. My mother had, naturally, trained us in the belief that make-up was wicked. That is to say, she had hardly ever said so. It was such a basic belief that even to state it was to weaken it, seeming to admit other possibilities. I realised this on my own account when I was reading a book that was supposed to be edifying and a man in it said to his daughter, 'Don't let me ever catch you putting on rouge.' I was horrified; it suggested that somebody might, that she might and that perhaps he might not have been so outraged after all.

This particular cold evening when we arrived at the Hall and went into the unfamiliar labyrinth at the back of the stage, I had no sooner hung up my hat and coat than I saw in one of the rooms a sight which terrified me. Three or four girls were sitting on chairs, holding up their faces to three or four strange women who were smoothing rouge, dabbing powder and drawing lips on to them. There was a mist in the air and a sweet tempting smell, and it seemed luxuriously warm. This was evil indeed, and it was clearly going to happen to everyone taking part; I could see the girl who was the daughter in our play. I turned and ran to my mother, who had, of course, brought us and stayed with us. She was chatting vivaciously in yet another back room with some of the teachers and broke off with a very bad grace to listen to me. I explained, quite distraught, the deadly peril that was lying in wait for me and have never been so confounded as when she gave me an impatient push towards the terrible chamber and said, 'Oh, go along.' I did go along. My principles could not shine on their own; they were borrowed light. But when the time came I clamped my lips together so that as little lipstick as possible got on them.

My mother was always there, all through the Council School. Whether or not in her professional training she had met the idea of teachers being substitute parents, she was certainly on her guard against any such state of affairs. Co-parents they might be allowed to be, and, indeed, they could be very useful in such a capacity.

From the start she got to know the teachers, and Miss England and Miss Britain were soon family friends, going to the beach with us on summer Saturdays, to Point-in-View with us on fine Sundays, meeting us in the holidays. The preferential treatment this resulted in was something I did not then resent. I suppose if anything I welcomed it. The fact that Miss Britain and Miss England knew that anything unfair or severe or incompetent on their part would go straight back to my mother outweighed the fact that any misdemeanour of mine could go straight back to her too. Perhaps I realised they were less likely to tell tales than I was, and in any case with a conformist like myself there would be nothing very dreadful they could say about me.

Anything nice they said to my mother about us she

repeated as soon as they were out of the house, and this was most pleasant. One compliment which sticks in my mind for several reasons was Miss Britain's saying approvingly that Sheila and I spoke without a Devon accent. The remark, and my parents' pleasure at it, showed me for the first time that to have one was a crime and was the first murmur of one composite voice which resounded through my schooldays, culminating in the comment made when I was preparing for University entrance that I would never get far with that accent. I wonder at what point I started talking with a Devon accent. The simplest explanation is that I always did – after all it was the only accent I ever heard during my formative years – in which case Miss Britain was merely trying to be pleasant. Or perhaps 'compliments' of that sort made me unknowingly intensify my accent and subconsciously cherish it as something precious. Perhaps it was my one act of nonconformity, made possible only because I did not realise I was doing it.

Mother's friendship with the teachers meant that we could never by seeming accident step out of our Plymouth Brethren attitudes, never take advantage of a misunderstanding. The teachers knew only too well what our principles were and respected them with irritating scrupulosity. One day some intriguing cardboard clocks were being given out, and the teacher of another class was explaining to us how we had to set ours at a time of our own choosing, hand it in with a small sum of money, almost certainly in aid of the Cottage Hospital, and then wait to see at what hour a master clock ran down; the nearest would be the winner. This seemed very exciting, and I was eagerly putting out a hand for mine when Miss Britain intervened with a few tactfully muttered words to the other teacher, who with a kind and conspiratorial smile to me took the clock away. Plymouth Brethren did not go in for raffles and games of chance.

At about the same time a woman known to Mr Barrow was setting up a dancing class, and he came to school one morning to enlist support for it. He described how attendance at this class would make us dance like fairies, and walked up and down the aisles asking us individually if we did not wish to dance like fairies. I became very uneasy as he approached me. This did not sound like Country Dancing, which had nothing fairylike about it and which in any case we did already. Sure enough, Miss Britain again intervened in her tactful murmur, and I saw Puck's eyebrows rising rather crossly. Plymouth Brethren did not dance.

Every Christmas there was a school party to which my mother was invited. She delighted in doing all the undignified sporty things that you could not expect many grown-ups to do. There was one game where someone led a procession, waving one of the huge bunches of school keys which every teacher seemed to possess. The procession wove all over the room till the leader threw down the keys, at which point everyone flopped on to the floor, and the last one was out. Mother took pride in excelling at this. It was almost her favourite image of herself if I may judge from the frequency with which she used to tell Sheila and me how a boy she had taught on her very first school practice had remarked afterwards, 'How that Miss Jeffery could run and never showed her britches once.' We liked this story.

I enjoyed the school parties, which I always recall whenever I see tinsel. We sang:

> The more we are together, together, together,
> The more we are together
> The merrier we shall be,

with Miss Webster's variation in the second part. She maintained that 'For *your* friends are *my* friends' had an ugly ring to the vowel-sounds and made us substitute

'For *their* friends are *our* friends', which according to her was more melodious. I still find this an interesting point. We played 'Naming the Doll'. I got very superstitious and rigid about this and stuck to the name I had picked on even the third time round when it had already been twice rejected, which was idiotic behaviour. Cynthia Boswell, though not academic, was much more intelligent. When it was Miss Britain who had chosen the name, Cynthia guessed Jean and won the doll the first time round. When I congratulated her afterwards she said, 'Well, I knew her niece was called Jean', and I dared not admit that I had known too.

But the sight of tinsel always reminds me, too, that as the evening went on I was usually attacked by the most painful anxiety, which grew like toothache, the worst pain I knew, to become misery and uncontrollable panic. I was sure it was later than anyone knew and longed to be at home. If only they would have given me the key I would have walked past the Exeter Road pubs and up through Withycombe Village in the dark by myself. No one realised how late it was. On one occasion the intensity of this feeling made me burst into desolate weeping without, for once, any regard for anything that anyone might think or say. I could not explain what it was about, and everyone assumed I must have broken something.

I suppose it was rather surprising, sheltered and kept apart as we were, with my mother presiding over everything, that we managed to make friends, but we did. Sheila was more successful than I was, as she grasped the idea from the first that a friendship need not be exclusive, whereas I believed for some years that it necessarily meant a close relationship with one person, a bosom friend, to protect and be protected by, whose company and secrets one could command in return for one's own. The girls at the Council School were amiable, but as I found none, except one weakling, who thought as I did on this point, I gradually modified my ideas.

There was a family called Tucker, who lived in Norfolk Terrace, just round the corner from Bradham Lane, and with the two younger girls, Peggy and Joy, we were on friendly terms right through Council School and Grammar School. We walked there and back with them year after year and played with them in the evenings and at weekends as much as we were allowed to play with anyone. Sunday, of course, was out of the question. Here my mother's religious beliefs coincided with her notions of gentility: Plymouth Brethren did not go out to play on Sunday, and neither did young ladies. She herself was for some time friendlier with Mrs Tucker than she was with anyone in Exmouth.

I was proud of the Council School, as I was later to be of the Grammar School, and gave it my unthinking and absolute allegiance. It was not compulsory to wear uniform, but regulation tunics and hats were available at a local store, and strong pressure was put on parents to get them if they possibly could. The day when Sheila and I appeared in ours was a happy one for me. We were noticed and approved of in Assembly and given a pip to wear. These pips looked like vegetable laxatives, and we stitched them on to our tunics in a row, if we were virtuous enough to have a row and lucky enough to have a tunic to stitch them on to. I had a chestful by the time I left.

So for three years we were trained not for life but for the Scholarship. Nothing was ever said, or, I am sure, thought, about the suitability of Sheila and me for the Grammar School. The will to pass the examination and the necessary industry were considered more important than intelligence or an academic disposition. My mother maintained that another qualifying factor should be what the pupil concerned intended to do from the point of view of future career, and here, of course, we were safe. She instanced Viola Carter, who had asserted all along that when she left school she was going to work in the Co-op, which she eventually did with obvious contentment, though she was top in all Devon in my sister's year, with Sheila just behind her, and took up her place at the Grammar School and did well.

It was assumed that Sheila and I would *pass*. To be first was the only anxiety. Sheila nearly was – Mother talked her way round the 'nearly' to Mrs Martin and all the rival mothers – and I actually was. As far as I know, none of the parents ever questioned the way in which the selection was made. It seemed to them the best way of doing it. Those who failed and minded about it put the news around that they had failed by one mark. Once Sheila and I were both safely through, my mother used to observe that she had yet to hear of anyone who had passed by one mark.

CHAPTER FIVE

Doctors and Nurses

THROUGHOUT my childhood I thought I had consumption and often turned sick and stiff with terror at nights before I went to sleep, especially if it was a fine light evening with a great deal of pleasant life going on outside, and sometimes when I heard my father winding up the clock the horror of feeling I should not be living in time much longer would have been past bearing had there seemed to be any alternative. I need hardly say I told no one of my fears. A medical investigation would have proved that either I did or did not have the disease, and I have no idea which diagnosis I secretly dreaded more. I used to tap my chest in bed, and there was one place which always sounded hollow, where, underneath, I imagined the illness to be burrowing away. Occasionally it sounded rather less hollow, but at the worst it echoed cavernously. If ever I was ill and had a hot-water bottle I clutched it to the hollow spot hoping the warmth might help.

In those days tuberculosis was a killing disease. I knew it from books. Stories where someone went into a decline – it was always a female; men did not seem to get it in books – were highly recommended reading for Plymouth Brethren, and, whether the victim was sweetly saved or rebellious to the last, the end was inexorable. It happened in secular tales, too. Ruby Gillis, the empty flirt of the *Anne* books, contracted galloping consumption; after a few weeks she could no longer bear the weight of the hairpins in her long fair hair, and soon her friends were looking down on her as she lay in her coffin, her face ennobled as it might have been by womanly joys and sorrows had she lived. And I knew it from life as, years before I heard of the Brontë sisters or the Keats brothers, I used to hear of a family of my mother's cousins living on the moors who died of consumption one by one, rhythmically and without exception. As the parents had once had a baby without fail every year, now they buried a grown-up.

The great sanatorium Hawkmoor, on the edge of Dartmoor, was a dreaded place and, though the verb 'to hawk' was in common use, I never knew anyone find the name funny. It was a moment of liberation in my adult life when a friend from another county laughed heartlessly and said, 'Oh, but it ought to be called Hawk*less*.' It was not so much that the treatment was thought to be painful or gruesome, though it was an often-told story of my father's that an office friend of his visiting a patient had seen grown men weeping with the cold; it was just that it was unmentionable. The next most terrifying building was Digby's, the lunatic asylum deeply hidden in trees, not far from Exeter; but whereas people might half-humorously lament that the vexations of their lives would land them 'up Digby's' they never suggested that their fatigues or chills might lead them to Hawkmoor.

In point of fact I must have been rather a healthy child. I had a bad start, it is true, being two months premature. My mother strained herself mangling the clothes one Monday, and I was born early on Tuesday morning. My father used to enjoy describing my dramatic smallness and ugliness. 'Like a tadpole. Only your mother could have loved you,' he would say, in a tone which suggested that even she did not thoroughly rise to the challenge. 'You just turned the scales at two and a half pounds,' was another favourite statement of his. I do not know if this was true; I was born at home, and I wonder if without benefit of incubator or other hospital appliances I could in fact have survived at that weight.

I had a very difficult first year, yelling all the time, my mother said. I could not feed properly, being tongue-tied. However, at last I had the necessary treatment, and when I had got over the novelty of being able to put my tongue out and pull it in again, which I did incessantly at first, I grew up quite normally. I was pale, it is true, and healthy children were supposed to have scarlet faces, and I was what my grandmother called 'poony', whereas a healthy child would have been grossly fat, and so I was commonly considered to be delicate. I traded on this by being fussy about my food. I knew they would not risk letting me go without a meal, and so I frequently found myself eating bananas and cream while Sheila, who was good, worked through her rice pudding. However, I got my come-uppance at night, being forced to eat a bowlful of Slippery Elm Food, which my mother bought from a herbalist in Kingskerswell. It was credited with magical properties for rearing the delicate, though I should think it might very well have killed them with retching, as it was the most disgusting mess I have ever experienced or imagined, consisting of unexplained globules and sudden patches of warm slime.

The herbalist was an honoured figure in the villages of my youth. She was more accessible than the doctor. In the case of Mrs Trigg of Kingskerswell you just opened the back door and shouted. She was more like one of us. She lived in the same sort of house, spoke with the same accent and used the same vocabulary. Her diagnosis and prescriptions were chatty rather than bleakly authoritative. She opened the way to discussion and personal taste. Women could tell her all about their periods when there might be nobody else to tell. Husbands were supposed not to be a suitable audience for this topic. My mother and aunts employed strange circumlocutions and euphemisms in the family circle, but when there were only women present it was a subject to which they brought great vivacity and descriptive gifts. (When they got carried away by the theme they seemed to lose all sense of modesty; at the time I started menstruating, my mother, who, as I say, would not have spoken openly to my father about it, gave Mrs Tucker a full account of the event in the back seat of Abbott's bus, at a pitch which carried at least half-way up the bus, which is where I myself happened to be sitting.) The herbalist had more remedies for period pains than for any other complaint, though some of the potions were generally adaptable. There was something called Kasbah, which my father took for his backache.

The chemist was above the herbalist in the hierarchy, being accounted learned and professional in a way she was not. Even as a child I was appalled and furious at the reliance which was placed on his judgement, far beyond what could be justified by any knowledge he might have or any investigation he could make. I have known people ask him over the counter if he thought they had cancer. They did not use the word, but that was what they meant. And he always told them, whatever it was, that they had not got it, and they went away greatly cheered.

Both the herbalist and the chemist had the more endearing qualities of the magician. The doctor stood aloof and unloved in his aura of medical endowment. There was a paralysing respect for the doctor among members of our class in those days. Apart from his power to cure us, he was our one contact with the upper classes, with his cultured accent and strange mealtimes. Most people had the Vicar as well, but, of course, he was denied to the Plymouth Brethren. So we changed all our underclothes for the doctor, washed ourselves thoroughly, swept the stairs and dusted the bedroom if he was calling, spoke in refined voices, and above all listened with heart-pounding deference to his opinion and repeated his compliments about the wallflowers or the raspberries for days.

He was a totem rather than a person. It is significant that I cannot remember the name of a single doctor who attended any of us during the fourteen years of my childhood. There was no objective standard of comparison either, as to gradations of skill. The doctor was the doctor, and if Mrs Tucker thought hers was better than ours, well, she naturally would, in the same way that she maintained her coalman made less mess delivering than ours. It proved nothing except possessive partiality.

The doctor's authority was in no way undermined by the old wives' tales about illness which proliferated precisely among those who held him in the humblest respect. There was no idea among the old wives that native wisdom should prevail, but neither did the tales vanish in the bright light of his greater knowledge. There must have been some area of reconciliation at a very deep level.

There was a time in my childhood when I wanted to be a doctor myself. My mother seized on this ambition with great enthusiasm and would tell Miss Phear about it at the School Sports. Miss Phear was the sad relic of the lords of the manor after whom Phear Park had been named, but she represented the gentry still. The amazing thing was that anyone should have taken my ambition at all seriously. I had none of the capabilities and nothing of the disposition which would have made me an even moderately competent doctor, and it was not as if healing the sick was regarded by my parents as an ideal; we had both been briskly headed off that at the time when we had wanted to be nurses. But to be a doctor was the height of genteel aspiration; it was better than being a teacher. Doctors were gods. I was well into adult life before I realised that the medical profession, like every other, had its fair proportion of exceptionally stupid members. Even the circumstances of my mother's death did not enlighten me.

I was always conscious of sickness and disease all around me. It was perpetually there, lying in wait. The impression began at home in a simple but symbolic way with the boil-bag. This was an old pillow-case, kept in the medicine-chest in the front bedroom and filled with lint, cotton-wool and everything thought to be needed for the treatment of boils and styes, including a brilliant orange ointment called Lion Ointment, which was supposed to draw them out. Someone always had a boil or a stye. My mother was especially connected with styes in my mind, chiefly because she was dedicated to squeezing them out, usually long before they were ready, but also because, as she often told us, she had had a huge stye on her wedding day.

Boils did you good, they were such a wonderful clear-out: this was universally believed. I suppose the idea was that we all had a certain amount of pus in us, constantly sluicing about, and a boil siphoned off that much of it. Once when my father went into the office with a carbuncle on his neck, a fellow clerk told him he would gladly give five shillings for one of them. Father replied he could have it for sixpence and for days was greatly pleased with this retort.

My mother had a way of inventing illness if the fancy took her. At one point a simple spot on my neck made her think of impetigo, which presumably she had seen cases of in her teaching days. Without waiting for any further confirmation or development she kept me away from school with strict injunctions not to tell anyone why – impetigo was as disgraceful as nits – gave me a separate towel and drenched the spot with iodine four or five times a day. Sure enough, the inflammation spread and the skin began to peel off; it was certainly impetigo. At last she took me to the doctor, who gave one look at my neck and said humorously to me, 'Tell your mother not to burn holes in you with iodine.' We went home. At his command all treatment was stopped, and soon there were no marks on my neck at all: the original harmless spot had long since disappeared in the general fiery glow. Mother took her defeat with resilience and even good humour.

Talk of illness was always in the air. As we walked through the village, little girls playing doctors and nurses on doorsteps would be saying, 'This time it's going to be a f-i-t,' spelling it out in lewd undertones, and gossiping women on the pavements would be giving each other mysterious advice at the tops of their voices, 'I reckon 'tis eggs. Keep her off them for a bit and see if 'tis eggs.'

Theorising about disease formed a large part of the conversation at any gathering. It was both ignorant and ingenious. A friend of my Torquay aunts was in hospital getting thinner and weaker from visit to visit in a way which appalled them, till someone in the Meetings explained that this was being done on purpose by the doctors and the hospital staff, as their aim was to break her right down before building her up again. It made her sound like a wall or a chimney, but the theory was so plausible that, even when she died a few days later, we felt that what had happened was that the doctors had missed the right moment and carried on the first part of the treatment just a little too long. This particular theory had been harmless, as no one who held it had been in a position to act on it, but much of the folklore that went round and round the gossiping groups was potentially very dangerous. The adage, 'What's movable's curable', for example, a favourite of my grandmother's and generally popular, often stopped people with shooting pains from consulting the doctor and was part of the so-called wisdom that later kept my mother from getting a proper opinion until it was too late.

Constipation was a perennial talking-point and ranked as a disease: if even one day passed without your going to the lavatory you were ill. My parents and relatives discussed their own functioning or lack of it in great detail, usually at mealtimes. The good effects of going to the lavatory were supposed to be instantaneous; when Sheila or I came downstairs from a visit we would be congratulated on a new brightness of eye, freshness of complexion and added vitality, and the consequences of not going were correspondingly obvious and basic. My father dwelt more on the subject than anyone and used to repeat conversations he had had in the Goods Office; apparently they all thought they were rotten inside and that even if their bowels were working quite regularly, some taint must still be left. One of the clerks recommended a self-administered enema, and Father described to us all that evening, luxuriously, how you just lay back and the fluid rose up inside you, floating out all the impurities. His sensuous enthusiasm was revolting; I felt sick.

It was the namelessness of so much illness that made it particularly terrifying. Soon after Grandpa Jeffery's death, my baby cousin Jeffery – that was his Christian name – was taken ill and died, and no one ever said what of, not just to spare us children, but because they did not seem to find it relevant or helpful. He was dead, they had noticed his symptoms, and what was in a name?

Later, when I was at the Grammar School, a girl in my form died in the same unspecified way as Jeffery. After being marked absent long enough to cause speculation, she was taken to the hospital, we heard, and then one day my mother said that Eileen could see anyone now at any time and eat anything she fancied, as there was nothing that could be done. And the whole grapevine of Exmouth mothers got no nearer to the facts than that, nor appeared to want to.

Mrs Croft, who lived a few doors down from us in Bradham Lane, had two nieces called Warcup who came to stay with her whenever they were ill. I suppose their mother thought as highly of Exmouth as ours did of Torquay. For half a year Betty Warcup lay on Mrs Croft's sofa, eating cream and other fattening foods, while her aunt kept the conversation going by telling visitors in the usual verbatim way how Mr Warcup, Betty's father, had been consulting a doctor about a condition of his own, which seemed from her account not only to be nameless but also to have no symptoms. However, the doctor had said in fine authoritative style, 'It will never kill you, Warcup.' But whatever it was, it did kill him, we heard, quite soon after Betty had gone home, and that was all we ever did hear.

Sometimes, even when the disease remained anonymous, an explanation of its origin would be given, and perhaps this was the most frightening thing of all, as it seemed that simple everyday things with innocent names and harmless functions could kill you. A nice young woman who served in Thomas Tucker's, the draper's, and always spoke cheerfully to Sheila and me, died without warning, and my mother said it was probably something she had picked up in the stock-taking. The ribbons, the tape, the stockings and the buttons of my favourite shop, and especially the overhead railway that carried the bills and the change, had suddenly become killers, and for years I took very shallow breaths in Thomas Tucker's. This idea that people caught things from the objects they worked with was prevalent and, I suppose, could sometimes have been true, as in the case of a clerk in my father's office who died of anthrax, allegedly picked up in the goods shed, an event which understandably plunged my father into a long bout not so much of distress – he had not been particularly close to the man – as of resentful sulks.

I can quite see why people did not badger the doctor as to what precisely their relatives had died of, but I cannot imagine why no one ever read the death certificate where everything was set out in black and white. For years after my mother's death one of her family maintained it had been due to a 'growth' – the word 'cancer' was never used – although the real cause, something quite different, had been plainly stated at the time.

I imagine that this reluctance to name illness was due partly to ancient superstition and partly to unfamiliarity with and perhaps distrust of words themselves, but I have sometimes wondered if, in the case of my own family, the vagueness and archaic phraseology of the Bible had not also something to do with it. In the Old Testament people were mostly slain in battle or by each other at home, or else carried off by the Lord's Will in circumstances where no further specification was needed. But, in the New Testament, sufferers were being cured of actual complaints by Jesus Christ, and the reports that they were sick of a fever, or sick of a palsy, or that they had an issue of blood, were so unsatisfactory, and yet, of course, so sacrosanct, that the very meaninglessness, to us, may have had an influence. I was grown up before I knew or cared that an issue of blood meant a haemorrhage; I dimly supposed that the woman whom Christ healed of it had up to that time made an issue of her condition, which possibly she had.

I had very few illnesses myself, and those I did have were in quite a different category from the ones I feared. They seemed much less real. The fact that they had already struck before the imagination could shape them and arrange some response to them meant that they got off to an excellent start, with a naturalness and spontaneity which was cheering, almost gratifying.

We were so sheltered and protected that I did not catch measles till I was in my teens, nor mumps and chickenpox till I was grown up. The infectious diseases of childhood, incidentally, were allowed names. Whooping cough, however, I did not escape, and I have a clear memory of waking myself up one night with whooping, and feeling a mixture of fear and complacency at the firelight in the bedroom, at the hastily-lit candle and the bare feet making sucking noises on the lino as they came to my assistance, and at the compulsive din I was making, which my parents' comments to each other assured me was genuine whooping. I was not to be one of those children, it seemed, who failed their families by not whooping so that in later life they never knew whether to put 'yes' or 'no' on medical forms.

The really dreaded infectious illnesses of my youth were scarlet fever and diphtheria. I was always sure I would get them. The books we read were as loud with their menace as with that of consumption. 'How can you touch that letter,' demanded a mother of her daughter, 'written as it was in the house, perhaps in the very room, where there is scarlet fever?' But in fact they only came fairly near. Once everyone was sent home from school because a girl had scarlet fever, and Sheila and I walked up through the village, excited by all the mid-morning activity we usually did not see and calling out to anyone we knew, 'We've just escaped scarlet fever,' chiefly for the drama, but also, in my case, because I really felt it to be at my heels.

Later one of my aunts got diphtheria, and this at first seemed like a death in the family. We all knew that with diphtheria something white grew in your throat and choked you; it featured in local lore as well as in Plymouth Brethren reading. The whiteness was the terrifying thing, and, when suffering from childhood sore throats, I often looked gaping-mouthed into the mirror and, seeing nothing but a painful purple, rejoiced at my deliverance. Once when I had a particularly sore throat I got Sheila, who did not share my neuroses, to have a look, which she did most perfunctorily, saying off-handedly, 'Oh yes, dreadful. All white.' I felt like killing her.

My aunt was taken to the Fever Hospital on the Newton Road. This was the first time the terrible ambulance came anywhere near me. I was sure no one could be taken off in one and live; it was as final as a hearse. I was disconcerted when my aunt eventually returned home, perfectly well, and was just as afraid of ambulances as before.

The Fever Hospital was bad enough, standing for exile and a deadly separation. As a matter of fact my aunt seemed to adjust to her stay there quickly, but the rest of us remained bent on communicating with her from the outside world. The Torquay–Exeter railway line ran through a cutting on one side of the hospital, and we, who had rushed down to Torquay for the emergency, hung out of the train and waved to her on our way home. She had had a message got to her in time and was stationed at a window waving back, quite vigorously, though the white linen and nightgowns of the ward behind her suggested a background of grave-clothes and made me think of Lazarus. The road to Newton Abbot ran by the other side of the hospital, and my uncle used to spend a great deal of time cycling about outside, waving to her.

One of my first memories of my mother is of her having pneumonia. I think she must have had it badly. I can remember nothing concrete about her illness, but I have a sudden brilliant isolated glimpse of crossing the bridge over the Teign in a taxi on the way to Torquay where she was being taken to convalesce. Up to then I had only seen the bridge from the train, as the railway kept to the west bank of the river, and to swing out at right angles like this on to a frail construction over blinding water brought home the outlandishness of going by road, the rich man's way of travelling, and of going so far in a taxi. This awareness lasted just as long as the bridge; the solidity of the opposite bank must have reassured me, as I remember not an inch more of the journey.

Nurse Goodman's sister died. I liked Nurse Goodman; she was the midwife who had attended my mother at Sheila's birth and at my own. She was gaunt and cheerful. Though she did not belong to the Brethren she was broadmindedly credited with being saved, and my mother described how in the days following both her confinements they often sang hymns together, the baby sleeping soundly throughout. We always kept in touch with Nurse Goodman, and it was natural to visit her sister when she was ill, though I hardly think the sick woman got much pleasure from it. She was thin and withdrawn and had to keep spitting into a basin. I used to gaze at her so fixedly that my mother had to say with bright embarrassment, 'Pat's taking in every detail.'

My mother paid these duty visits, but on the whole had little sympathy to spare from her own family. Once, when a lad who lived at the top of Bradham Lane was pitched through the windscreen of a car and killed, she hinted that people who dashed about in cars were asking for it, and when a woman in one of the Torquay Meetings hanged herself, my mother stated outright that Sister Curtis could not really have been saved after all, as the Lord would never have let one of his own do such a terrible thing. In general, however, the Brethren did not think of illness, accident and death as a punishment for sin. With the case of Job vividly in our minds, we were more likely to interpret it – if we did in fact take it other than straightforwardly – as a distinguishing and honourable trial of faith.

In the middle of all my anxieties and terrors, almost the only actual pain I experienced was at the dentist's. In those days, in Devon, dentists really did hurt. There was no idea of injecting before drilling, even for the deepest cavity, and our only too regular visits were a genuine ordeal. The first dentist we went to, Mr Clift, had a beautiful chow dog which lay on the surgery floor near the chair, occasionally flexing his purple tongue. The ideas of painless normality which the sight of him conjured up, although he was so exotic, were an aggravation of the torture to come.

The dentist we changed to later on, I do not remember why, was Mr Esselman. We were about twelve and thirteen at the time and were urgent with my mother to let us go on our own. She was very dubious about this and seemed quite alarmed at our independence. We must have been unusually insistent because, instead of straightforwardly refusing, she described how in old days young ladies of good family never, never went to the dentist or any other professional man unchaperoned for fear that he might do something unpleasant. When this neither scared us nor moved us to snobbish emulation, she gave way. In the event Mr Esselman did do something unpleasant: he slapped my face when I yelled, which, ironically, I imagine he might not have done had my mother been present. He went on drilling, and I felt his hand getting cold against my cheek as my face flamed. I do not know how I should have reacted if he had started on any of the liberties my mother had in mind, but I could hardly have felt more outraged.

When we were young all conscientious parents arranged for their children's tonsils and adenoids to be removed. Sheila and I had been made aware of these harmful sets of organs, one pair that you could see and one pair that was invisible, spongily lurking in some crevice, by the incessant salt-and-water gargling of our childhood which had made every scratch on the bottom of the kitchen sink so visually familiar, and we had always known that they would have to come out. Father haunted the Devon and Exeter Hospital in order to arrange it and saw a Mr Worthington about six times. Mr Worthington never saw us, at least not until he got us on the operating table, so it must have gone through on my father's say-so. Sheila had hers out when she was nine and I a year later, when I was nine too.

My mother would not come into the hospital with me on the grounds that it would be too upsetting, so Olly took me in and left me with a parting gift of half-a-crown, a very encouraging sign of her belief that I would come out alive to spend it. As a matter of fact I was quite phlegmatic about the whole thing, after five minutes of unpleasant flutter when the summoning letter arrived, and suffered little.

A rude boy in the ward kept shouting, 'Nurse, nurse, I want to pee', which shocked me, and on other occasions 'Nurse, nurse, I want to –' and then a two-syllabled verb I could never make out. It did not sound like any of the forbidden vulgar words I knew and so, though it was decidedly onomatopoeic, I did not mind it.

It was a small square ward, and in the bed in one corner was Nellie Williams, the little sister of a young woman in the Exmouth Assembly. Of course I did not know what was the matter with her. I did not even know who she was until Miss Williams came to visit her and spoke to me. The first morning, as the trolley with instruments and bottles came rattling into the ward, Nellie started to cry. The trolley was followed by fat, complacent Sister who said, 'Now don't be a baby, little girl.' The screens went round her bed, two doctors arrived and went in behind them with Sister. And then Nellie started screaming. I had never heard such screaming, and indeed I have not to this day. The only words she uttered were, 'Put on my nightie. Put on my nightie.' All the rest was pure screaming, high, sustained and shattering. I did not look at any of the other children, and I am certain they did not look at me. This happened every morning.

A few weeks later, when I was perfectly well again, I met Miss Williams in the Exeter Road. She asked me very kindly how I was and then said, 'Our little Nellie died, you know,' quite brightly, not wanting to upset me.

Behind all our fears about illness stood the knowledge that we were poor. Money would get you the best, and we had too little. When my mother was known to be dying, my father kept saying, 'If only I could afford the Pencarwick.' This was a posh nursing-home overlooking the estuary. In fact, it was probably terrible, and there were known to be beetles in the beds, but I saw my father's point. At the Pencarwick, as you were rich enough to pay the fees, they might at least take the trouble to find out your name and use it when you were in pain, which they had not bothered to do with Nellie Williams. And nobody in St Marychurch thought it odd or offensive when the parents of a boy who lived in Petitor Road offered the doctor a hundred pounds to cure their son of his pneumonia. It was regarded as an appropriate gesture by a loving father and mother in dreadful extremity, and, absolutely vast though the sum appeared to us, we wondered, when the boy died, if perhaps it should not have been raised to two hundred.

CHAPTER SIX

First Love

WE were bound to be bookworms. Both heredity and environment made it inevitable. We read, were read to, asked for books for Christmas and birthdays, and were given them, as far back as I can remember. We were never allowed to go out and buy books for ourselves; we never knew the pleasures of deliberation and free choice and frivolity in this respect. Even when I won a pound's worth of books in a *Girls' Own Paper* competition, Mother chose them, on strictly educational lines.

Her censorship was by no means as rigid as it might have been, however. If we had been entirely governed by the views of the Plymouth Brethren we should have been starved indeed. They did permit novel-reading, it is true. Plays of all kinds were taboo because they told lies: if someone came on to the stage and said, 'I am thy father's ghost', this was obviously untrue; but novels, though they probably told more lies per hundred words than any play – and this was characteristic of the woolliness of Brethren thinking – were acceptable, provided they passed certain tests. There were gradations of opinion here. One of our Sunday School teachers, Mrs Widdowson, used to impress on us that we should read no book unless a little girl was saved in it. This was perhaps the narrowest criterion of all as she seemed to rule out even the salvation of little boys. More liberal mentors declared that if anyone at all was saved the work was suitable.

The attitude of both Mrs Widdowson and the liberals was not exactly moralistic; there was no demand that a work should be edifying, merely that it should be founded on the basic doctrine that no edification was possible apart from salvation through the blood of the Lamb. So large a group thought in this way that there existed a series of booklets produced with them in mind called The Lily Library. Every cover carried the Library's slogan, 'Pure as the flower whose name they bear.' The series must have been peculiarly vapid, because I do not remember any of the stories or any of the titles.

We came into close contact with these views in Brethren circles, of course, but at home my parents were amazingly permissive. I can think of only two forbidden books. One was *The Blue Lagoon*, but even so it was in the house, actually in the bookcase, though at a great height on the top shelf, and in any case it was forbidden to children of godless homes as well. When we were at the Grammar School, the English master's daughter, who was in the same class as Sheila, told us that her father had read *The Blue Lagoon* and thought it very beautiful. We were greatly impressed. It seemed the height of sophistication to get beyond the excitement of reading a description of sexual intercourse – this we knew was the point of the ban, though Betty Martin informed us that it only said 'locked in each other's arms' – and to be able to use the calm Olympian word 'beautiful'.

Another book which was proscribed, though for quite a different reason, was *Ben Hur*. I am sure that in The Lily Library, Jesus Christ was mentioned in every fifth sentence and assumed in the intervening four, but in *Ben Hur* he actually appeared, which was blasphemous and made it a very wicked book indeed. I believed this judgement implicitly, and on one occasion, in my first year at the Grammar School, it stood me in very good stead. We were having a discussion about books in the English lesson and had been dragged and cajoled to the conclusion that some books were good and some bad. Examples were asked for at this point, and, as an instance of a bad book, I sternly named *Ben Hur*. I was not required to give my reasons, and Miss Rafter seemed struck by this demonstration of literary taste: an eleven-year-old had seen that as a historical novel *Ben Hur* was inferior to, say, the works of Scott.

Apart from these two books we could read almost anything, though girls' school stories came in for heavy and sustained attack, and at one stage in my life I painfully hankered after them. There was one in particular, *Ursula's Last Term*, which was in the school library and which I ordered almost every week on my library list and read in secret. It was an addiction. Once when the library monitor made a mistake and another book arrived in its place, I suffered what must have been withdrawal symptoms. I can still see one of the illustrations, 'Full on the playing field fell the bomb', but whether the girls went on playing hockey round it, or whether Ursula made amends for something by rescuing someone from under it, or was mutilated by it as a punishment for past wildness, I do not remember. Aplomb, compensatory heroism and the administration of come-uppance were all three popular themes in these books, and it may have been any one of them.

Only once did my mother catch me reading this book. She made a long scathing speech about it, called it trash, and ended up, more ambiguously than she meant, I imagine, by asserting scornfully, 'I could write that kind of thing myself.' I was so worked up by this attack on an idol that I retorted, 'Then why don't you?' an extremity of defiance which shocked both of us. I had never answered her back so roundly before or openly questioned any of her attitudes. Not only was she furious, but Jesus, it seemed, was grieved. I was duly crushed and humbled, but it never once occurred to me that my mother's point of view about *Ursula* could embody any integrity or taste. I assumed absolutely that the fame and glory of having a book published would and should override all principles and induce anyone to do so given half a chance.

I have no idea why my mother took such a firm stand against school stories. I have wondered since if it may have been because all the girls in them went away to boarding schools and were out of their mothers' clutches. Certainly, I fervently wanted to go to boarding school myself and might well, after a period of conditioning to middle-class ways and speech, have been very happy there. Perhaps Mother sensed this wish and disposition.

Throughout our childhood, Mother read aloud to us, usually at the kitchen table but sometimes, as a treat, in the front room and sometimes, on warm summer evenings, in the meadow beyond the garden. But, whether we were propping our elbows on well-scrubbed wood, or sprawling on the mock-leather suite, or sitting in deep grass with our backs against a log, we were always a group of three. It was a ritual, with Mother up at the altar. Father always seemed to be excluded. He would be somewhere else, doing something to maintain the house like putting up wallpaper or mending a bucket. I have never been able to recall Mother's voice, but it must have entered most profoundly into my consciousness.

Sheila and I enjoyed these readings. We had to be very attentive, of course. Once when we said something to each other in the middle Mother stopped dead and waited for the silence to break us down. We stuck it out for what seemed like a manfully long time but then apologised, and the reading continued in a reproachful tone. But it was gratifying to have the whole of Mother's concentration and effort trained on us.

She enjoyed these sessions, I am sure. She believed

that it was good for children to have books read to them, and she genuinely had our welfare in mind, but I also feel reasonably sure that it was no arid duty for her. In the first place it meant that she had us under her eye and under her influence for long stretches of time; to read to people is an excellent and fairly innocent way of dominating them. And she must have found it an indulgence to savour in our presence, if not exactly to share with us, the books that meant most to her.

I cannot imagine how she had the nerve to call school stories trash. The books she chose for these readings were, I now see, startlingly bad. Two of her greatest favourites were *Coming Through the Rye* and *Freckles*. The first was a tale with a middle-class Victorian background showing true love thwarted by a designing woman. 'You will never be Paul Vasher's wife, never,' said this woman to the heroine Nell. And she never was; the designing woman married him. He and Nell had first realised their feelings for each other when they met in a field of rye, and at the end of the book when Paul Vasher lay mortally ill with a fever, he suddenly sat up in bed and said, 'Coming through the rye. God's rye, Nell,' after which he fell back and died.

My mother always wept at this bit. Her chin started to wobble and dissolve, her face reddened and her voice broke, but she read on. It was embarrassing but also exciting to watch her. But there was a passage at the end of *Freckles* which overcame her so that she could not continue. Freckles, the Irish waif who guarded the Limberlost, whatever that was, for his beloved boss, Mr McLean, who loved him like a son, had been horribly crushed by a falling tree from whose path he had rescued a beautiful girl, the Angel, whom he loved. He seemed to be dying, but the Angel, realising what was on his mind, sought out information about his long-lost mother and brought it to him, together with a photograph of her, which he seized with broken exclamations of 'Me little mither.' This was the point at which the reading stopped.

I think I can see now, though I never thought twice about it at the time, why these two passages affected my mother so extremely, beyond others which seemed equally pathetic to us. With regard to *Freckles*: she had always wanted a son. She often said so, and at local Music Festivals or the School Sports, if some boy of about Sheila's age and looking rather like her distinguished himself, Mother would fairly groan with longing. She gave Sheila the nickname 'Dick'; I was allowed to stay female, not being handsome or amiable enough, I suspect, to be worthy of such a metamorphosis. So Freckles, the boy who craved for a mother as much as she craved for a son, met her half-way. He had the right kind of disposition too. I suppose that Sheila and I seemed affectionate enough, but certainly neither of us was the type to murmur 'Me little mither' or its Devonian equivalent.

Coming Through the Rye may have summed up her other longing, for the exciting, masterful mate, and also her sour acceptance of the fact that she was not likely to have him now. Somehow I do not feel that the idea of coming through God's rye helped her much. The Bible said only too plainly that there was no marrying in heaven, and a love affair was not quite what she wanted, either here or there.

Occasionally the readings produced an enjoyable little conspiracy. Although the implications of many passages in *Coming Through the Rye* and *Freckles* were both highly erotic and godless, there was nothing either of lechery or blasphemy that you could put your finger on, nothing to be left out when reading aloud. But in *The Scarlet Pimpernel* there was the key line, 'That demmed elusive Pimpernel'; and, of course, 'demmed' would never do, so Mother substituted 'awful'. I think she deliberately chose a word which did not scan and which obviously was not the original one. We knew perfectly well it was 'demmed', and when that particular session was over we went off to find Father and quoted to him the whole verse, 'We seek him here, we seek him there', with Mother's emendation and in her hearing. He also knew it was 'demmed' and must have realised from our self-conscious voices that we knew it too. It was a pleasant family plot, with all of us in it together, for once.

The Scarlet Pimpernel, incidentally, was another great favourite of Mother's. For one thing it was by a Baroness, and so both begetter and begotten were of noble blood. We all identified absolutely with the persecuted aristocrats of the story. It seemed not to occur to one of us that had we lived then we should by reason of our social status have been *sans-culottes* dancing round the guillotine, rather than *vicomtes* escaping in carts. I remember the book for another reason as well: it was one of the few from which Mother drew a moral. In general she was willing to let the narrative and the sentiments speak for themselves, but on putting down *The Scarlet Pimpernel* she explained most impressively that the French soldiers had allowed Sir Percy to escape because they were obeying orders blindly instead of using their own judgement. I thought this was an excellent moral to draw; I still do, though I cannot help reflecting that it was an odd precept, coming from my mother. I wonder if, secretly, she was as irked by our slavish obedience as we, secretly, were.

On the whole, reading aloud seemed to have little to do with books. They were the occasion, certainly, but the other elements in the activity were more important. It was the books I read to myself that formed my real experience of reading. However much Mother might recommend them, approve of them, and suggest to my aunts that they would make acceptable presents, she did not greatly impinge on my relationship with them, and many of them became part of my life in a way that the books she read aloud did not.

I must have had a natural taste for the second- and third-rate myself, as I cannot even remember reading the well-written, imaginatively conceived books, such as *Alice*, which I must have met in childhood. My recollection of *The Pilgrim's Progress* is a little clearer, as it was the inspiration of much physical activity and play, such as springing out at Sheila from dark corners pretending to be Apollyon. For some reason we were never confronted with the famous animal books in childhood – neither *The Wind in the Willows*, nor *Winnie-the-Pooh*, nor any Beatrix Potter – and when I did meet the works of Kenneth Grahame and A. A. Milne, at the age of twelve or thirteen, I was past them to the extent that I read them from a height, like a connoisseur, with no involvement, accepting with sophistication rather than naïveté the clothing, the speech and the human motives of the animals.

Either at school or at home I read all the classics considered necessary for children: *Treasure Island*, *Kidnapped*, *Little Women*, *David Copperfield*, *Ivanhoe*, *Robinson Crusoe*. I suppose I enjoyed them; I certainly did not resent or avoid them. Very occasionally some incident would seem to connect with my own life: the doings of the Spanish Inquisition in *Westward Ho!* for example, fitted in exactly with what I had heard about Roman Catholics. But on the whole the themes appeared completely abstract and impersonal, even when the author intended a message to strike home. *Uncle Tom's Cabin* did not cause me a moment's concern for the plight of Negro slaves in America, and neither did *The Water Babies* for the sufferings of the child chimney-sweeps, not because these situations had been done away with, but because no book stirred me in that way.

Once or twice some description of physical pain broke

through my detachment: the detailed account of the binding of a young girl's feet in a missionary book about China, or the evocation of the agony, like walking on a thousand knives, endured by the mermaid who was given human legs. The story of *The Little Mermaid* was in fact one which did make me feel and understand. The hopelessness of a relationship between two people born in different elements was somehow an emotion which I could grasp to the point of distress and one which came back to me in adult life with a sense of complete continuity. But this understanding was almost an aberration. In *The Ugly Duckling* the meaning was something that in my own way I thought about much of the time: I was destined for a higher sphere and would be appreciated when I achieved it; and yet I did not see it in the story or make the connection at all. In fact I interpreted it in the most banal and inaccurate fashion as saying that the plain would become pretty.

Of course, the book I read most consistently throughout these years was the Bible, but its influence on me, though obviously great, was not directly literary. I never thought of it as a book at all: as far as I was concerned, it might well have been called *The Bible Designed NOT to be Read as Literature*. In the quizzes, questionnaires and competitions that I frequently went in for, a common question was 'What books have most influenced you?' but I never dreamed of putting 'The Bible'. Much of the feeling of magic which the Bible would have inspired in me had I really taken it as literally as I believed I did, and as I had been taught to do, I had to look for in fairy tales, where the difficulties of ordinary life could indeed be overcome by spells, enchantment and something like prayer. I needed to believe in magic, but I could not find it in the Bible after the day when God had not mended a torn picture-book overnight for me.

I can see now that there were three distinct epochs

in my own personal reading life as a child, when certain books provided the distinctive colour, the emotional tone of my existence, and gave me the archetypes and the objects of identification that I needed. Up to the age of ten or eleven I moved in a world evoked by a series of volumes published by the Religious Tract Society in the Edwardian period. The outstanding authors on the Society's list were Hesba Stretton, Mrs O. F. Walton and Amy Le Feuvre. I knew nearly all their books, but three of them stood out, and I remember them most vividly to this day: *Little Meg's Children*, *Jessica's First Prayer*, and *Christie's Old Organ*. Most of the titles, incidentally, were phrased possessively.

One of the chief themes of these books was poverty. The poor were poor indeed. The children were always stunted, with shrewd, anxious faces. They habitually wore rags; some might have red dresses and bonnets hidden away to be worn on the annual occasion of a sailor father's return from sea, but, if he was delayed, they had to pawn them. They went barefoot even in hard frost. Their feet turned blue and so numb that if they hit them against doorsteps, badly enough to make them bleed, they could hardly feel it, and their characteristic gesture of putting one foot over the other provided only the illusion of warmth. Their arms were blue, too, but this might be because of bruises.

They ate almost nothing except crusts and stale buns which people threw at them. They lived in airless attic rooms off grimy courts, reached by steep, crooked staircases. The rain came through their roofs into broken tubs. Their ceilings were weather-stained and their floors rotten. They slept on straw or on rough mattresses with improvised pillows, and had only a handful of coals, if that, to warm them.

There was no solidarity among the poor. The inhabitants of the courts were always a 'bad crew' who drank, brawled and cursed. They neglected the sick of their community, leaving them to die with no food, no covering and no light, and if any inmate's children appeared decently dressed they would be stripped before they reached the shelter of the larger streets so that their clothes might be pawned for gin. The women ill-treated and over-worked any child who might be running errands or drudging for them.

The poor were automatically objects of suspicion. Everyone, even the most charitable of ministers, assumed them to be thieves ('I shall be sure to know if you cheat me') and in the matter of their possible possession of religious faith or any principles, there was a simple formula which dealt with that: no shoes or bonnet = heathen.

A companion theme obviously had to be riches. The rich were not as rich as all that – a description of one of their houses might make it sound no bigger than the villas on the Salterton Road – but they were superior beings, marked out by their manners and their attitude to life, particularly their attitude to the poor. They had been brought up on the motto, 'Remember the poor', and the good rich did remember them, systematically, though they found it difficult to remember their names: even Miss Mabel, when she knew Christie quite well, tended to address him as 'organ-boy', while Miss Winnie and Miss Jane always called Jessica 'little girl'. It was only the good rich who appeared in the books; the bad rich were suppressed.

The rich were sumptuously dressed. The rustle of silk was a sure sign that they were approaching, and the silk itself would certainly be red or pink or some other bright impractical colour. Rich women did not walk; they swept, even into Chapel, with their velvet mantles and the long, rich feathers on their velvet bonnets taking up the whole aisle. Rich boys tended to be dressed as little Highlanders and to show off their kilts, dirks and pouches to fond mammas and nursemaids.

The rich were patronising. It was not just that they threw pennies out of top windows and expected the poor to root about in the flower-beds to find them; it was rather that even the nicest of them kept harping on the difference in station. Miss Winnie and Miss Jane read texts aloud to each other in front of Jessica about not rebuffing the poor, and made signs at her all through the service as to when to stand up and when to kneel, which she could perfectly well have observed for herself. Even the minister, searching for an analogy to show Jessica the need of preparation for the Kingdom, turned instinctively to the fact that if – the most bizarre of hypotheses – he were to take her into his own house to live with his daughters she would have to be washed and dressed properly. Salvation did nothing to obliterate these differences. When in later life Christie and Miss Mabel, now young Mrs Villiers the Rector's wife, were both engaged in the Lord's work and happened to meet by sickbeds in dismal lofts, he, though no longer 'organ-boy', was always 'Christie' and she was always 'ma'am'. And although all were equal in the sight of God, it was an alarming triumph for democracy when Old Treffy and Miss Mabel's mother, who died on the same day, entered the City together.

But they were not as revoltingly snobbish as some people in a mid-way position credited them with being. Mr Daniel, the Chapel-keeper who ran a coffee-stall on weekdays to make more money – he was not only mid-way socially but also mid-way in his Christianity – was desperately anxious that the grand congregation should not find out about the stall, as they would think it low and mean of him and might even dismiss him. But in fact when the truth finally came out no one turned a hair.

And they were sustainedly compassionate. At the

artless remarks of the poor, they were for ever putting handkerchiefs to their eyes and being able to say no more. It never once occurred to them, as it never occurred to me, or to my parents, or to Hesba Stretton, Mrs O. F. Walton and Amy Le Feuvre, that anything could or should be done beyond tears and the hand-out and the prayer in the wretched attic. Into neither the world of books nor the real world in which I lived did ideas of socialism and social reform ever enter. The authors of the books not only believed, as did the Brethren, that being washed in the blood of the Lamb was the only thing that mattered but also that God Himself had ordained who should be rich and who should be poor, so that to tamper with the existing social order would have been both a frivolous sideline and a grave sin, and no one brought up on Brethren methods of thinking would reason that it could not possibly be both.

Whereas it had been perfectly easy to identify with the émigrés of the French Revolution, with these books it was rather a puzzle to know who one was. The poor children, Meg, Robin, Jessica and Christie, were the obvious choice; they were the heroes and heroines, and after terrible struggles and perils they all won through, Christie to be a Scripture Reader, Meg and her brother to start a new life overseas, and Jessica to help Mr Daniel with serving coffee at the stall and cleaning the Chapel, though I admit I felt this last to be a poor reward. There were other elements in their histories, too, which made them very congenial. For one thing, their parents failed them; there was nothing in the tales to remind one that such a thing as a human father existed for the poor, except the one appearance of Meg's sailor father, and he did not cut much of a figure, having left them in unsavoury lodgings to starve, while mothers were produced only that they might immediately die or go off on a permanent spree, abandoning their children to destitution. For another thing, nearly all the children at some point lay seriously ill with the nameless, killing fever which was my own constant preoccupation.

There was a conflict, however. Although we were poor, we were by no means as poor as that, and in fact were being carefully brought up to be as like Miss Mabel, Miss Winnie and Miss Jane as our circumstances allowed. To go barefoot seemed as disgraceful to us as it did to them, and if Father had described himself as a servant, meaning of the Southern Railway, our horror would have been equal to theirs when the minister referred to himself as a servant, meaning of God. There were no poor in Withycombe or Exmouth for us to be bountiful to, but we did our best by looking down at the occupants of the council houses at Littleham, especially when one of them, who went to the Meetings, borrowed a pound from Mother and never gave it back.

It was surprisingly easy to fit in the picture of London which these books gave with the London I really knew. The city which Meg and her children saw from her attic room, the vast stretches of roofs, and the masts of dockland and the occasional church spire which they could pick out in the thick atmosphere, unless the fog was so dense that they could not see even the stars or the street lamps, was more than a mile to the east of St Paul's Cathedral. Down at street level, in even staler air, were the dark gullies, the labyrinthine alleys and courts, where Jessica and Christie lived as well. The buildings reeked with the fumes of gin and tobacco and rang with the sound of groans, curses and sobs.

Sometimes the children worked their way to the edge of this maze of lanes and stood looking in awe at the broad streets where well-dressed people visited handsome shops. And it was precisely here that my path crossed theirs. The terrible slums of London were as dear a myth to Devonians as were its fogs to foreigners. As a family we were more familiar with the handsome streets of London than our fellow-countrymen were because of the free passes which enabled us to go to London as much as three times a year. We would mix with the fashionable people in and out of the well-appointed shops and then, when we got to a suitable place, stand fearfully at the street corners beyond which the slums were supposed to lie, peering into the dark world of Meg, Jessica and Christie, at much the same spot where they had peered out into our lighter realm and with equal panic. What went on in these poor districts was thought to be unspeakably evil and menacing, and was therefore, by definition, unstated, but the mere impression was enough to keep us safely out of its clutches.

I smile nowadays when I recall where some of these danger-spots were actually supposed to be, but it was no joke then. We caught the six o'clock train back to Exmouth, and so it was usually dark as we made our way to Waterloo. Father had warned us solemnly again and again that, if by any mischance one of us were to get separated from the others, whoever it was must always remember that once she had crossed Westminster Bridge, she must take the second turning to the left to arrive safely at the station, *not the first*. Down the first turning to the left there apparently lay a black and vicious district where rape, robbery and murder were almost inevitable. Father was not as specific as this, but I have to be, in order to do justice to the gravity and innuendo of his tone. His admonitions were certainly crowned with success; Mother, Sheila and I were all three much too frightened to make the fatal mistake of taking the first turning to the left, though our friends Meg, Robin, Jessica and Christie must have been down there somewhere.

The wickedness of London was something we believed in as firmly as we believed in the slums. Here again the books both shaped and bore out our forebodings. Girls like Mrs Blossom's Posy came to the city to go to the bad; apparently it could not be done in the country. Of course, what Posy actually did was not stated, but even in my ignorance I realised that the drunken disorderliness for which she was sent to the House of Correction, and which should have seemed quite evil enough, was in fact by no means all. Men came into it somehow, as Posy herself hinted; when Meg's father failed to come home on the day his ship docked, Posy went off to find him in the confidence that she knew what men got up to when they came ashore. What Posy knew, Mother at least suspected; once, when the three of us were waiting for Father at Tottenham Court Road underground station, she was deeply worried about a group of men, who, according to her, were eyeing us lustfully. I heard her telling Father about it later. It was very exciting, though I could not determine whether it was Sheila and me, or herself, that they were after. The men of Exmouth never acted like this.

I am sure it was plain to any Londoner who cared to give the matter a moment's thought that we were up from the country, but we would not really have had it otherwise. In the books you could tell a countrywoman by her fresh, rosy-cheeked comeliness, and I certainly had no objection to being so recognised. Country people carried with them the aura of lanes, roses and honeysuckle, and birds that were cleaner than the black sparrows of Meg's rooftops. I was largely blind to the charms of all these things when I was at home, but they somehow did me credit.

In later life, I remember, I was cheered to find in print opinions which were the reverse of all that I had been taught, but at this stage it was comforting to find them all confirmed. Apart from the paid ministers who appeared in the tales, everything was just as the Brethren said. The books were like a Gospel Meeting with a story. Heaven was our home, and we could only get there by the way of personal salvation. Those who had been washed in the blood of Jesus would be welcomed into the Heavenly City, and all sorrow and sighing would flee away. I believed the Brethren when they told me this, but it was a luxury to find it between hard covers as well. My reliance on God the Father, with all the radiance and cosiness he provided, was still absolute. It was only recently that I heard, with horrified surprise, *Christie's Old Organ*, *Jessica's First Prayer* and *Little Meg's Children* described as goody-goody children's stories. Well, perhaps, but I was a goody-goody child, and they were my native air.

After the age of ten, I turned to a series of works which were no less goody-goody, though the saving blood of Jesus had been transmogrified into a more abstract sense of decency. All the good characters in the *Anne* and *Emily* books of L. M. Montgomery were churchgoers, their religious beliefs clearly being basic to their mode of life, and the hard-hearted ones finally came to their senses and worshipped God again just like the backsliders I was used to, but the old evangelical terminology and concreteness had gone, to be replaced by a sentimentality which, in its own way, was even less true to real life. I now became as immersed in the world these books generated as I had been in the slums of London and the Eternal City. At first I was worried by the lack of explicitness about the way of salvation; Anne and Emily were obviously saved, but I would have felt easier in my mind if Miss Montgomery had said so. However, once I had surmounted this anxiety, by the joint help of time and habit, I rather enjoyed not having the blood of the Lamb washing over me perpetually. It was a pleasant change, too, to find at last, instead of the struggle to keep circulation going and clothes out of pawn, the normal preoccupations of the sort of girl I was and, more thrillingly still, the woman I was to become.

To crown it all, Emily was a poet. Anne was a creative writer, too, in a way, but I dismissed her early on as, by her own admission, she only wrote things that little children were fond of and, much worse, she gave it all up, quite cheerfully and automatically, when she got married. I greatly disapproved of this, not from any feminist point of view, but because, even then, I did not believe it could really happen. Mother's repeated laments that all her talents had gone down the kitchen sink never convinced me, as she could offer no proof of what they had been, and I knew perfectly well that if she had been a real writer – this was the only talent I could imagine – she would have gone on being one. I *knew* she could not have written even *Ursula's Last Term*.

Emily was a professional; her attitude was quite different. She had a vocation in the pursuit of which she suffered and made sacrifices, as the shrewd, drunken schoolmaster who first recognised her talent had foreseen she would. ('She will pay for it.') The actual theories about writing, however, that were embodied in the novels, I found disquieting. It is very surprising I should have done so. I had swallowed whole and without a qualm all the religious attitudes of Hesba Stretton and her sisters, but when it came to L. M. Montgomery's attitudes about poetry, although they were precisely what I had had authoritatively presented to me in school, I did begin to stir. What makes it odder still is that Emily's actual verse, plentifully quoted in *Emily of New Moon* and *Emily Climbs*, was much like mine – rhyme, metre, cliché, poetic diction and all – but I can honestly say I was uneasy when Emily rejected some words as ugly and explained that she never used them in her poetry. The best-selling novelist, Owen Ford, in *Anne's House of Dreams*, was just as bad, with his ideas about inspiration coming from beauty and his spooky notions about the central theme of a book which would beckon and allure, only to bob come-hitherishly out of his grasp, but at least, although one was supposed to admire him, one did not have to identify with him.

In the early books Anne and Emily were the same age as I was. I was quite unmoved by their childhood woes, which, I now see, were presented with the highest degree of unrealism; Anne, before the age of ten, had undergone a series of rejections from which no real child could ever have recovered. In sequels they both grew up, and it was when they were older than me that I became thoroughly involved with them. Emily's happiness, meaning her marriage, was long delayed, as you would expect with a poet, and her belated engagement, when she was too old to have her age specified, was the last we heard of her. Anne, however, got married at the very beginning of *Anne's House of Dreams*, and the book was devoted to feminine mysteries, feminine rather than sexual, to which I was now romantically introduced for the first time. The honeymoon passed without a murmur of sex, but the baby, from the first innuendo about what spring might bring to the House of Dreams, through whimsical hint to final outspokenness, was played up for all it was worth. The agony of motherhood was emphasised more than the ecstasy and I certainly found it more thrilling. The ecstasy was present but was described in sexual terms which seemed, even to me, to belong elsewhere and therefore to sound wrong in this connection. There were references to the holy passion of motherhood, and, once the infant was born, Anne and her woman friend were said to indulge in 'shameless orgies of love-making' when presumably they were just cuddling and admiring the baby.

The descriptions of the agony, however, were all that could be desired, and it was not only Anne who suffered.

Everyone was in agony: Gilbert's face was grey and haggard, Marilla paced the garden path muttering prayers between set lips, Susan sat in the kitchen with cotton-wool in her ears (a very exciting touch) and her apron over her head, and Leslie, who lived up the brook, saw that every window in the House of Dreams was lit and did not sleep all night. Actual quotations come back to me with the same vividness that speeches and sentences from *Jessica* and *Christie* do; Anne's 'pale face blanched with its baptism of pain' I shall remember, I suppose, as long as I remember 'And the Minister said Amen to Jessica's first prayer' or Treffy's despairing cry: 'Only another month. Only another month.'

This presentation of what the books called 'womanly joys and sorrows' now took over from a decade of my mother's and my aunts' whisperings to each other about the waters breaking and stitches. I enjoyed reading about these tortures, but I did not in the least want to be tortured myself. The raptures of motherhood sounded poor compensation, and I realise that, on the whole, I must have pitied Anne, for I began to include her regularly in my evening prayers, in the tone of self-conscious compassion that I kept for such unfortunates as Lawrence of Arabia's mother when her son was killed.

The content of the *Anne* and *Emily* books, mawkish and sentimental as no doubt much of it was, caused me not the slightest embarrassment, not even when the forty-five-year-old Miss Lavender pretended to be seventeen again, but the style sometimes did. Hesba Stretton and Mrs O. F. Walton, I still think, wrote rather well. They waded purposefully into their descriptions of London and of poverty, they called a slum a slum, and if there was anything they could not write about straightforwardly they left it out. L. M. Montgomery was often coy and circuitous, even when there was no need to be, and some of her sentences were mosaics of cliché, idiom and euphemism. They might have been phrases from collections of colloquial English expressions for foreigners. One example still sticks in my mind: 'The latch-string of the little house was always out for the race of Joseph.' It reminded me of 'The hand that rocked the cradle has kicked the bucket', which made me laugh in an English lesson at school.

But no ineptitude of style could seriously mar the world of Prince Edward Island, whose fresh air and agricultural society now replaced the slums of London. The distinction between rich and poor was ousted, too, by a way of life where everyone did chores. Even the most prosperous in the community skimmed milk, scalded dishcloths, bleached bedspreads and peeled potatoes. There was no hint of a better world where people were waited on. Neither did education unfit anyone for her original sphere. The 'eddicated' and the ignorant never got on each other's nerves or ceased to be equals. What should have been more like the world I knew than a big city could be was in fact much less like, but of course this was no drawback. I thought I was alone in my addiction until one day in school someone asked Mr Earp where Prince Edward Island was, and I guessed then that there were many of us.

It was after our second family holiday in the West Highlands of Scotland, when I was thirteen, that someone recommended that we should all read *The Flight of the Heron* by D. K. Broster, as it dealt with that part of the country at the time of the '45 rebellion. My mother bought it, and the most exciting period of all my reading life began. I was possessed by a rapture, an ecstasy, for which nothing in all my experience, and certainly not religion, had prepared me. I remember the actual surroundings in which I sat reading the book, on a bench in Phear Park for example, on a sunny Saturday morning. I can quite see why I had to escape from the house, though I wonder how I managed it, as my mother distrusted and discouraged solitary wanderings and expeditions.

Merely to enjoy the book was permitted, even approved. Mother read it with pleasure, but not with the passion I felt but which it seems I successfully hid from her. She soon got on to the sequels, *The Gleam in the North* and *The Dark Mile*, and mentioned casually one day that she had glanced at the last page of *The Dark Mile* and seen that 'he was mashing someone called Olivia'. I recoiled. Mashing. My faithful Ewen, who had married Alison in the first book. But it was all right. It was his cousin Ian. Mother could not tell the difference.

Sheila read *The Flight of the Heron*, too, but was less impressed. I think she realised how I felt; she once teased me about it. There was a stirring scene in the book where Charles Edward turned angrily on Ewen, who, as his aide-de-camp, had discovered that the Prince intended to go out into the streets of Edinburgh at night and was trying to persuade him not to, saying that he had not realised when he appointed him that he was hampering himself with a s———, biting off the offensive word half-way. Sheila knew I had got to this passage and said airily, 'Do you think the Prince was going to call Ewen a shit?' For a second I was horrified and affronted, and then we laughed together till we cried, taking care to keep fairly quiet. I am still not sure what the word really was. I presume it was not 'shit'.

Ewen Cameron was my first love. My interest in the process of having babies was superseded and swept clean away by this pure infatuation. Fortunately for me, he was not very interested in women. Alison was pretty and loving but no rival. His real feeling, I could see, was for men, and it was his relationships with them that made me tingle with an excitement that had no envy or possessiveness about it. He loved three men: his chieftain Lochiel, Lochiel's brother Archie, and Keith Windham, the English officer with whose fate his own was so mystically intertwined and who died holding his hand. All three of them were so attractive that I could love them too. The most emotional passages in the book showed Ewen involved in erotic situations with them – held in Lochiel's arms after saving him from the shell of a six-pounder at the siege of Fort William, lying in bed at Ardroy after the defeat with Archie bending over him, clasping the dying Keith against him on the white sands of Morar.

Ewen loved his native land, too, better than he loved Alison, as she herself coyly pointed out, and here again I could feel with him. Loch na h-Iolaire and Beinn Tigh, with their mists and their heather and their shapeliness enchanted me as they did him and threw the green fields of Prince Edward Island and the dark alleys of London right out of my dreams. I have seldom been as moved by anything in literature as I was by the description of how Ewen, on what seemed to be his last journey, gazed in farewell at the lakes and mountains of his home, as he rode past them, tied to his horse, on the way to Carlisle gate. I studied the map of Scotland with a raptness which might have been good for my Geography if we had ever done the West Highlands, though perhaps it was as well we did not, as I could hardly have borne to hear Mr Earp talking about it.

I first saw Ewen naked. He was swimming in Loch na h-Iolaire two hours after sunrise on a beautiful July morning and, in order to find out what his foster-brother Lachlan was up to, he came out of the water till he was waist-deep and then, after a titillating pause, came right out, splendidly made, and threw himself down unconcernedly in the heather. The word 'unconcernedly' added just the right touch of embarrassment. All the time he was sitting in the heather and bog-myrtle, clutching his bare, bent knees, I was conscious of his bare bottom on the scratchy plants. ('Dhé, how these vegetables prick.')

Looking back on *The Flight of the Heron* I feel sad. The feelings it roused in me were not about anything real, yet I have experienced nothing stronger since. Loch na h-Iolaire and the house of Ardroy, Ewen Cameron and Keith Windham never existed, yet they brought me a unique joy. I have never known a greater love for any person or any land, nor half such an ardent loyalty to any cause. Naturally I was a Jacobite.

CHAPTER SEVEN

Thou Shalt Not

It is not easy to say what being a member of the Plymouth Brethren actually involved. Nothing could be simpler than to describe what Meetings we went to and the form they took or to define the articles of our belief; on both points everything was as rigid and prescribed as could well be; but to indicate the ways in which our beliefs and our routine of chapel-going moulded our morals and our attitudes I find almost impossible, and I suspect it may be because not much moulding in fact took place. Examining my own conscience I cannot see that my years of worship and faith affected my soul at all, certainly not for good. Being saved did not prevent me from being mean and selfish; I was possibly no worse than most children, but considering my lifelong dedication to a loving Lord I should presumably have been better.

I really cannot think of any virtue, as opposed to outward behaviour, which the Brethren extolled or tried to inculcate in their children and practise themselves. I am not saying that there were no examples of courage, humility, kindness, cheerfulness and tolerance in the Assemblies; many of the Saints had these qualities, sometimes to a heroic degree, but it must have been because that was the sort of people they were. These virtues were never presented to us; I do not mean that they were not presented attractively or in a manner that would win us to emulation; I mean they were not presented at all. Two of them indeed – cheerfulness and tolerance –

would not have been considered as virtues. And no one was ever assessed by the criterion of spiritual gifts; it was always a question of conduct. A brother would be rebuked and shunned if he went to the races, but if he was haughty or even cruel no one would think the worse of him as a Christian, though they might dislike him as a person.

Our code of behaviour was entirely negative, a complex system of prohibitions. I have already mentioned three things I was not allowed to do because I belonged to the Plymouth Brethren: I could not go on roundabouts, take part in raffles or games of chance, or do any dancing except Country Dancing. These were by no means the only taboos. There was almost nothing Brethren *were* allowed to do. Any pleasant activity was by definition worldly pleasure and therefore ruled out, and although the term 'worldly pleasure' suggested that there must somewhere be some unworldly pleasure, of a higher and more satisfactory kind, I never experienced it, and neither did anybody else, as far as I could see.

Many of the taboos were concerned with entertainment. The most dangerous ogre of all was the cinema, which was only a little younger than the Plymouth Brethren movement itself and had all the menace of novelty. The theatre was just as bad, of course, but there were hardly any theatres in Devon, so the temptation was not on the doorstep, and in any case it was a more respectable temptation connected with a much older tradition, added to which everyone knew that films were more entertaining, less heavy-going, than plays, which automatically made them worse. The cinemas of the thirties, even the Tudor at St Marychurch, always looked so glitteringly evil, too.

Early in life, of course, I asked why I could not go to plays and films and was given two reasons. The first I have quoted elsewhere: plays and films tell lies. Ironically

this is my own chief complaint against them today, but
I do not mean quite what the Plymouth Brethren meant,
that is, that the actors were stating that they were people
who in real life they were not, and were talking and
behaving in sustained pursuit of this falsehood. The
second reason was that actors and actresses led immoral
lives. I found both these reasons infuriating, but they were
difficult to combat. In reply to the first, one could only
say that of course they did, but they deceived nobody,
and why did it matter, which sounds quite convincing
now, but would have cut no ice then. Any possible retort
to the second was undermined by the fact that the
Daily Mail, which my parents took, seemed always to be
full of accounts of the divorces and other escapades of
film stars, and I suppose that the climate of Hollywood,
both geographical and moral, did make their sex lives
more eventful than they would otherwise have been,
and who was subsidising them in their wickedness but
the patrons of the Tudor? I see now that the second reason
was particularly perverse, in that, just this once and just
to be awkward, the Brethren were, however crazily,
envisaging the responsibility of the individual for his
fellow men. At no other time, in politics, civil affairs or
anything else, did they allow themselves any such wild
trains of thought.

So we grew up without ever seeing a film, though something of the culture got through to us. In infancy, I was
given a celluloid figure called Jackie Coogan. In girlhood,
friends spoke of Jessie Matthews and Shirley Temple.
At school parties guessing games were often based on
theme tunes from films. It was very distressing indeed
to be unable to identify any of them.

My mother, in her near-isolation, did not experience
these social embarrassments, but once she was on the
verge of yielding to temptation. *Cavalcade* came to
Exmouth, and everyone went to see it, even those who

never gadded as a rule, even Nurse Markby, the gaunt, wild, elderly occupant of the house two doors down from us in Bradham Lane. She called afterwards on purpose to beg my mother to go, and was so eloquent and so coherent that my mother very nearly gave way. But the moment passed, and on the whole I think she had no particular wish to go to the pictures.

As far as I know, none of the Brethren did transgress. For one thing it was so public; Sister Somebody would have been sure to see you going in. But a very tricky situation arose at St Marychurch when a Brother took the job of commissionaire at the Tudor. Times were hard, and many people were out of work, including several of the Saints, but this was felt to be no excuse. Yet they could not exactly turn him out of the Assembly. I believe he was spoken to by the Oversight, but he held on to his job and could be seen in his livery of sin night after night, gloomily but obstinately ushering the beaming unsaved in to their worldly pleasures.

The wireless was a newer temptation even than the cinema, showing how the Devil was always at it. My father and mother would never have a wireless in the house, they said; as though most people had them in the garden, I spitefully thought, longing for one. But some of my Torquay relatives weakened surprisingly soon, and in general the Brethren gave way to the wireless, even while I was a child, in a way they never did to the cinema, though in fact much the same objections might have been raised: the wireless told lies, and probably a few of the announcers led fairly immoral lives. As it was, in the course of the thirties, the nearest some of the Brethren got to a game was to have a wireless but to put it under the table when a really strict visiting Brother came to tea before preaching the gospel and to tell everybody afterwards how he sat there with his feet on it and never knew it.

Plymouth Brethren did not drink. For one thing, few of them could have afforded it, and indeed this was perhaps one factor in their condemnation of play-acting and the wireless, though it was never admitted. Social occasions had to warm up without alcohol, which was possibly why they did not warm up very much. Even Christmas parties rose to no more than non-alcoholic ginger wine, and even that only as a stirrup-cup, as though one thing might lead to another if the guests were not on the point of going away. But the Brethren inconsistency operated in this field too. My mother and aunts would frequently order cases of stout to be delivered to the house, to be kept in a dark corner of the larder and drunk ritualistically last thing at night as a tonic.

Although Brethren did not drink, however, they could not condemn alcohol outright as a matter of principle; not only was there no text in the Bible to support such an attitude, but there were even verses which positively promoted liquor. Paul recommended drinking wine for the stomach's sake, and the Good Samaritan used it medicinally, though whether he poured in into the wound or into the mouth of the man who fell among thieves was not clear in the translation, and it was not our way to inform ourselves about first-aid practices at the time of Christ. It was easy to ignore the fact that Jesus drank wine. He was such a law unto himself that much of his behaviour, for example, remaining celibate and being rude to his mother, could be denounced in his own name when imitated by, in the first place, Popish priests and, in the second case, Sheila and me.

They did not therefore encourage members to sign the pledge or even provide the opportunity for it. There was something worldly about the procedure; it smacked of organisation and of being a movement, and moreover was based on a social experience of the demon drink which may not have been very up-to-date but was more realistic than the Brethren quite liked. As a matter of fact I did sign the pledge when I was about nine, at Point-in-View, the little Anglican chapel in the fields just outside Exmouth. I read out the oath very solemnly in my best voice, getting even the word 'beverages' right, but totally misunderstanding what I was swearing as I thought that renouncing alcoholic liquors 'as beverages' meant 'such as beverages', not 'except medicinally', and was left with the impression that as long as I kept off beverages, whatever they were, I was remaining true to my word. On that occasion, as so often, my precocity at reading deceived myself and everybody.

It must have been the jolly social aspect of drinking that repelled the Brethren, and of course the buildings in which it took place. Pubs were disgraceful, and you drew your skirts aside and averted your eyes as you went past, leaving the sinners to it, not going in after them like the Salvation Army. Mother, however, seemed to like catching people out, once they were safely in the street. One day some girls of about our own age, whose family Mother knew, were seen coming away from the off-licence of the pub at the top of Jubilee Terrace, carrying a basket, and Mother practically crowded them into the gutter in her curiosity to see what was at the bottom of the basket; in vain, as a newspaper was spread decently over the contents. I wonder how she would have reacted if it had been stout.

It is very difficult to say what the Brethren thought about sex. Whereas my mother, as an individual, said a great deal, the Brethren as a body said almost nothing. The actual composition of the Assemblies was likely to produce a rather balanced approach to the subject. The numbers of men and women were about equal, and I cannot remember any pious frustrated spinsters of the type I noticed in such abundance later on in the Church of England. There was a decidedly family atmosphere, though it was brought about by a preponderance of married couples rather than by a plethora of children. Many couples had one child, few had more than one, and there was a considerable proportion with none at all. This tendency to unfruitfulness, though obviously I cannot examine it now with any sort of accuracy, would seem to have been due to dislike of children rather than dislike of sexual intercourse. One pair of newly-weds, the Middletons, who worshipped in one of the Torquay Assemblies, openly told anyone who would listen that they had deferred their marriage until the age of child-bearing was past. They had left a wide margin for safety too, Sheila and I thought. They looked very ancient indeed, but appeared at the Breaking of Bread shining with an unmistakable radiance which had not been there in the decades of their engagement or at least such few years of it as I had observed. In general, the Assemblies wore an air of longstanding and reasonably happy marriage.

Mother was against sex. She said that she had never – the verb was in the past tense – enjoyed it herself, or rather, to quote accurately, that *that side* of marriage had never meant anything to her; but this, like so many of her attitudes, was probably inspired by notions of gentility rather than of Puritanical religion, though, as I have mentioned, the two often went hand in hand. Women, not so much of the class she belonged to but of the class she aspired to belong to, might at that time be supposed to think like this. Many of my mother's views in general had, I think, been filtered down to her from the real ladies for whom my grandmother, when she was in good service, had worked: notions of delicacy and refinement and the nicest way to do things. Ladies did not enjoy sex, so she was damned if she was going to either. Certainly in her mind most of the feminine vices coincided with sexual generosity. When some famous slut, whose lavatory smelled and who threw socks away when they got holes in them, remained over the years the object of her husband's devotion and interest, Mother would explain this injustice by saying, 'Well, of course, if he can get *that* whenever he wants it . . .'

It was the bearing and bringing up of children, however, that brought out her real bitterness. There was nothing affected or cerebral here. Betty Martin told me at school one day all about the trousseau of a cousin of hers and was particularly vivid about the dressing-gown, which was made of light blue velvet and had a Medici collar. I had no idea what a Medici collar was, but it sounded lovely, and I repeated the description to Mother when I got home. She fairly spat out: 'Yes, it'll look marvellous when the babies start peeing all over it.'

I wonder whether I was, without conscious intention, meaning to taunt her, because by this time – I was at the Grammar School – I must have been sufficiently aware of her views to realise that descriptions of honeymoon clothes, especially bedroom wear, would be red rag to a bull. I remember very well one occasion when I was quite small and was in Mother's bed one morning when she was getting up. As she sat on the chamber-pot – genteelly and idiotically called 'chamber' when it was not vulgarly called 'po' – she told me how, ever since my birth and because of its difficulties, she had had trouble in passing water. 'That shows,' she concluded, 'how much I love you.' This provoked me to one of my few open displays of defiance as opposed to the withdrawn sulking which was my more usual weapon. I sat straight up in bed and glared at her. 'Well, you needn't have had me,' I said. That time I won, I have no idea how or why. She was not especially reproachful, and there was not a single reference to the grief I had caused Jesus.

My mother had some rational grounds for disliking children. I was born only fourteen months after Sheila, which was sooner than they could afford or than her health and nervous protectiveness of us could stand. It was a mistake, she often told me, meaning not that it turned out to be a mistake, but that my conception was against their intentions. As far as I can assess my reactions to this piece of information, it did not make me feel unwanted, more like a clever survivor. The chores which our first years involved Mother in seem to have irritated her terribly. She always took great pains to dress us well and keep us clean, and I can understand her furious despair when, according to her, we waited until we were got up in outdoor clothes, knitted romper suits and all, before thoroughly wetting ourselves. In all her family there seems to have existed this animus against child-bearing. When Olly was pregnant she had bad bouts of sickness, and often when she was retching in the scullery my grandmother would come out, not to hold her head or do anything helpful, but to comment sourly, 'The joys of matrimony, my dear.'

I had certainly adopted the Jeffery viewpoint about the rigours of married life at an early age. There were two women of much the same age in the Exmouth Assembly: one, who was drawn and haggard, was called Western, and the other, who was rosy and placid, was called Colson. I knew one was Mrs and the other was Miss, and in view of their appearance assumed that they must be Mrs Western and Miss Colson. I was extremely surprised to find that it was in fact the unmarried lady who looked as though life had been too much for her.

I never had the impression that the Brethren, as a community, thought that sex was especially dangerous or fraught with temptation, so probably here again it was Mother's own personal attitude, though on this point she was wholeheartedly joined by my father. He was often eloquent on the perils which awaited young girls when they went out into the world. He explained to us that men offered girls drugged cigarettes which would make them unconscious and therefore easy prey. 'We don't smoke,' I said pertly. I never minded answering *him* back. 'No, I know,' he replied resourcefully. 'They'd have to put it into chocolates for you.'

Mother seemed to enjoy alluding to sexual crimes. Exeter gaol lay alongside the railway line just outside Queen Street Station, so we had to pass it on our way back to Exmouth. There was sure to be someone in there for rape or something similar, and she would tell us about it as the train went by. Once it was a man who had raped his fourteen-year-old niece and got her pregnant. 'Her uncle!' Mother glared at the prison. I thought of my favourites, Jack and Uncle David, but shuddered.

Modesty meant only one thing to the Brethren, and to my parents: the avoidance of any display of the body. My father and mother went through the most ingenious contortions while dressing and undressing in our presence, and I am sure they kept it up when they were alone together. Things were made easier by the fact that we all wore our vests in bed, so there was always one basic layer covering the worst areas. My father's procedure was to sit solidly on the edge of the bed – we would be in the bed, so he was turned safely away from us – bending forward so that his shirt spread over his thighs, under which cover he exchanged his pyjama trousers for his long pants like some elephantine conjuring trick. My mother was much more nippy and deft. Standing up, she could put on almost everything under her nightdress, whipping it off at the last moment as though she were unveiling a plaque.

This idea of modesty naturally extended to the sort of clothes we wore and the way we wore them. Anything tight-fitting, flashy or low-cut was out of the question. Within these limitations, however, the Sisters of the Assembly dressed rather well. (Of course, we always saw them in their Sunday clothes, hardly ever during the week.) The material would be of good quality and carefully chosen; they took trouble. Respectability demanded it as well as suitable deference for the Lord's Table. We were all very respectable, and the ample cut of our clothes had a dual purpose: anything skimpy would suggest not only lechery but poverty. But though the local Sisters could look quite comely, the lady missionaries labouring for the Lord in the foreign field really were freaks. Lantern slides and photographs arrived from abroad showing them dressed in baggy blouses and skirts, looking like piles of laundry dumped down in the middle of groups of shapely natives.

As a child I felt very much the lack of fashion and elegance in the Assemblies. I hated my own clothes, which was ungrateful, as Mother made them herself and put a lot of work into them, and in fact Sheila and I had more new frocks than anyone else at school, but they seemed so dowdy and bunchy that it was difficult to be even decently appreciative. We were dressed alike, too, which made us stand out like a miniature set of something and emphasised the home-made character of our outfits. Graham Martin, Betty's younger brother, once made a remark which I found devastating, though Mrs Martin repeated it to us in all good humour. He had seen us on our way to the Gospel Hall one Sunday in our new summer dresses, and had said to his mother, 'Do the Beer girls always wear yellow?' There was something in the question which nettled me for years.

Mother and all the Sisters, not surprisingly, had strong notions of respectability on the subject of underclothes: they must be stout, infinitely concealing ('those filthy French knickers'), and either whole or properly mended; but Mother went further: they must match. She put as much weight on this criterion, snobbishly, as she did, moralistically, on that of decency. When we went bathing with a girl from the Meetings called Sylvia, whose blue princess petticoat was seen to be accompanied by knickers which, though directoire, were pink, Mother said loftily afterwards, 'Oh well, 'tis probably things people have given her.'

Comely was the politest word you could use for the Sisters, and then only of the ones who had definite natural advantages. No help was at hand for those with shiny cheeks, red noses, grey lips or ferrety eyes. Make-up, as I have said, was such a basic taboo as to be virtually unmentionable. Glasses and false teeth were allowed, and indeed were very popular with the Sisters, who often had recourse to them before it was actually necessary. I suppose such aids would feel excitingly like personal adornment if you were allowed no other kind. Aesthetic considerations did not enter into the choice, however. In fact, the most hideous and ill-fitting on the market seemed the favourites.

Sheila and I were untroubled by all this, obviously, during the years when we needed no make-up, but when Sheila was fourteen and I thirteen we fought a long and bitter battle with my mother on the subject of underarm hair. We both had luxuriant crops, and, as we did a lot of bathing and often wore sleeveless dresses, which were considered permissible for the little girls we were still considered to be, this was most embarrassing. Mother at first categorically forbade us to do anything about it. She and her sisters had never seen the need to do so, God had put it there, and that was that. For months, on and off, we miserably and resentfully studied the advertisements for Veet which described so mellifluously how the paste dissolved the hair roots, leaving the elegant uncluttered armpits that you could see on the girl in the illustration. We became quite obsessed. It shows how much under my mother's thumb we were that the possibility of buying a tube of Veet out of our pocket-money, using it and then asking Mother what she was going to do about it never crossed our minds. We had just enough courage to persist in our entreaties, and that was all. Even our best arguments we dared not try on her, but rehearsed them grumpily to ourselves, as on the day when we were climbing up from Petitor Beach and Sheila suddenly exclaimed that it was all right to say that God had made underarm hair, but he had made Veet, too, or allowed it to be made. Not long after this, however, Mother recognised the emergency enough to suggest that perhaps a heavy application of talcum powder would hide the hair. Victory was in sight. A few weeks later she bought us a tube of Veet.

It was the same with Odorono and brassières, only not so drawn out. The question of brassières was Sheila's worry principally, as she was very well-developed and in a mixed class at school where the boys shouted, 'Here comes Venus!' when she entered the formroom, but I backed her up as well as my less pressing needs warranted. The argument against deodorants was much the same as the argument against brassières, and both resembled the one employed in the underarm-hair controversy, that is, they were neither appointed by God nor used by Mother in her youth, and the features they were meant to control were natural. The outcome of the discussions was similar, too. Mother let us discard the clumsy underarm shields which we had sewn into our dresses and which used to become clammy in the first five minutes of wearing, and she made us brassières. They were prettily done, out of odd scraps of flowery material. They did not outline or support the bust; they acted more like bandages, but for the moment we were satisfied.

There was one battle we never won. It raged for years, and even after her death Mother's known wishes prevailed. This was the question of long hair. Paul had said that a woman's crowning glory was her hair and that it was a shame for a woman to be shaven and shorn. None of the Saints knew or cared that he was speaking to specific loose women who were letting down the tone of a particular church at a definite date in the first century. The words were enough. No Sister must be shaven or shorn. Up to the decade of my childhood his remark had been irrelevant because no one had dreamed of being shorn, but at this time bobbing and shingling had not only come into fashion but were so widely practised by women under fifty that to have long hair was equivalent to wearing a crinoline. I did not much want to be shingled. The girl who sat in front of me at school had this extreme cut, and the sight of the spiky hairs just emerging from the over-pale skin on her neck and half-way up her head rather put me off, but I passionately wanted to be bobbed. It was probably the most intense sustained feeling of my childhood.

At one point Sheila and I were the only two girls in the whole of Exmouth Grammar School, except one notorious frump, who had long hair. We wore it in pigtails. Sheila's looked quite pretty, as a matter of fact. Her hair was curly, and the loose tails that came below the ribbons went into natural corkscrews, and the short ends that would not go into the plaits turned into ringlets at the nape of her neck. My hair was straight and did neither of these things. It was long and heavy, and the weight of the pigtails pulled it right back off my forehead, which was too high in any case. I looked terrible.

Paul having said what he did, I knew Mother would never relent. We were fortunate, I suppose, that he had not mentioned Veet, Odorono and brassières. It is a good indication of my angry confusion of mind that I felt that God might help. In books girls frequently had their hair cut off in high fevers. This would be a way out, I thought, though I may have been wrong in my assumption that

Mother would regard a high fever as *force majeure* when such an important principle was at stake. So night after night I prayed for a fever. As most of my time I was neurotically terrified of getting one, this shows how fierce my wish was; I would almost have died to be bobbed. God did not answer my prayer, I need hardly say. It would have been very odd if he had.

Mother realised how strongly I felt. She could hardly have helped it, even though I told her nothing about my prayer, and she did what she could to alleviate the situation. It was not in her power to reprieve the condemned man, but she could at least provide a hearty breakfast. Sometimes when she had washed my hair she brushed it thoroughly and took me into her bedroom, where she had arranged two mirrors so that I could see how nice it looked hanging down my back. 'There,' she said, 'that's to help you along the road of not being bobbed.' I felt trapped and hopeless. It was kind of her to take the trouble, and my hair did look beautiful, but it was simply not the point, not the point at all.

When she resorted to logic, however, it was worse. In her girlhood young ladies had taken great pride in their long hair; their maids brushed it for hours. Even in the lower echelons of society it had been a good thing to have it long; one girl in her class, who had lice, had come to school cropped, and the others had danced round her shouting: 'Shaved for the maggots.' This was not the point either.

But the bitterest part of it all came years later, when I realised it was not a question of principle at all, but of the passage of time. The Brethren moved with the times in the worst possible sense: they did not rethink their rules in a mood of enlightenment working on social change; they just gradually stopped forbidding. By the end of the thirties, though Paul was still thundering away about the shame of being shaven and shorn, the Sisters of the Assembly were as shorn as anyone else if they wanted to be, without a blow struck. I have lost touch now, but I dare say they go to the cinema and wear make-up, though probably they have not caught up with the contemporary fashion for long hair. They may even forbid it.

For the first few years of my chapel-going life, my parents worshipped at the Gospel Hall in Exeter Road. This was a rather fine grey and pink stone building with tall sash windows and one little circular one. It had a porch at one side that linked it with the house of the caretaker, Mr Edds. Outside, next to the notice-board, was John 3: 16. We always spoke of texts by their reference like this. For one thing it was quicker, for another it sounded initiated. This particular text was the first I learnt by heart, the first of many. It was basic to our beliefs. 'For God so loved the world that he sent his only begotten son.' Inside, the hall was light, large and impressive, and full of other basic texts: 'By grace are ye saved through faith.' 'The wages of sin is death.'

I have little more than a composite memory of the Brethren at the Exeter Road Meeting. Only two personalities really stand out, Brother Jones and Brother Johnson, Brother Jones was a barber; he had a shop just opposite the station with ERNEST H. JONES above it, looking like an alias, so different a life did he seem to lead during the week. He was grander and more used to mixing with the world than most of the Brethren, yet he roused none of the resentment that he would have done had he been for example as rich as Mr Sercombe, of the Exeter Assembly, who sold bananas, or as professional and middle-class as Dr Sims, also of Exeter. He was smooth in his manner, and popular, a natural headman. He officially ran the Sunday School, and, unofficially, the whole Assembly. His wife was very strong-minded and reasonably benevolent. I remember her being always there. My father referred to her behind her back as

Maudie, which sounded like an alias, too. Brother Johnson was waspish and domineering. No doubt he had many other sides to his character, but this is all that ever struck me, and it struck me very often.

When I was about ten, the Oversight proposed a dramatic step: to open a new Gospel Hall in the middle of a growing council estate at Littleham. Several members of the Exeter Road Meeting lived near the proposed site and were sounded as to their willingness to form the nucleus of the new Assembly. My parents were the first to be approached, as Withycombe and Littleham were neighbouring villages. From our house we could clearly hear the bells of Littleham church when the ringers were practising on Friday evenings. Originally there had been a couple of miles between the two places, but now they had spread till they were as nearly joined as Withycombe and Exmouth. Bradham Lane was the direct way from Withycombe to Littleham, so we were the obvious choice as pioneers.

My parents agreed. It would have been difficult not to, but in fact it suited them quite well. The walk to Littleham was shorter and pleasanter than the walk into Exmouth, which was an important factor as we did it three times on Sundays. It consisted simply of going up Bradham Lane, which was still peaceful and leafy, and turning to the right at Littleham Cross. The new hall was to be just off the Salterton Road, in the newer, poorer world which had sprung up behind the prosperous villas. I think my parents liked the added prominence it would give them, too. Certainly they achieved a position which would have been impossible in the Exmouth Assembly, especially for my father, who as a Saint was very much a newcomer.

I wonder now who put the money up for the new hall and how it was all managed, but I had no curiosity of the kind then. There must have been a great deal of discussion and organisation, but all I know is that the new building took shape quite quickly. It was more a hut than a hall, rather like Hebron Hall in Torquay. In view of its position, in the middle of the new estate, the Brethren imagined that it would grow on more evangelical lines than the meeting in Exmouth could, set as it was in the middle of a community of those who had made up their minds long ago whether to go to the Baptists, the Methodists, Holy Trinity or nowhere. There was a Brother called Widdowson who had just come to live in Littleham and who was very enthusiastic and evangelically minded. My mother, who was not (she would never go to Open Airs), used to say scornfully that he had visions of himself putting out extra chairs to accommodate the throngs pressing in to the Gospel Meeting and crying, 'Another soul saved. Glory, hallelujah.' If he did have such a dream, it never came true.

The new Assembly, though it remained small, was a pleasant and prosperous one, however. Brother Widdowson, even with his hopes cut down to size, was keen and hard-working. His wife, who looked just like the traditional sentimental picture of an almswoman, taught very sweetly in the Sunday School. Brother Palk had been in the War with Uncle David and had two sons, Percy and Harold, who Sheila and I used to think might do for us, until our growing educational aspirations made it clear, to us, that they would not, quite apart from the fact that they took not the slightest interest in us; I have the impression that they both married widows. Brother Scott and Brother Restall were new arrivals in the district and brought considerable glamour and sophistication to our gathering. Of Brother Restall I have to say more later; he was very important. Brother Scott was a lively and amusing man with a wife who was pretty in a worldlier way than the Sisters we were used to. All our family liked the Scotts very much. Indeed my mother took up the cudgels very decidedly for

Brother Scott, who was the subject of some criticism among the Saints, because he travelled for Imperial Tobacco. Brother Palk was her chief adversary on this issue. I am not sure what she actually said to him, as they happened not to discuss it in my presence, but I overheard her telling my father in an unguarded moment – normally she avoided coarse language – that Brother Palk would travel for Imperial Shit if they paid him enough.

It was axiomatic that Plymouth Brethren did not attend services or other functions, even garden fêtes, held by Anglicans, Baptists and Methodists; an exception was sometimes made in the case of the Salvation Army, who could hardly be accused of not stressing the cleansing blood of the Lamb. Sheila and I had a fierce battle with Mother on one occasion when we were at the Grammar School. Withycombe Parish Church was holding a pageant in the Church Hall, and nearly all our schoolfriends were to appear in some scene or other. We begged Mother to let us go; she objected, principally on the grounds that a collection was to be taken in aid of the Church Missionary Society, and she could not possibly support the propagation of Anglican doctrines, opposed as they were to the Word and to God's plan of salvation – a perfectly logical conclusion if you happened to believe the premises. However, we pleaded so hard that she gave way but insisted on accompanying us; I suppose she aimed both at snatching us away from any too insidious persuasions in time and also at showing the neighbours that we had not flouted her authority, but were present with her dignified assent to watch the poor heathen at their antics. In the event it was an uncomfortable evening, as Mother sneered silently throughout, especially at points where we showed signs of being most impressed, as for example when a procession of monks shuffled slowly up the central aisle towards the stage, chanting an approximate plainsong.

It is the more remarkable, therefore, that for all the years of my childhood that I can remember we used as a family to attend the afternoon service at Point-in-View on summer Sundays. Point-in-View was an Anglican chapel surrounded by almshouses, little more than single rooms, the whole forming one low building with a central spire on which seagulls perched and squawked. It was set in the middle of a field. We knew its history; it had been projected and endowed by two maiden ladies who had lived in a grand though small house in the middle of the next field down. This house was called À la Ronde; it was years before I discovered how the name was spelt or what it meant. Of course, the house was not open to the public in those days – it is now – though the maiden ladies were long since dead, and it was regarded with respectful bewilderment. Everyone could see it was circular (no one knew quite why) and the rumour went that the individual rooms were shaped like pieces of pie, but instead of being taken as an oddity proceeding from the semi-cultured minds of two half-educated spinsters, it was looked up to as being the sort of thing the gentry did.

Point-in-View was almost engulfed by the most beautiful meadow I remember, with the longest, lushest, warmest grass I knew. At the far side of the meadow stood an elegant white manse, home of a series of very old mild clergymen: in view of the gentle nature of his responsibilities – half-a-dozen almswomen's souls to look after and one service a week – the incumbent was always very ancient indeed. The first one that I remember was Mr Ellis, who was so old he could hardly speak, and the only eloquence he ever had the strength for was summoned up by the subject of Queen Victoria, in whose reign he was clearly still graciously living. To this day I can hear his ghostly remnant of a voice in the hot sleepy stillness talking about her as though she was a young and vulnerable girl whom he would have defended to the death had he himself been young again. 'She was a flower,' he quavered. 'She was a flower.'

I loved Mr Ellis so much that I called my first doll Ellis. It seemed to me perfectly natural to do so, until people started saying that surely I meant Alice, and then, when I corrected them and explained the origin of the name, throwing up their hands at the quaintness of the fancy. Sheila, who had called her doll Muriel, was spared all this, so I soon learnt from her and rechristened mine Ruby.

The services at Point-in-View were above all relaxed. The chapel was tiny, full and hot. The spire, under which the miniature pulpit and organ stood, consisted chiefly of leaded triangular windows, through which the sun shone suffocatingly, and, as there were only five narrow pews on each side of the aisle, even a small congregation could pack them lethargically tight. The almswomen who attended simply walked in from their stuffy clean bed-sitting rooms next door, but everyone else had come on foot either from Exmouth or Withycombe, and was only too ready to sink down into sweating repose. Our own way there was a particularly beautiful one, through three overgrown lanes, dark green and heavy with heat.

The service itself was far from taxing. It was very Low Church indeed and was conducted on the simplest of lines with no sign of mummery or mumbo-jumbo. The message was perfectly orthodox according to our views, but the tone was more restful than that of our own Gospel Meetings: there was less insistence on the activity of getting saved, which the Plymouth Brethren could make sound so athletic, and the references to the afterlife, whether spent in Heaven or in Hell, represented it as much less strenuous. The hymns were often from the same stock as the ones we sang in the Assemblies, but they were chosen for their cheerful conviction rather than for their dire warnings to trembling sinners. There was one, 'Praise Him, Praise Him, Jesus our Blessed Redeemer', which had a really frisky tune and rhythm, and which I connect especially with Point-in-View, particularly the lines:

> Christ is coming, over the world victorious.
> Power and glory unto the Lord belong.
> O ye saints, that dwell in the mountains of Zion,
> Praise Him, Praise Him, ever in joyful song.

We made friends at Point-in-View. There was a family called Down, who came from Exmouth, whom we got to know and like better than any of the Brethren. They were open and good-tempered. Nellie Down, the schoolteacher daughter, played the organ, which Daddy Down, as we called him, pumped, sitting beside her. It was no doubt hard work to blow this organ systematically and reliably, but he always made it look a pleasure, though important, too, as he swayed forwards and backwards, singing heartily at the same time, his hymn-book held unnaturally in his free hand. There was cheerful gossip and greeting in the meadow afterwards and visits to Mrs Down's sister, who was one of the almswomen, and who always had a kiss for us children that was as stuffy and clean as her room.

The sheer prettiness of Point-in-View made it a welcome change from the Gospel Halls; it had panelling and painted lilies, hassocks (these were regarded suspiciously by my mother at first, but in fact hardly anyone did kneel to pray, so that was all right), and curly pew-ends with built-in collecting-boxes. Even the texts were more social and less personal than we were used to: 'O Israel, thou shalt not be forgotten of me,' and 'The labourer is worthy of his hire.' But basically I suppose it was the fact that neither our nor our parents' real responsibilities lay at Point-in-View that made it all look and feel so enjoyable.

From the time of the move to Littleham there was a growing anxiety in my mind: the prospect of baptism. As I have said, total immersion was the only way in which people could be fully received into the Assembly, that is, be allowed to break bread. The Brethren made certain that no one should approach the Lord's Table unworthily. When holiday-makers came to the Meeting on Sunday mornings they had to produce letters of introduction written by the Oversight of their own Assembly. These letters were stereotyped and couched in New Testament language. They nearly always ended with the command, 'Receive them as becometh Saints.' Apparently the behaviour thought to become Saints was not very hospitable; the visitors occasionally got asked to tea, but never by my mother.

There was no detailed tradition about the baptism of believers' children, because the Saints were so unfruitful, but in outline the procedure admitted no deviation at all. Young people were supposed to be quite ready by the age of fourteen to testify to their faith in the waters of baptism. If anyone had let it drag on till he was seventeen, for example, although for the sincere reason that he did not feel prepared to take such an important step, there would have been continual scandal, back-biting and nagging, and this would have come most heavily on the parents of the rebel. Their methods of upbringing, even their own personal salvation, would have been called into question. I knew this, and it alarmed me. Mother was the last person to have her authority doubted. She would never have supported any scruples of ours in the face of the whole Assembly, or indeed, to give her credit for consistency, at home.

By the time I was twelve remarks were beginning to be made, all addressed to Mother in our presence, never to us directly. Some were no more than friendly hints, but by the end of the year Brother Johnson had begun to turn nasty. (Exmouth being a small town, the Littleham Assembly was constantly under the eye of the Exeter Road Brethren.) One afternoon we met him in the lane on his bicycle. He drew up and asked Mother straight out when we were going to be baptised. 'Well, not *just* yet,' said my mother. He sneered at us over his handlebars, then turned to her and said: 'Oh, are they afraid of three feet of water?' in a most unpleasant voice. I realised it could not be long after that.

What precipitated it at last was the arrival of a letter from Torquay, written either by my grandmother or by one of my aunts at her instigation. It said that Reen was ready to be baptised – I imagine that the same sort of softening up had been administered to her – and that it would be a good idea if all three cousins were baptised together; in Torquay, of course. The letter came while Father was upstairs shaving, and we were having breakfast in the room below. Mother read it out, took our agreement for granted without even a questioning glance, and swept on into making arrangements about the date, what we should wear and so on. Father heard all this from upstairs, and for the only time in their life together, as far as I ever observed, he rebelled against Mother's strident disregard of any schemes but her own, in this particular case on a point which he at least realised was one of some delicacy. He came downstairs, half-shaved, stood in the doorway and looked angrily at her. 'When you've got everything settled, Queen,' he said, 'just send me a postcard, will you?' He then went upstairs again.

My mother must have felt the justice of his comment. There was a touch of guilt in her manner as well as a great deal of outrage and injury and scornful amusement, as she followed him up to the bathroom. I heard them arguing, but not what they said. She must have won. I never heard him protest again, about that or anything else.

Plans for the baptism went forward, smoothly except for the miserable conflict in the mind of at least one of the candidates. Sheila, and indeed Reen, too, may have felt just as I did, but we never spoke of it. I was deeply uneasy. I must already, and without acknowledging it, have realised how much my faith was a matter of pure conditioning with no natural source in any part of my personality. I obviously suspected that I should never be able to keep it up and that to be baptised was for me morally wrong, but I could not act on these suspicions; I could not even honestly formulate them to myself. There was only one way out of this irritation of spirit: to condition myself even more thoroughly than others had conditioned me. During the weeks before the baptism I systematically attempted this and with quite a degree of success. I brainwashed myself into something like holiness and belief.

I suppose, if I had approached my baptism with the sincere and natural faith which alone could have justified it, the whole process would not have seemed so embarrassing, though there really were sources of genuine embarrassment inherent in the situation. It *is* humiliating to be pushed under water, deliberately, in full view of a hundred gawping spectators, whose main motive in attending must be vulgar curiosity (there was no such turn-out for any other type of meeting), especially if you are a young girl self-conscious about your figure. As it was, in my case the embarrassment became an active, corroding shame, a prolonged violation.

Sheila and I had to be interviewed by two Brethren of our own Assembly before any further step could be taken. Brother Palk and Brother Widdowson conducted the examination, perfunctorily, as we were hardly likely to utter heresies about God's plan of salvation after thirteen years of sustained indoctrination. When we had glibly passed this test, the Assembly at St Marychurch took over the organisation of the ceremony itself. For me, the fact that it was going to be in Torquay made it worse. It was too much a part of my mother's perpetual whipping us away from the surroundings we loved. It made it too much of a widespread family affair, too. It was bound to be my mother's baptism in any case, but in St Marychurch it would belong to her family as well. Uncle David was to officiate.

Mother decided that we should wear white dresses. She ignored the fact that this was the sort of worldly symbol that the Saints despised and shunned, and moreover that it had strong Popish associations. It was her big production, and she was going to choose the costumes. Underneath, she decided, we would wear our bathing-dresses. Two days before the ceremony Sheila's period unexpectedly came on, but Mother rose to this emergency like a Victorian bride's mother. She whispered mysteriously and lengthily to Uncle David that he was to read Sheila's text as she was going down the steps into the tank and not keep her standing about in the water for any longer than was absolutely necessary. He took these hints, which presumably he interpreted correctly, so much to heart that when the moment came he was so brisk that he did not get Sheila's face completely under.

There was a special hymn which the Brethren usually sang at baptisms. It was not particularly appropriate in subject-matter, but it had a confident thumping rhythm and a rumbustious tune which expressed something of the tone of the occasion, from the point of view of the spectators, that is. It was ideal for singing while the baptised persons dripped and flapped and stumbled into the outer room, one verse for each candidate. It would have drowned anything short of really wild screams.

Reen was first:

> Praise the Saviour, ye who know him.
> Who can tell how much we owe him?
> Gladly let us render to him
> All we have and are.

Sheila was next:

> Jesus is the name that charms us
> He for conflict fits and arms us.
> Nothing moves and nothing harms us
> When we trust in him.

It was my turn. I was used to water with the fearlessness of an experienced swimmer. I had been underneath time and time again, but that had been salt water not fresh, cold water not warm. The sheer obscenity, as it seemed to me at that moment, of having warm, fresh water meeting over my face sent me padding to the outer room in a clumsy rage, that and the fact that my red bathing-dress was showing ludicrously through my wet frock.

> Keep us, Lord, oh keep us cleaving
> To thyself and still believing
> Till the hour of our receiving
> Promised joys in Heaven.

Mother was waiting in the outer room, in the middle of a group of Sisters, emotionally clutching a towel and showing off like mad. Reen and Sheila had already been rubbed down and were dressing. It had all gone off beautifully. And outside they bellowed the last verse.

> Then we shall be where we would be.
> Then we shall be what we should be.
> Things which are not now nor could be
> Then shall be our own.

CHAPTER EIGHT

Worldly Pleasure

Considering how we were denied all worldly pleasure, the world seemed a surprisingly pleasant place. I look back on my childhood as a time not only of chapel-going but of treats and outings as well. My mother could not let us go to the Fair or to the cinema, because she had to save us from ourselves; the privation was in our own best interests. But in anything that was permissible to the children of God she was an enthusiastic organiser. It is true that she always went with us, she always presided, but though this may have cramped our development, it did not hinder our enjoyment.

Exeter, the big city, was the glamorous centre of many of our excursions. We lived only ten miles away, and with the privilege tickets that Father got for us the train fare was no obstacle to our going there frequently. We went so often that I cannot now work out how often it actually was. It seems, in memory, like every few weeks. The branch line from Exmouth ran alongside the river, through Lympstone and Topsham. The river kept appearing and disappearing, white boats and seagulls dotted about on it like sheep and lambs, and the strips of mud when the tide was out looking quite improbable, neither hard nor soft. The line ended at Queen Street, as Central Station was then called.

My father worked in the Goods Department of Queen Street, and sometimes, when we were expected, he would come down a side path, for employees only, on to the platform to meet us. If he could not get away, we went up to his office, the office in which he worked for fifty years. It was a small building, approached from Queen Street, the road as opposed to the station. We turned off at the Clock Tower, a red and white composition of turrets and fountains, with intriguing groups of the front halves of wildly struggling horses which seemed to have far more knees than two each, they were so rounded and raised. We passed the weighbridge with its cottage and went down a slope.

The room in which Father and the other clerks, about five of them, worked, overlooked on the far side the shadowy goods shed where the trains were loaded and unloaded. On the near side it looked up the slope, and, if Father himself did not spot us, one of the others would point us out. He would get up from his table in the corner and cross the room with its tall stools and sloping ledgers to the porch in the corner where, through a sash window above a counter, the public was dealt with. Here he would chat to us, listen to our plans, give us our pocket-money if it was Saturday, and send us off to the enjoyment of the city. We had a round of sights that we did every time: the Museum, the Rougemont, the Cathedral, St Nicholas Priory, Matt the Miller. I never got tired of them. Each one was important to me.

The Museum was half-way up Queen Street. As a building seen from outside, it was my ideal of elegant architecture. It was made of bright red stone, in a rich fantasy of pinnacles, arches, pillars, rose windows and every kind of ornament and decoration. Above the entrance, at the top of quite a stiff flight of stairs, were carved the words ROYAL ALBERT MEMORIAL.

I realise now that the Museum must have had a good collection of archaeological and anthropological specimens – there was room upon room of them – but there were only certain limited areas that interested me, though it was not mere interest they aroused, it was devotion.

Downstairs to the right, in the doorway that led to one wing of the building, stood a moose. He was too mighty and baleful even to seem to be beckoning, but he did exercise a morose hypnotism, and I always went in past him to the suite full of stuffed animals over which he was presiding, and here I stayed.

The rooms were mostly lined with large cases of assorted animals, arranged regionally, in every attitude of stalking, leaping, sniffing and staring. Higher up, the walls were covered with stuffed heads: of hyenas, buffaloes, wart-hogs and others. These animals seemed to belong to people, for they bore possessive names such as Kirk's Dik-dik and Thomson's Gazelle, as though the owners might one day come back for them. Altogether they suggested plenty and wealth, but nevertheless were a mere background to the large individual specimens standing out in the room, squarely on the floor, with only little stands or plinths to keep them in place. These were the personalities, the best-loved objects of my childhood.

The giraffe dominated the main room in those days, though he achieved this with his bottom half only. He was so tall that his head emerged into the floor above; he could be seen from mid-neck upwards later in the visit. The ceiling of the room where he stood was made of thick glass, almost opaque; you could see the soles of the people standing on it in the room above, though nothing else of them at all. Their feet came and went quickly and lightly, more like birds. One of the sections of glass had been removed for the giraffe's head to go up through; as it arrived upstairs, it was enclosed in a transparent glass case. I hear he has now been moved into a room with a gallery. He was a fine giraffe and the only animal in the museum to have kept his genitals. They were outdone by his tail, which had a handsome flue-brush knob at the end, but still he had them.

There were two elephants, one Indian, one African. From studying them I deduced that Indian elephants have small ears and African elephants large ones. The two specimens in the Museum seemed to bear it out with all their might. The Indian elephant's tusks drooped in sour humility, his little eyes were spiteful, and he exaggerated the smallness of his ears by pinning them right back. The African elephant appeared to smile, his eyes were large and generous, his tusks were curled flamboyantly upwards and outwards, and his ears were wider spread than the wings of even the grandest Biblical angel.

Smaller, but just as impressive, were the hippopotamus and the rhinoceros. They, too, formed a contrast. They both stood solidly with their front legs planted firmly apart, as though the only real view of them was head on, but, whereas the rhinoceros kept his mouth resolutely closed, the bottom lip tucked firmly inside the top lip, like someone desperately trying to keep a secret, the hippopotamus held his mouth wide open, in a square shape, with all the waxy pink inside showing. He looked rather desperate too, and reminded me of my father singing a solo.

The other free-standing animal which I greatly admired was the Polar Bear, though in this case I should say 'animals', as the label said 'POLAR BEAR in the act of killing a COMMON SEAL'. The Polar Bear was magnificent, with whiter, nastier teeth than any of the other predators. He stood on a white plinth, which seemed to be made of icing-sugar. It was very realistic; you could see the footprints he had made before he took up his final position. They were rather firm, measured steps, it is true, for someone actually engaged in killing, but the Common Seal did not play a very important part in the group. It was half slipping off the plinth in any case, and had apparently passed from its death-throes straight into rigor mortis with no intermediate stage of going limp. The bear did not seem particularly proud of his conquest. He kept one foot firmly on the Common Seal, but he was already looking into the distance for something else to kill.

Some of the single animals in cases were almost as stirring as the free-standing ones. The pride of the collection was a 'TIGER shot in Nepal by KING GEORGE V' and presented by him to the Museum. As a small child I found it confusing that KING GEORGE V was printed in bigger capitals than TIGER. I already equated savage beasts with regal authority, divine or human. In one of our encyclopaedias there was a picture of a lion standing behind a bush while a procession of fleshy people carrying baggage walked unsuspectingly towards him, somewhere in Africa. The picture was entitled 'The King waits for the Train'. In the Gospel Hall, too, we were used to hearing the King of Kings referred to as the Lion of Judah; there was a hymn which said:

> For the Lion of Judah shall break every chain
> And give us the victory again and again.

Furthermore, I had often seen royal personages in showcases, for example, on the occasion when the dairymen of Devon made a statue of the Prince of Wales in local butter. The King/Tiger was beautiful, set with verisimilitude amongst tawny native grasses in which his tail curled and disappeared. His head was thrown back. One paw was up on a rock, but he had tucked the other one up in a harmless kittenish way.

There was no whole lion in a case, but there was a handsome head and shoulders, so arranged, in more tawny grass, against the wall that it looked as though he was charging into the building and that the rest of him would be following immediately.

Another favourite case of mine showed an informative

tableau labelled 'Group of Arctic Animals in Winter Dress'. Again on an icing-sugar background were arranged, on top of a rock an ARCTIC FOX, and, lolling in false security under the rock, an ARCTIC HARE. In the right-hand corner was an ERMINE creeping up on a group of innocent PTARMIGAN. The animals were familiar ones, a fox, a hare, a ferret and partridges, opulent in white, and translated into a snowscape. The tableau was well composed and implied a great deal of drama. All of a sudden there seemed a relationship between some of the animals, beyond that of their presence in the same room. For a moment the interdependence and mutual awareness of this group seemed to affect all the others, as though one day the rhinoceros might conceivably impale the hippopotamus, the hippopotamus shut his mouth at last on the elephant's leg and the elephant wind his trunk round the giraffe's neck.

In the middle of all this convincing semblance of life — it convinced me entirely — were a few skeletons and skulls. I did not know what a *memento mori* was, of course, but I felt these exhibits to be inappropriate in the face of these stuffed, immortal survivors that I loved, who would stand around for ever.

When I could tear myself away from them I went upstairs as a sort of epilogue, past a figure in a niche labelled ALBERT, through a clicking turnstile and into the art gallery. I remember only two things here, and these two seemed to stand for all the rest. One was a statue of the Queen of Sheba, and it represented for me what sculpture really should be. It was brilliantly, translucently white. The draperies were meticulously done, their braid and lace rendered faithfully stitch by stitch, their folds photographically caught. Underneath were realistic arms and legs, the flesh looking accurately firmer than the garments. If I had had to comment I would have used the words 'lifelike', though the statue looked like nobody I had ever seen, and 'beautiful' because this was how people ought to look.

The other exhibit was Benjamin Robert Haydon's 'Curtius plunging into the Gulf', by far the largest and most impressive picture in the Museum, and this was what I felt oil-painting should be. The verisimilitude of the top of Curtius's toes coming over his sandal convinced me again that this was realism, although within my experience men did not leap into gulfs on horseback. The horse himself seemed more lifelike by the fact that he was obviously from the same stable as those on the Clock Tower. On every visit I gazed in admiration at both Curtius and the Queen of Sheba. I was then ready to leave the Museum.

The Cathedral seemed the only grey building in a red city. Though I spent so many hours in it, over a period of ten or eleven years, I never learnt anything about it in the sense of being able to describe it architecturally or to give any part of it the correct technical name. I suppose, however, I must have really experienced it, in some inarticulate way. I must, from an early age, have grasped what a cathedral was and have taken in some concepts of space and size, if only from observing, for example, that the sort of chair which looked a normal size in the Gospel Hall here shrank to dolls' furniture.

It was the fittings of the Cathedral that I enjoyed, especially those that had anything to do with people, and the majority had. Outside sat Hooker, reading aloud, with one finger on the page, as though it did not come easily to him. My own early prowess at reading aloud made me notice this. Inside, the tone was chiefly military. There were avenues of faded banners, and monuments to soldiers who had fallen in every war for the previous hundred years or so· in the Crimea, in India, in the breach at the siege of Badajoz, leading the charge of the Devons on Wagon Hill. The Devons had a chapel to themselves, but memorials to our fighting men spread all over the Cathedral as well. On every wall, in almost every niche, could be found these resolute figures, sitting on horses under palm trees, lifting their chins authoritatively at tribesmen or lowering them over fallen comrades. It seemed quite natural. I had been used to hearing about our Empire not only at school but at home: Mother was fond of singing Kipling's *Recessional* at the piano in the front room on summer evenings, and I knew of our far-flung battle-line and how, under God's awful hand, we held dominion over palm and pine.

But I preferred the domestic tragedies, of which there were such vivid accounts, as, for example, in the memorial to eighteen-year-old Mrs O'Brien, whose clothes caught fire, but whose one instinct had been to save her baby – though it irked me that by the very circumstances in which these stories were presented none could have a happy ending. I should have liked Mrs O'Brien to be rescued. The tombs and plaques of the Cathedral bore witness to an overwhelming amount of precocity and fortitude: a boy who had died at the age of seventeen had been Master of the Music at Canterbury *and* Exeter; a helmsman, who reminded me of my great-grandfather, had last been seen calmly awaiting death as the waters closed over the ship. To a young hypochondriac, the district sounded dreadfully unhealthy. Familiar and, one had hoped, harmless names kept appearing: 'departed this life at Dawlish', 'departed this life at Sidmouth', 'died of consumption at Lympstone', 'sank into a rapid decline at Budleigh Salterton'.

St Nicholas Priory provided the same sort of human interest. Through visit after visit I remained quite insensitive to the construction of the building and the function of the individual rooms. They were low, cool, flagged spaces where nobody lived or did anything except show or be shown around. But the custodian was fascinating. She was a Roman Catholic who proclaimed her faith in and out of season, just as the Brethren were exhorted to do, and wore a large felt hat, also in and out of season. The highlight of the tour for me was the point at which she described how, a few months before, on a holiday abroad, she had seen the Cross being carried through the streets and how everyone had knelt down. How wonderful it would be, she concluded, when this happened in our own beloved city. Mother, calm, I suppose, in the assumption that nothing was less likely – it *was* difficult to imagine – listened tolerantly, because after all this was education, and quite often afterwards made her rash statement about the possibility of our meeting Roman Catholics in heaven. The final stage of the tour was to step out into the courtyard to see the ravens, 'the monks' birds', the guide said, from which I concluded that they had been there since the Middle Ages. They looked old, patchy and very cross, and moved little more than the animals at the Museum. I was told they later got bombed, which I was very sorry to hear.

The Rougemont was the reddest building I had ever seen, fiery, carroty red. It was not really a building at all, more a set of walls with paths hitched on to them, but its original presence was strong still, and it gave me the same feeling, both adventurous and sheltered, that I had when playing under the table at home or crawling down to the bottom of the bed. We always entered it from the wide lawns of Northernhay, up through a crooked little path, tangled with shrubs and bushes. At the top the path tunnelled right into the castle wall through about twelve feet of scarlet stone. Inside, what had been the moat was covered with bright, short grass that looked wet even when it was dry, and that curved and swelled and dipped where the old contours, though planed down into peacefulness, still gave the place character. There were a few brilliant flower-beds and a great many big trees. It was neither a park nor a garden nor grounds. It was beautiful and well-mown and set apart, like Paradise.

We always had tea at Deller's, which has now gone for ever, bombed the same night as the ravens. It was the apotheosis of a café, glorious and exciting beyond anything I have seen since, and permeated by a smell of coffee, which was a drink we never had at home. It was circular and had three floors; the top two had galleries that looked down dizzily into the central well where the palms stood and the ladies' orchestra played. When my father was in his Mr Worldly-Wiseman vein he would describe how a man could have a large meal on the top floor, go down to the lavatory on the bottom floor, have a cup of tea at a nearby table and then go out on the ground floor where the cash desk was, paying only the tea bill.

There was an enchanting hugger-mugger feeling about Deller's. Hardly a table stood out in the room open to view. They were all tucked away, in niches, cubby-holes and cubicles. Some even had curtains. You had to pack yourselves into the seats as though entering a miniature train. The waitresses appeared mysteriously from doors that were indistinguishable from the walls, but you could get glimpses of them in rooms beyond, through apertures shaped like crystallised lemon-peel, and one of them, who dispensed sundaes with dashing new names like Knickerbocker Glory, actually pushed them out through this opening, which I liked to imitate at home in bed with the pillow in a crescent above my head. We had tea and toast, which came from scalding heavy silver receptacles on to our cool dainty plates and into our cups. On my first visit I said 'Thank you' for every single thing the waitress put on the table, sugar-bowl, teaspoons and all, till I was checked by Mother.

The last thing we did before we went back to Exmouth

was to go down into a narrow lane at the bottom of the High Street, to see Matthew the Miller. This was a striking clock on a church tower, so it was obviously to our advantage to get as many strokes as we could, usually at six o'clock. It never occurred to me that Matthew did not look much like a miller, chiefly because I had never seen a miller. He must have been a king or a knight; he wore a plumed helmet and golden garters. On either side of him stood a younger person, a son or a servant, dressed in a red belted tunic. These two announced the hour by hitting out chimes on little bells beside them. He then nodded his head for each stroke of the hour as it sounded from the belfry behind him.

These visits to Exeter represented for us the peak of entertainment, the high life. There was another source of enjoyment, however, of a more everyday casual nature, which perhaps was even more basic to our way of life, and that was the walks Mother took us on, through the countryside surrounding our home. We were good walkers; we had to be, so it is lucky we really did like it. We had to be for two reasons: the first was that Mother felt it was a wholesome, unworldly form of recreation, in the course of which, moreover, we were as much under her control as though we had been on the lead, and the second was that there was little in the way of public transport. There was *some*. Two rival firms, for example, ran buses between Exmouth and Withycombe: Abbott's and Harris's. Abbott's buses were blue and Harris's brown. In shape they were very far from being anyone's idea of a bus and they rattled dreadfully. One of the games Father played with us when we were small was called Abbott's bus; it consisted of his taking us on his knee and joggling us up and down till our teeth clashed. But the buses had real personality, as indeed had the drivers and conductors, who became prominent in the lives and conversation of everybody using the service.

At one time there was a conductor on Harris's bus who always shouted theatrically, 'Hold very tight! O.K.' as a signal for starting, there being no bell. Sheila and I made up a clandestine riddle about this. The question was, 'What would a bus conductor do if he suddenly wanted to go to the lavatory?' to which the answer, of course, was 'Hold very tight! O.K.'

The buses operated on the informal lines of the traditional village bus. The starting-point for the return journey was the corner of Bradham Lane and Norfolk Terrace, and the bus never actually set out without at least six children appearing from various directions with cries of 'Mummy's coming!' to Mr Foster or whoever was driving. I thought that Mr Foster, whom I remember particularly, had superhuman powers of divination. The children always used the same formula, though in fact the grown-up who finally arrived was often Auntie or Granny or even Daddy, but Mr Foster knew exactly when to move off. As the two buses were rivals, people sometimes took sides, but Mother was above loyalties of that kind and we patronised them both impartially, though infrequently.

There were some buses that went to East Budleigh, to Budleigh Salterton and to Ottery St Mary. One private firm ran a service, and there were a few Devon Generals, but we never used them. They seemed eccentric and irregular, expensive and unnecessary. If we wanted to go to these places – and we did – we walked. Our attitude to buses as a whole was, in fact, one of dubiety and caution. We were not happy with them. For one thing, they were an innovation. When my parents settled in Withycombe, there were none at all, and now they seemed to desecrate the countryside rather than provide an amenity. To Puritan consciences, too, there was something suspect about being carried when you could walk. A great many hymns used this metaphor, always attributing virtue to the very act of plodding, marching and toiling along, as opposed to being wafted. Certainly to take a bus to the Meetings, supposing there had been a Sunday bus service, would have been quite out of the question for even the oldest and most crippled. As usual, too, financial and religious considerations went hand in hand. We could not really afford bus fares.

None of these arguments applied to trains. To begin with, we had privilege tickets. And the railway had been in the district for so long that it almost seemed God-appointed. (As I have mentioned, the Brethren were greatly influenced by the passage of time.) It had its prescribed track, too, which everyone had grown to accept, and would not suddenly come lurching and roaring round a corner. Beyond all this, we were a real railwayman's family in that we felt loyalty to the railway, or at least the Southern Railway, not only because we lived off it, but because we felt true affection for it. It therefore did not seem like luxurious self-indulgence to go by train; it seemed normal and sensible.

My favourite line was the branch line from Sidmouth Junction to Exmouth, a single track running mostly through water-meadows, which carried a few passengers to and from stations that were little more than focal points at the sides of fields, out of sight of the villages they were named after, with empty roads coming suddenly up to them from over humped bridges or between high hedges. Our longer walks were planned to end up at one of these stations.

Ottery St Mary, for example, was the terminus of our grandest expedition, the thirteen-mile walk over Woodbury Common, on the high windy ground between one grey river and the next. I did this walk first at the age of nine and repeated it often. Once when Guy Fawkes' Day was on a Saturday we got there in time for nightfall, in order to see the blazing tar-barrels rolled down the hill. In fact we did not see them. Either something went wrong or we had to leave too early, and they have gone down in memory with other abortive quests of childhood: the excursions to hear a nightingale that never sang, and to watch an eclipse of the sun from Blackhill one early morning when the mist never lifted. We did see the bonfire at Ottery St Mary, though. It was large, noisy and powerful. The heat could be felt so far away that I understood how the martyrs could have been burnt alive, which was difficult to grasp in terms of sluggish garden bonfires.

East Budleigh was the station for the walk to Hayes Barton, birthplace of Sir Walter Raleigh, and to the coast at Ladram Bay, where Spanish sailors had been washed up after the Armada (my father used to say that the word Ladram meant 'the grave of Spanish sailors', but I never heard his reasons) and smugglers had hidden contraband in caves. It was also the starting-place for the best walk of all: down the banks of the Otter to Budleigh Salterton. The River Otter, which had come zigzagging into the fields just after Ottery St Mary, had by now settled down on the left of the railway, running parallel to it under a bright red cliff with thick trees on top and ivy trailing down the side, and so it went on till it came to the sea. The lavish growth of the meadow trailed over into the water. The river moved quite strongly, and long plants with yellow flowers stretched out downstream like horses' tails decorated for the Carnival. Some which had recently gone in were field-green and -yellow still and recognisable, but there were also thick coagulated clumps, dark green like yew trees and much the same shape, which had been floating for some time. The reflection of the bright red cliffs bobbed brilliantly along with them.

Each station had a personality of its own and events connected with it. Tipton St John's was the junction for Sidmouth, where we often went to walk on the pebbly beach and look at the houses with their elegant verandahs. On our way home we liked to watch the train going back to Sidmouth for the night, while we waited on the platform for the Exmouth coaches to come in from a siding. The hill was so steep that the train seemed hardly to move for three or four minutes. Then it suddenly blinked out under a red bridge. It looked as though it had dropped over the edge, but in fact, though now hidden in trees, it stayed on the heights, as the station at Sidmouth was far above the town.

Budleigh Salterton station was the biggest on the line and the most sophisticated, with porters and taxi-drivers, the travellers talking in middle-class voices while assembling leather luggage and being greeted by confident residents. There was something like bustle, such as you never saw at the other stations, but the passengers and their hosts soon cleared off down the hill in the taxis or in cars. The railway left the station on as steep an incline as it had approached it, and trains that had not stuck on the first hill often stuck on the second.

Littleham was the station we knew best. It was near the top of Bradham Lane, and my father usually came back this way from his work at Exeter, simply changing trains at Exmouth. There was a little gate for pedestrians beside the level-crossing, and we often stood on the bars, ready to wave to him as the train came by, monstrously near. We knew the names of the stationmaster, the signalman and the porter. We thought they exchanged tablets better than any other railwaymen along the line. As the railway was single-track, the driver had to be in possession of some unique symbol to show that he alone had the right to be on that stretch of line at the time. When he went on to the next portion he surrendered the tablet to some member of the station staff to be handed on to the next tenant, who would, of course, be going in the opposite direction. So, at Littleham, Mr

Trigg would stand with the tablet labelled LITTLEHAM—
EXMOUTH hooked over his arm to give to the south-
bound driver in return for the BUDLEIGH SALTERTON—
LITTLEHAM one, which *he* held similarly hooked over
his arm as he leaned out of the cabin. As this was always
done with dramatic intensity and a fine swinging action
while the train was moving quite fast, it needed real
bravura, and we loved watching.

As a result of all our walks and expeditions I got to
know thoroughly a wide area of country, wider certainly
than that known to most of my schoolfriends, yet I do
not feel that I was really a country-bred child. Our house
backed on to a meadow with a brook running through it
and other fields beyond, so that from babyhood it was
natural for us in good weather to go right out into an
open and luxuriant countryside which had not yet begun
to shrink away; and in front of the house lay the cultivated
fields where every year we watched the corn coming up,
growing and being cut down. But the rhythm of country
work and even of the seasons themselves was something
that did not seem to enter into my thinking and feeling,
any more than did the names of all the trees and flowers
and birds that I saw, except as an occasional academic
piece of information, for example that barley was the one
with the beard. As a family we cherished no traditional
country lore; we had no expertise in predicting the
weather; we looked out of the window and grumbled or
exclaimed at what we saw, like town-dwellers. Sheila and
I took no interest in Father's garden except for the fruit:
he grew really fine raspberries, loganberries and goose-
berries. Yet I truly loved the country. It was not only
that I realised that certain aspects of nature had to be
admired, though certainly I was trained to that idea.
I had real feeling for growing green things and open
spaces in the sense that they were necessary to me.

Often our walks took us to the sea, even in winter, as

when we went to Sidmouth or Budleigh Salterton, but this was a very different activity from 'going to the beach', which we only did in summer, different not only because from June to September we could bathe, but also because from late spring onwards we obeyed an entirely different set of conventions. For the few warm months of the year, the life of everyone in Exmouth and the surrounding villages was focused on the Saturday afternoon by the sea. (For the godless it was Sunday afternoon, too, I suppose.)

The beach at Exmouth was a two-mile stretch of sand from the Harbour to Orcombe Point. Along it there was an almost continuous line of beach-huts. In those days they were placed on the beach itself with their backs up against the sea-wall and with the road behind them; year after year owners who had left them there just a few days too long, because of a seemingly endless summer, were surprised by the autumn tides. These huts had glamour and conferred great prestige on both proprietors and guests. They were not beautiful, but they were well-kept, gaily curtained and, above all, lavishly equipped. It would have been thought rather shameful not to have the apparatus to serve huge, elaborate teas for a large number of people. Mothers of families seemed to go to the beach only to provide such teas; they never took off any of their clothes and were to be seen all the afternoon inside the huts, cutting and buttering and arranging. To be invited to a person's hut was often more solemn and significant than being asked to the house.

As a family we had no hut. This lack must have been taken for granted, as I never heard the matter discussed. Though I do not know the reasons, however, I can guess now that there were two: firstly, we could not afford it, and secondly, it would have seemed too worldly, too much like belonging to a community of the unsaved; the hut-owners certainly had a marked community spirit, and, equally certainly, I never knew a Saint to own a hut.

The Tuckers had one, and they often invited my mother, Sheila and me; my father may have been included in the invitation, but he never came. Their hut was about three-quarters of a mile from Orcombe Point. It was called *Talawa*, which Peggy and Joy told us was the name of an Australian town.

The naming of the beach-huts was a subject in itself. Like most subjects it had both conventions and categories. There were the poetic names: *Blue Haze, Sea Spray* and *Clear View*. There were those which were romantic, too, but a shade more folksy: *Step Aside* and *Downalong*. Then there were the French names, both serious and facetious: *Bon Ami* and *Skwattee-voo*. But above all, there was the enormous category of humorous names, names which would never have been used for the person's house, but which were justified presumably by good weather and holiday mood and hospitable meaning: *Osokozee, Omefromome, ICDC, Duz-e-Gude* and *Fitzusall*.

The huts were quite small, not much bigger than the changing-cabins I have since seen on other beaches. They were about the size of our bicycle shed at home. No one but the hostess stayed inside, though there would have been room for one other person, fairly comfortably. The fronts of the huts opened right out, and the grown-ups sat in a group round the door. They remained fully clothed, and even we children wore bathing-dresses only to bathe: when we came out of the sea we put our frocks on again. Sun-bathing was not fashionable in those days, and in any case would have presented a practical difficulty: bathing-dresses were thick and ample and took a long time to dry, so that it was horribly clammy to keep them on after a bathe – I tried it once – and nobody had two.

We always bathed as soon as we got there. The rest of the time we spent playing behind the huts. We hardly ever went out into the scene or in pursuit of any part of it. Very occasionally we walked along to Orcombe Point, a promontory built up in bright red layers with a clump of vegetation on top so matted that it seemed to be wearing a hairnet. Even less often we went to the Maer Rocks, a long spur exposed at low tide, covered with lush and glutinous seaweed and full of rock-pools over which swarms of enquiring children bent and into which they peered and poked for hours. I found rock pools uninteresting and rather offputting, and so apparently did Sheila and the Tuckers.

The curved lines of huts formed a miniature street in a wooden village, charming with its gables and its neatness. Between the backs of the huts and the sea-wall was a long lane about two yards wide, private, clean and excitingly cut off, and here we played all afternoon, mostly a game called 'Statues', which was the merest excuse to enjoy the inexhaustible pleasure of jumping off the sea-wall into the powdery sand.

In a way the best moment of these particular days on the beach was going home. Mother, Sheila and I returned to Withycombe on foot: it was a walk of about a mile, which was nothing to us. We left the sea-front and struck up through Douglas Avenue and Cranford Avenue towards Littleham Cross, which was at the top of Bradham Lane. These two avenues contained some of the most prosperous houses in the town: simply to go past them evoked a soothing awareness of wealth and ease. That is to say, I found it soothing: Mother, I suspect, may have felt resentful, but I was supported by the conviction that I would end up as well off as any of them. The glare of the sun had gone; our skins were rough and cool with salt and sand; we had jumped and shouted and were glad to be quiet. Beautiful smells were coming from all the prosperous gardens and from the eucalyptus trees in one of the avenues.

The Tuckers invited us frequently but not, of course, every Saturday. We had a family routine of our own,

which was to spend the afternoon at Straight Point.
This was a beach about a mile along from Orcombe
Point towards Budleigh Salterton. Considering its nearness to Exmouth, it was amazingly deserted: sometimes
we were the only family there. It was not too easy to reach,
however, and the path down from the cliff-top needed a
fair amount of agility: there were no ropes or steps, and
it was both slippery and steep. We always called it
Straight Point, which was the name of the headland, but
many people referred to it as Sandy Bay. I felt very
strongly about this, after the age of ten, on what I
thought were grounds of literary taste. 'Sandy Bay'
seemed to me banal and pretty-pretty and feeble, whereas
I felt that 'Straight Point' was decently and austerely
descriptive. (I hear it is now universally called Sandy
Bay and that there is a caravan site on the cliff-top.)

We reached it by going through Littleham Village and
across the fields, a walk of about two miles. Sheila and I
always got our weekly pennyworth of sweets at the last
little shop in the village before striking out into what
seemed like very deserted land indeed: deserted, though,
not waste, as the path lay through fertile fields where the
corn whispered, and even clapped, in the sea breeze
louder and louder every week as the summer advanced.
We could first hear the sea itself, and clearly enough to
tell whether it was calm or rough, at the farm which was
the last homestead before the lonely stretch of fields,
and from then on the seagulls, which screamed quite
loudly over our own house, got noisier and noisier.

It was at Straight Point that I learnt to swim. My
father who nearly always bathed too – my mother never
did – gave me a few unsystematic lessons, but I really
taught myself at the age of about five. It was a safe beach
with no currents, and once I was in the water I was left
alone, and in any case my father, without his glasses,
could not have told either of us from a dolphin. I first

of all discovered how I could support myself, and even move, by a kind of dog-paddle, and on to this I later superimposed a few more or less conventional strokes. I never became a good swimmer in the sense of winning races or displaying beautiful style, but in an unambitious, inelegant way I *was* a good swimmer, if that could mean being thoroughly at home in the water rather than master of it.

I greatly enjoyed swimming, but I dreaded the initial getting wet. I was thin and had a poor circulation, and the water always seemed icy, even in August. I was invariably the last to get under, which was psychologically painful, too. I knew quite well as I watched my friends and relatives swimming and splashing that the agony of plunging would be less if I could ever be the first to endure it. We all ran down to the sea together, so I had a perfectly fair chance, but I never managed it. I tried everything: letting the water creep up by millimetres so that my body hardly noticed the encroachment, sprinkling a few drops over my shoulders and chest to anticipate and so lessen the final anguish – nothing worked. I should really like to know whether I *was* more cowardly and less resolute than the others or whether, in spite of their shrieks and exclamations, they in fact suffered less.

Brilliantly through all my happy childhood memories shines the one worldly pleasure we were allowed to experience. This was the Carnival, and I still cannot imagine how it got through the net year after year, as it had not just one or two but all of the elements that made the Fair, the cinema, dancing and make-up so sinful. In the twenties and early thirties the Carnival really went with a swing. I have heard that the Second World War killed it, but in those earlier days it had enough life in it to impress people far less naïve than ourselves. The excitement was felt throughout Littleham, Withycombe and Exmouth for weeks beforehand, and on the night everyone who was not actually dying came out or was propped up in the window to watch the procession. Able-bodied people could watch it several times by means of nipping from one vantage point to another.

For us in Bradham Lane the Carnival started as soon as it got dark, with the arrival of the *tablows*, as we were careful to call them, from Littleham. They had to come down our lane in order to get to Phear Park just beyond which the procession formed up; and it was a thrilling moment when we heard them rumbling over the hill and saw the lights approaching through the trees. The Littleham contingent was always particularly good. They sent in at least six *tablows*, which were usually poetic and pretty, rather than satirical and humorous as the Exmouth ones tended to be. A typical Exmouth entry was *Rent in Arrears*, where, in the middle of a room that indicated direst poverty in every detail, a woman had her son across her knee repairing a split in the seat of his pants. Two Littleham contributions I remember very well were *Tiptoe Through the Tulips* and *If Those Lips Could Only Speak*. In the first a Littleham lady, lavishly painted and powdered and dressed as a Dutch girl, teetered on the spot all evening through a clump of artificial tulips. In the second, a Littleham man sat gazing at a picture frame in which simpered the live face of a woman who was almost certainly his wife.

The *tablows* were nearly all mounted on horse-drawn carts. My old acquaintances, Prince and Farmer, were usually somewhere in the procession; I could not imagine what they made of it after the cornfield. It was most unusual to see motor vehicles, which were not so suitable, as they stopped and started much more jerkily than the horses, and with their engines running during the halts they seemed more impatient of the inevitable hold-ups than Prince and Farmer and their stablemates, who appeared to welcome them. But the carts did shake terribly, and to stand on anything like tiptoe for several hours, or even to sit looking at a picture, must have been a great strain.

When the Littleham carts had creaked round the corner to join the Withycombe entries and the lane was dark and quiet again, we set off to walk into Exmouth. By this time the roads beyond Phear Park were as brilliant and noisy as a fairground. The bands were forming up, the Exmouth *tablows* were coming in thick and fast, the Littleham and Withycombe ones were just arriving, and the adjudication was beginning. This was taken seriously; the judges went to a lot of trouble, if dashing up and down was anything to go by, and everyone in the *tablows* took up his best pose, but paradoxically no one seemed to mind greatly what the result was or even to remember it. For the next twelve months outstanding entries would be referred to, quite regardless of whether they won or lost.

We passed all this and hurried down a parallel street to take up our positions in the Exeter Road. The pavements were packed by this time, but we usually found somewhere to stand between All Saints and the Council School.

The Last Trump, which I was brought up to think of as the acme of joyful noise, could not be half as exciting as the sound of the first band – there were usually five or six – turning into the Exeter Road as the procession started. I can still hear the tune and recall the thrill. On came the procession. It was headed by the Carnival Queen and her Ladies-in-Waiting. These were three girls from the town's primary schools, one from each. We were pleased when the Queen was a Council School girl, which happened every three years, as the matter was arranged in strict rotation, though there was always the pretence of a contest, with pictures in the *Exmouth Chronicle*. They looked wonderful, elegantly grouped in a garish light, heavily made-up into an unhealthy waxen beauty. Sheila and I used to call to the girl from our school, whether Queen or Lady-in-Waiting, but she never heard. (One year it was suggested that Sheila, who was by far the prettiest girl in the Council School, should be put in for the contest, but those who knew my mother's views quashed the idea before it came to anything.)

After the first group of *tablows* and the second band came a cluster of decorated bicycles. These were handsomely upholstered with foliage and coloured paper and flowers so that they looked unnatural and puffy and as though they could hardly move. However, they did move, quite briskly, their fat wheels spinning round till the decorations on the spokes became a blur. Later in the procession came the children's fancy-dress section, for which all the most lively and attractive girls in the town had gone to great pains to present themselves as evil or stupid or senile, in the guise of witches or dunces or very old ladies. The homely ones tended to be powder puffs or Madame de Pompadour.

The procession seemed to be going by for hours. The last *tablow* was traditionally an Exmouth entry, and for several years running it was *The White Slaves' Final Appeal*: a line of three of four bakers in white aprons and hats rolling pastry. We always shrieked appreciatively and clutched each other. They looked so like my Uncle Jack: they had just his air of cheerful dexterity. After them the crowd closed in, and we walked back to Withycombe. But I followed the procession in my thoughts as it went flaring and rumbling on through the crowded darkness. It would pass the Gospel Hall and Brother Jones's barber's shop, and I wondered if Brother Edds, the caretaker, was peeping through his curtains or if Sister Jones was perhaps watching, standing well back in the shadowy bow-window of the shop. No one ever mentioned the Carnival at the next Morning Meeting, either in prayer or in conversation, but it is quite possible that others, as well as myself, had that night been given a lifelong taste for worldly pleasure.

CHAPTER NINE

Arising from Vicissitude

I CANNOT imagine where I got the idea of becoming a poet. It was certainly not from my father and mother, whose ambition for me, though it later adapted itself to the new concept, did not spontaneously take any such form. My father, as I have said, thought in terms of my being a headmistress. My mother lifted her eyes to the Houses of Parliament: she actually said so once, when we were going across Westminster Bridge after one of our days in London when I had been particularly intelligent and keen about the sights I had been shown.

Certainly I felt the need to be famous; I cannot remember a time when I did not. It was a need more than an ambition, and it was strongest in face of my fear of death. I could not contemplate dying: I could not conjure up any reflections which made it seem at all tolerable. My belief in God's plan of salvation and my knowledge that I was redeemed came nowhere near the problem. But on one particular day, when I was about eight, a solution occurred to me: if I were to become famous, really famous, world-famous, there would be a crowd outside the house as I lay dying; messengers would hurry backwards and forwards, and their words would be eagerly listened to; the final news would draw a long sigh from thousands of people, who would be even sorrier than I was. It sounds as though I were adapting some impression I had received from a Royal Death, but this cannot have been the case as, though the house in which I lay dying bore a very decided resemblance to Buckingham

Palace, the only king who was to die during my childhood, George V, did not, in fact, do so till some years later.

I was determined to be rich, too, and quite convinced that I would be. I felt this conviction, as I have mentioned, every time we walked through the grand avenues of the residential districts of Exmouth. I felt it even more with regard to motor-cars, which in those days were a sure sign of wealth. We very seldom went in a car, and the idea that we as a family might own one was so ludicrous that once when we were asking the way from a shopkeeper in Scotland and he enquired of my father, in order to give directions more clearly, where he had left his car, Sheila and I could hardly get out of the shop without exploding into laughter. The only person we knew who even had access to a car was Brother Restall, who sometimes borrowed it from his rich relations. Occasionally, after the Sunday evening Meeting, he would take us for a drive, up to Blackhill perhaps, skimming in five minutes over the rising ground that took us half an hour to cover on our walks, scouring the familiar lanes with his headlamps and even raking the woods where Marley and Bystock stood so grandly and so secretly. The very first drive he took us on, which I feel sure must have been the first time I was ever in a private motor-car, my mother, who guessed my ambitions – we were alike in many ways – turned to me and said, as we purred up the hill, 'Are you going to have a big car like this when you're grown-up?' 'Much bigger,' I said firmly, not meaning to be rude, but, since asked, ready to state a fact.

So there is no doubt of my determination to succeed and shine and no mystery about it either, but I *am* puzzled as to why, in childhood, it took the form of deciding to be a poet. As I say, it was not suggested to me by my parents. It can hardly have come from anything I had read, either. I had the notion firmly in my head from a very early age, long before I arrived at the *Emily* books, for example, with their portrait of the young girl as poet. Nothing of what I read before the age of ten can possibly have persuaded me to such a sense of vocation. Yet I clearly remember standing on the downs above Petitor Beach, one day when, again, I was about eight, a little way away from the others and seeming to look out to sea, and facing squarely what struck me as a basic dilemma: the choice between being a poet and being happy. (Happiness for me, at that age, meant marriage.) I thought it over carefully there and then, staring at Tide Rock, and decided, not without serious misgivings, to be a poet. I am certain that I had never met the romantic theory of the inevitable sufferings of the poet, and I have no idea why I should have assumed the two states, matrimony and poetry, to be mutually exclusive. It is true that my mother had brought me up to believe that a woman's talents were all brought low by marriage, but even so, why poetry? I was the kind of bright child that showed promise at several skills: I could draw and paint; I could sing. But I never felt for a moment that either of these gifts would require that I should dedicate myself to, or renounce, anything.

Neither had I had set before me the sort of poetic feast that would inspire an impressionable and competitive child to emulation. The only poetry book I owned at the time, as far as I can remember, was *The Book of the Flower Fairies* and the only poems I had presented to me at school were such pieces as *Abou Ben Adhem*, *Nod the Shepherd* and *The Highwayman*. I was fond of the *Flower Fairies*. I thought the pictures were absolutely beautiful – the Hazel Catkin Fairy looked very like Sheila – and I admired the inventiveness with which a different fairy was wrested out of each flower, and the accuracy too: flowers which blew in the wind, like daffodils, had fairies that bent and leaned and swayed; those which were sheltered, like wood-sorrel, had unruffled, placid fairies who had clearly never moved in their lives. I liked the characterisation: the Daisy Fairy was a baby, fat, dimpled and pink-and-white; the Dandelion Fairy was a cheeky little boy; the Wild Rose Fairy, in an ankle-length pink silk dress, was the Carnival Queen herself. But I was not at all excited by the verse. I know this because I have looked at a page or two recently without the faintest feeling of recognition or remembered pleasure; it was not a bit like looking at *Jessica's First Prayer*, for example. The illustrations to the *Flower Fairies*, as I saw them again after thirty-odd years, did call up a long-buried glamour, the text none. Here is *The Song of the Convolvulus Fairy*:

> Wreathing the hedges
>   I ramble and twine;
> The roadside is tangled
>   With garlands of mine.
>
> I'm little Convolvulus,
>   Bindweed as well;
> I know all the secrets
>   The fairies can tell.
>
> I spread a pink carpet
>   For lightest of feet;
> I smell like blanc-mange
>   For princesses to eat.

Hymns were the first kind of poetry I heard, and I heard them in my cradle in the earliest days of my life, when Nurse Goodman and any visiting Saint or relative sang them with Mother in the front bedroom where both she and I lay. I heard them again when I started going to the Gospel Hall and from then on for the rest of my childhood. I need say nothing here about the general effect that the singing of these hymns had on me through all my formative years, but I do speculate about their influence as verse. They were certainly darker, stronger fare than the anaemic insipidities of the *Flower Fairies* and their kind; they may have been fantastic, they may have been mad, but they were not whimsical. They may not have been precise, but they were concrete: salvation was sweeping through the gates of the New Jerusalem, security was the City foursquare. What they said may not have been subtle, but it was not trivial either; it was grand and important. Perhaps most vital of all, for me, was the fact that these hymns were the only form of poetry I met (though I did not think of them as poetry; they were religion) that dealt with life as I knew it; the pearly gates and the golden strand were part of my experience in the sense that I believed they existed and that I was going to them. As a child I never read or wrote anything half as realistic.

Like many another person *vis-à-vis* many another branch of the arts, I thought and spoke of myself as a practitioner long before I actually produced anything. It was not until I was at the Grammar School that I began to write verse more serious than the toadying rhymes for the Christmas cards that our class had sent to Mr Barrow. And it was not until I was in my third year at the Grammar School that I began to love poetry. The poems we had studied with Miss Rafter, the teacher of general subjects who had taken us for English in the first and second forms, were a continuation of the *Abou Ben Adhem/Highwayman* tradition of the Council School, and I had felt much the same about them as I always had. But in the third form the teacher changed and the book changed.

The teacher was now Mr Heath, the Senior English Master. To this day I feel an unswerving sense of gratitude towards him and an unshakeable conviction that it was he who really started me off as a poet, though, of course, he was in no way responsible for my dreams of becoming one: I had had them for years, and they could hardly have been intensified. I cannot justify or explain this gratitude or this conviction; indeed, every fact I can remember tells against it. In the first place, I am sure it was not a question of personal magnetism: I admired Mr Heath, I attended to what he said, but I was not sexually attracted to him (and I *do* know what this could be like, as I felt it for the Maths master). Nor had he the eccentricity, the dash and the glamour, so often meretricious, that can inspire an impressionable child to enthusiasm and even to a semblance of talent. He was a well-built, pleasant-looking family man with two daughters at the school. His nickname, which he was proud of, was Bullo, though there was nothing at all bull-like in his appearance or behaviour; it must have arisen from some trivial, long-forgotten incident or remark.

He was a good and conscientious teacher according to the methods of the day, but he adhered so unwaveringly to those methods that he cannot have inspired anyone by unorthodoxy or wild flights. There were two grammar lessons a week; as we had already mastered the parts of speech at the Council School, these lessons were devoted to parsing and analysis. I rather enjoyed them; I quickly grasped the principles, after which it was simply a question of keeping the lines straight and the writing neat. There was one composition lesson a week. Composition was taught very formally: there was absolutely no question of self-expression, any more than there had been at the Council School. We usually read an essay first, from some anthology, and then founded our own compositions on that. If Charles Lamb whimsically described the discovery of roast pork, we whimsically described the discovery of roast beef. A vivid composition would receive praise and perhaps be read out – mine often were – but it would be 'corrected' purely with grammar, syntax and sentence-construction in mind. I was once reproved, for example, for writing 'Tennis would be more popular, with me at any rate, if . . .' on the excellent grounds that nothing could be popular with one person, and not at all for the facetiousness and ignorance of the composition as a whole, on 'Playing Games', which was even more facetious and ignorant than the anthology piece on which it was based. Yet somehow notions of style did come into it. I remember how a romantic atmosphere-choked account of some archaeological discovery led me to a description of a room where an Egyptian princess had, as I first thought of putting it, 'lived, moved and had her being' and how I decided to reject 'moved and had her being'.

There was one Shakespeare lesson a week. This often took the form of paraphrase. The art of paraphrasing, as we were taught it, or, to be just, as we understood it, was to substitute a synonym for every word of the original. If we were to put something into our own words it seemed to be the only way; it occurred to no one that we could not possibly *have* any words for something we would not have dreamed of saying. The method worked quite well for most passages of Shakespeare, which made little real sense to us either in his version or our own, but when Sheila and I were preparing for School Certificate English, the set play being *Coriolanus*, we ran into trouble over 'Farewell, my wife, my mother' which came into one crucial speech. Sheila's solution was to send the whole method up by brazenly putting 'Good-bye, spouse and mater'. Her infallible instinct for knowing when she could be cheeky stood by her once again, and Mr Heath merely asked her very mildly if she really thought Coriolanus would say that. She did not point out that Coriolanus was in fact quite likely to have said 'mater', and the incident passed.

There was sometimes more to the Shakespeare lesson than paraphrase, however, though it was really no more to do with Shakespeare's work than the paraphrase had been. Mr Heath had a way of making the plays interesting by weaving around the incidents a story of his own making, worded in terms which we could understand and to which we could react. The first play I studied with him was *As You Like It*, and I shall never forget his describing the arrival of Le Beau to tell Rosalind and Celia about the wrestling. He related how Le Beau came through the trees towards them, his bright courtier's clothes glinting among the leaves; he discussed the expression on his face; I almost think he mentioned the colour of his hair. It was wonderfully vivid. I was thrilled, and repeated it all to my mother when I got home with such enthusiasm that she was afraid I was developing a love for the theatre.

There was one poetry lesson a week and this consisted of working through Book III of Palgrave's *Golden Treasury*. One by one, in the order laid down by the selector, the poems were put before us by Bullo, read, discussed and often learnt by heart. (I enjoyed them all so much that I learnt most of them by heart even when not required to do so, and I can recite them to this day.) Educationists would think this was a terrible way to teach poetry; for me, it was pure magic, pure enchantment. I loved the poets' tone of calm authority; they suggested nothing, they stated, not aggressively but with conviction. It was like listening to an argument that had already been won, to a debating motion that had already been carried, to a recorded programme where nothing could go wrong. The poses and the gestures were as unfelt and insincere as the ones I was arriving at myself. When A. Pope, as Palgrave called him, wrote:

> Thus let me live, unseen, unknown;
> Thus unlamented let me die;
> Steal from the world, and not a stone
>   Tell where I lie,

I almost wept with agreement. And it was genuine agreement: Pope, I am surely safe in assuming, did not really mean these sentiments and I know I did not; on the contrary.

I particularly enjoyed poems about the death of the Brave, as they were called:

> How sleep the brave, who sink to rest
> By all their country's wishes blest!

and:

> Toll for the brave!
> The brave that are no more!
> All sunk beneath the wave
> Fast by their native shore!

As clearly 'Brave' meant 'those unfortunate enough to get killed in war or shipwreck' this did not come too near home, and neither were there any disquieting ideas of real courage or cowardice to upset me.

I loved W. Cowper's vein of melancholy in general. I think I may be excused for not having seen how desperate he was. I was especially moved by a poem of his which, without any idea of how silly it was to do so, I called *To the Same*:

> The twentieth year is well-nigh past
> Since first our sky was overcast;
> Ah would that this might be the last!
> My Mary!

It was sad, but the poet was sufficiently in command to put an exclamation mark at the end: I always felt that exclamation marks were a sign of control. And here, too, I think we were basically in agreement, though the circumstances were so different: one determined survivor was calling out to another across the natural wish to die.

I liked W. Collins's vein of melancholy, too. I had had
no articulate feelings about evening till I read his poem,
but after that I was prepared to see it as he saw it, in his
sentences that seemed never to end:

> O Nymph reserved, – while now the bright-hair'd sun
> Sits in yon western tent, whose cloudly skirts,
> > With brede ethereal wove,
> > O'erhang his wavy bed;

this was very different from darkness falling round the
house in Bradham Lane and all the better for it.

The anthology included a great many poems in
Scottish dialect. These I liked, too. Most of the lines
were either quite incomprehensible:

> > Grat his een baith bleer't and blin',
> > Spak o' lowpin ower a linn!

or suggested altogether the wrong image:

> > Ilk ane lifts her leglin and hies her away.

But though it was mumbo-jumbo, it, too, was authoritative and categorical: the poet clearly understood what
he was saying even if we did not. No one shrank from
reading these poems aloud. Certainly neither ignorance
of the meaning nor my own strong Devonshire accent
stopped *me*. It must have sounded bizarre in the extreme.
I was very fond of reciting *Mary Morison* to myself at
home, presumably *sotto voce* or Mother would have heard
me. But, loud or soft, I put my whole self into it.

> > Tho' this was fair, and that was braw,

I declaimed, as if 'braw' meant 'foul',

> > And yon the toast of a' the town,
> > I sigh'd, and said amang them a',
> > 'Ye are na Mary Morison.'

But the great love of my life — I use the expression seriously — at this time was T. Gray. I knew nothing about him personally; it never occurred to me to read a biographical study of him. I knew him only by his work, but this was most plentifully represented in the *Golden Treasury*: he was the undoubted laureate of Book III.

I was obsessed by his work and I have tried to understand this obsession. Though I do not remember its fading — and it *has* faded — I remember its onset; it was love at first sight, and was therefore called up by *Ode on the Pleasure arising from Vicissitude*, which was the first poem in the book. I have no need to look at it: I can recite it; and I think I can see where the attraction lay. It is perhaps best explained by the way in which his and my views on Nature were related. Although I dumbly and inarticulately loved the meadows and the trees of my home, this feeling lay beneath the level of conscious observation: I did not really notice the seasons, for example, till I was grown up. So when Gray spoke of the change from winter to spring he was both describing an experience I had not had and failing to describe an experience I had had. His accounts of the joys of spring:

> New-born flocks, in rustic dance,
>   Frisking ply their feeble feet;
> Forgetful of their wintry trance
>   The birds his presence greet:

and the pains of winter:

> Yesterday the sullen year
>   Saw the snowy whirlwind fly;
> Mute was the music of the air,
>   The herd stood drooping by:

corresponded with nothing I had actually felt or seen:

they were the purest invention, as far as I was concerned.
But at the same time as he was enlarging my experience
by describing reactions I had never had, he was leaving
peacefully intact my deep, lazy, mindless love of the very
things he was depicting.

I could say much the same about his pronouncements
on life in general. The verse I liked best in *Ode on the
Pleasure arising from Vicissitude* was the last:

> See the wretch that long has tost
>   On the thorny bed of pain,
> At length repair his vigour lost
>   And breathe and walk again:
> The meanest floweret of the vale,
> The simplest note that swells the gale,
> The common sun, the air, the skies,
> To him are opening Paradise.

I remember reciting it aloud as I walked up Bradham
Lane to do some shopping at Littleham Cross. He was
again enlarging my experience: I had had no long illness
and therefore knew nothing of the joys of recovery.
But he was also once again dodging, as it seemed, my
experience: no one knew better than I did the fear of
illness, if not the reality, and his words took much of the
sting out of it by making it sound like nothing at all.

How he pronounced! It was not his weightiest sayings,
those of the *Elegy*, for example, that I took to heart:
it was his minor reflections on the state of man and the
world:

> Beside some water's rushy brink
> With me the Muse shall sit, and think
> (At ease reclined in rustic state)
> How vain the ardour of the crowd,
> How low, how little are the proud,
> How indigent the great!

This seemed to me deliciously worldly. His portrayal of the woes in store for the pupils of Eton College when they grew up was something I was in no position to check, but his extraordinary contention that children were strangers to pain, that their tears were forgot as soon as shed and that their breasts were full of sunshine was a proven lie that would have shattered my faith in him completely if I had for one minute expected him to tell the truth. I welcomed these sage inaccuracies, these melodious garblings. What else was poetry for? I could hardly put *The Golden Treasury* Book III down.

I was certainly ripe for it. My earliest poems sound as though they had been influenced by a study of eighteenth-century verse, when in fact they were written some years before I came to the *Golden Treasury* at all. I have found one that I wrote at the age of ten and had published in the school magazine, *Exmothiensis*, in my first term at the Grammar School.

COTTAGES BY THE SEA

The morning dawns, the sun begins to peep,
    The smooth sand glitters in the dayspring light.
Each wave is murmuring secrets of the deep,
    Learnt in the moonlit silence of the night.

These little cottages are not perturbed
    By the fierce rush and bustle of today.
By traffic they are not at all disturbed –
    Their music is the murmur of the bay.

Where fishermen begin to ply their oars,
    And seagulls hover o'er the flashing foam;
The everlasting music of its shores
    Enfolds this place where Peace has made her home.

Later on, my verse deteriorated, not moving in the common way of adolescents from perception to would-be sophistication, but from relatively simple and sparse lack of perception to lush and romantic lack of perception. At the age of thirteen, for example, I wrote the following:

EVENSONG

The ocean heaves with gentle discontent;
  The lapping wavelets kiss the pebbled shore;
Day is dying, all her radiance spent,
  And dusky is the glorious robe she wore.

The fishing craft rock lazily to sleep
  With joyful wing the seagulls cliffward fly;
To rest are gone the toilers of the deep
  And scarce the echoes rouse to give reply.

But hark! a sweet, clear note is slowly tolling
  From the grey church beside the windswept bay;
Across the waves its gentle summons rolling
  Calls every faithful heart to come and pray.

I am appalled now by the sheer wanton inaccuracy of the poem. I knew perfectly well that by the time the toilers of the deep, whoever they were, had gone to rest, it would be much too late for even the most faithful hearts to get up a church service. I knew that the seagulls' wings were not joyful, that the ocean was not discontented and that the wavelets were not feeling affectionate towards the pebbled shore. Above all, I knew what the sea was really like. I do not say I was taught to write like this; it was more that I realised that it was the only style that could possibly win approval, or rather, more basically, the only style there was.

I was not alone. I was not even the worst. I would never have written, for example, the sheer gush which Ina Plimsoll allowed herself in her poem which ended:

> Ah, heaven,
> What joy to be alive – and young – in Devon!

I might not even have concealed my true experiences in the heartbreaking way that Mollie Lane did in her poem *Dunkeswell*, which began:

> Dunkeswell is my home, you know,
> > Far from everywhere.
> It's small and beautiful, and oh,
> > We are all happy there.

I knew Mollie well. Dunkeswell, a village near Honiton, had indeed been her home, but she had by this time left it for ever because of the death of her mother from cancer, and even before this had lived there fatherless; I do not know exactly what the circumstances were, but I asked her once if her father was dead, and she just said, 'I don't know.' Yet in the poem she described an idyllically happy scene, of which she was still a partaker, with the merry clamour of the blacksmith's forge, the visits of the genial vicar and his hospitable wife, and the jolly bee-like busy-ness of the miller and the carpenter. We all tended to hide our feelings in those days – it was the fashion – and especially we hid them in our so-called creative writing. A poem that dealt with what we really felt was quite out of the question.

Only an introduction to modern poetry could have made any real difference at this stage, and that was out of the question too. Teachers in East Devon in the early thirties, even if they had known Eliot's work, would have been unlikely to admire it, and they had every excuse for not even knowing about the work of Auden, Spender, Day Lewis and MacNeice, which after all had only just been published. In any case, I wonder if I, for one, could have borne the demands of contemporary poetry, as either reader or writer. I needed all the security that rhyme, metre, accepted diction and conventional subject-matter could give. We were taught that all these features were essential to poetry, and I was only too happy to believe it and to adopt them.

In fact what I was writing was not poetry, not even bad poetry. I was defeated from the start by having no idea that the real world could appear in literature at all. I had never met it there, in all my avid reading. I thought that what literature did was to invent situations and reactions and then talk about them with all the verisimilitude it could command. I suppose it was inevitable that I should hold this assumption: I had never read a story or a poem which presented life as I knew it. The people, the places and the emotions were all outside my experience; however much I might identify myself with their world, they never touched mine. It was I who made the effort, and successfully. I could change my entire disposition and upbringing to join in the adventures of middle-class girls whose parents had released them to boarding schools; I never met, and never expected to meet, a book about girls of working-class background with possessive mothers, and might have felt rather affronted if I had. I could completely revise my twentieth-century world to accommodate the exploits of the French émigrés and the Jacobite clansmen; I did not expect to come across my own age, as I knew it, in print. And this attitude applied even more to poetry: if I wished to enter into a poem, enter into it is precisely what I did; it never concerned itself with me. If I felt like sharing its sentiments, I had to invent some of my own to go with it.

On these principles I wrote my own poetry. I selected some idea or some scene which had interested me when I met it in a book, and re-presented it, not cold-bloodedly – there would be real emotion behind it, real affection for the idea – but with no kind of exploration at all, no contact with the actual world. An example of this is the following poem written when I was thirteen:

REFLECTIONS

> Fed by Nature's crystal fountains,
> In the heart of stately mountains,
> Smiles, beneath their purple hauteur
> A mirror lake of magic water.
> Calm, unwavering, limpid, clear
> Lies the deep translucent mere.
>
> The lofty pines, with calm precision,
> Contemplate the mirrored vision.
> The willows, under their protection,
> Peep to see their own reflection.
> The eagle views his vision there
> And screams derision to the air.
>
> E'en the mountains gaze austerely
> At themselves, reflected clearly,
> With their ever-changing tinting
> In that lake, serene and glinting;
> Their frowns relax to see their sweeps
> Engraved on those enamelled deeps.

This poem was written in the first flush of my love for Ewen Cameron and was based on Miss D. K. Broster's description of the lake that meant so much to him, Loch na h-Iolaire; this circuitous method of expressing my feelings for him was the best I could manage. It sounds, too, as though the poem was written in the first flush of my love for Longfellow, whose verse I remember I was greatly enjoying about this time; I had not met it at school, but had discovered it for myself at home, as the complete works were in the bookcase. But in spite of this genealogy – by Hiawatha and Ewen Cameron out of D. K. Broster – I felt the poem to be mine, I had put such devotion into it.

Certainly I was outraged when Mr Heath tampered with it. I had given it in towards the end of the Christmas term, and the magazine was ready when school reassembled in the New Year. Before the copies were given out, Bullo took me aside and explained that he had had to alter the last two lines of the first verse. I had written:

> Distant, calm, unwavering, cool,
> Shining like a polished jewel.

He explained that 'cool' and 'jewel' did not rhyme. (As a matter of fact they do rhyme in the mouths of Devonians, who say 'jool', but for him correctness according to Standard English was all.) So he had changed the lines and hoped I was pleased. I smiled gratefully and said I was, but in truth I was furiously indignant, with the fullness of anger that any dedicated professional might feel at having a carefully conceived piece of work messed about by an ignorant blunderer. I thought 'translucent mere' was a vile phrase; I still do. And though nowadays I would not go to the stake for 'polished jewel' either, I am convinced it is better than 'translucent mere'.

I was openly proud of my poetry, and so was Father, who lived in hopes that I would write a hymn, and so was Sheila, and Mother may have been proud in secret. I saw no reason why I should not show it to anyone who would look, without any drawing back or embarrassment. Even had I not liked being in the limelight – and I liked it very much indeed – there could have been no reluctance to overcome: as there was nothing to reveal there was nothing to hide.

CHAPTER TEN

Three Against One

ONE of the first things I remember my mother saying to Sheila and me was: 'You've got the best father in Withycombe.' She said it impressively and with feeling. I cannot remember what particular attitude or action of his caused the remark, but the affection behind it was representative of the harmony of their early years together. Perhaps even then my mother thought she was cleverer than my father – she was a teacher, he was a railway clerk – but she could still look up to his masculine qualities, his role of benevolent provider to the family.

We heard the same sweetness of tone in her accounts of Father's courtship, about which she used to tell us, often at our request, when we were young. At their first meeting he had been a widower; the people who introduced them to each other, she hinted, had done so with romantic hopes that something might come of it. He was eleven years older than herself, and at the point when something was indeed beginning to come of it and he had taken to calling for her after school, the children used to run to her shouting, 'Miss, Miss, your father's waiting for you outside.' There was some raillery in her voice, naturally, as she told this anecdote, but it was very pleasant raillery, and it was there again in her description of Father's proposal: they were out for a walk in one of the lanes, and he had stopped abruptly at a five-barred gate and said, 'I'm awfully sorry, Queen, but will you marry me?' She showed us a poem he had written for her at the time just before their engagement when they had gone for long expeditions on Dartmoor; it mentioned Haytor Rocks, Becky Falls and other beauty spots, and ended:

> We walked for miles. Time flew unseen.
> Shall I forget? Not likely, Queen!

Mother was proud of this poem, both for its sentiments and as a composition. I feel again all the old dread of her scorn when I think what her reception of it would have been in later years, if he had written it then, or if it had been something similar that I had written: how tartly she would have pointed out that time was not in the habit of flying visibly.

In those early days Father was in high favour with my mother's family. Her younger sisters respected him; he was nearly twenty years older than they were, and he seemed quite a man of the world. He had treated them generously when he was courting: they spoke of elegant gloves and handbags he had given them. He was earning five pounds a week, too, which at that time was very solid and prosperous and was twice what their own husbands were to earn when, some years afterwards, they themselves married. Later, when the scorn came into my mother's voice and increased, it seemed, every year, they began to treat him rather differently but never as anything worse than a lovable old fool; they never spoke to him coldly or with disrespect.

I did not realise how much I enjoyed the early state of harmony until it had gone, apparently for ever. I do not know when it went, I can only guess why, and I cannot be certain, of course, that it really did. My memories of the last six years of my parents' life together, it is true, consist of a long series of incidents marked by discord, frustration, bitterness and tension, but I have no way of knowing if things were, in fact, as bad as they seemed.

I cannot even say when the balance of power changed, or, rather, when we became three against one. I remember one episode – I must have been about six – which perhaps indicated the way in which the alliance was already beginning to form. My parents had been wrangling quite amiably about something and Mother turned laughingly to Sheila and me to get us to say that we were on her side in the matter. I joined in stoutly by asserting: 'Oh, yes, we'll all three go to Heaven. He can go to Hell, if he likes.' This remark should have seemed neither bizarre nor rude, coming from a child of the Plymouth Brethren. For one thing, I meant what I said about going to Hell quite literally, not metaphorically at all: the final respective destinations of the saved and the unsaved were to me perfectly factual, and it was as though I had said, 'At the bottom of the road we'll turn to the right, and he can turn to the left if he wants to.' In any case the remark was a joke: I was fond of my father and had no wish that he should really burn in the fires of Hell for all eternity. My speech caused consternation, however. I got told off with dreadful severity by my mother; she chose to take it that I had meant 'go to Hell' as loose and vulgar abuse, but it seems to me that the ganging-up must have already begun – and her excessive severity may in itself have been a sign – or I would hardly have said what I did. After all, literal or metaphorical, jocular or serious, it was fairly strong language. I think I had already decided where my loyalty had better lie, in the case of any division. I was, in later years, appalled at the way my mother used to speak to my father; I tightened and quivered with horror sometimes. But I was always silent: I never stuck up for him. Much as I dreaded my mother's scorn of him I dreaded much more that it might be turned against myself. I did not formulate the matter, but I see now that I made a choice. It seemed the most clearcut of issues: it was either Father or me. And I unhesitatingly threw him to the wolves.

By the time I was eleven there was no doubt about the fact that we were three against one. I can be precise about the date as it was at the time of one of our holiday visits to the West Highlands of Scotland that I was forced to realise the position. We were in the middle of one of the long wet walks which characterised these holidays when we passed through a village and Mother asked me to go and buy some bars of chocolate. I went off with the half-crown she handed me and came back with three bars. Mother asked me furiously where Father's was – she assumed immediately that it was his that was missing – and sent me back to buy a fourth. I felt aggrieved and, I now think justifiably: I had in fact been indoctrinated and then let down by the indoctrinator, who happened herself to be in the grip of a holiday mood. Looking back on it, I might have to conclude that it was my own original attitude, that I was the one who took the initiative in cutting Father out (certainly I used my recurrent insomnia and my agonising nightmares, usually of men with flaming red eyes lurking on the landing outside my room, as an excuse to get into bed with my mother so that my father had to spend the night in my bed), if it were not for the events of the next three years.

During these three years Sheila and I were both at the Grammar School, and Mother was beginning to fly high. She was becoming increasingly involved with our education. Sheila and I were now well on the way to the goal that Mother had set for us: we were getting good marks and were clearly going to pass School Certificate. From then on the path was plain: entrance to Teachers' Training College, qualification, a post in a good school, and so to the middle-class friends and the middle-class life she wanted for us, with perhaps even a little car at the end of it. She was not only rising with us, but rising on her own account: she had more or less abandoned Miss England and Miss Britain now and had become very friendly with the Headmistress of the Grammar School. I am not saying that this was pure social climbing on my mother's part: she and Miss Fleming did seem to get on well with each other, and indeed my mother could be very lively and amusing company. But she attached more value to the relationship than it intrinsically held, fostered it untiringly and imaginatively, dropped other friends such as Mrs Tucker in consequence and kept Father systematically in the background. Miss Fleming behaved most correctly: whenever she invited Mother, Sheila and me to a meal she always included Father in the invitation, but he was never allowed to accept, and indeed by this time things had come to such a pass that Sheila and I were astonished that he should be invited at all.

An unmistakable sign of his relegation at this time was his exclusion from the Lectures. The Lectures may not sound dramatic or exciting, but they were an important part of the social life of Exmouth and had gathered round them the sort of glamour that makes me link them in my mind with the Carnival. A series of public lectures was held every winter and there was enough support for the scheme for really eminent people to be engaged: people who had flown round the world, held key posts in the League of Nations, and made newsworthy discoveries about birds. I remember particularly Commander Campbell who in his talk *My Mystery Ships* spoke about the camouflaged vessels by means of which he had destroyed so many German submarines in the First World War. It was illustrated by lantern-slides, and in showing one of them he was forced to add that it was for this action he had been awarded the V.C. We all clapped and it seemed wonderfully sophisticated. I loved the Lectures: I loved the knowing jokes, for example, when one speaker alluded to 'America, that great country to whom we owe so much', though of course I would not have realised it was knowing had not everyone laughed appreciatively. It was exciting to do anything after dark in a town that seemed to go to sleep at dusk, and for Plymouth Brethren children who were cut off from so much, the massing crowds in the streets near the Hall were very thrilling.

For this annual series Mother booked three sets of tickets. Father was never included, though he loved information and great minds beyond anything. On some of the evenings when there was a topic he simply could not resist, such as *Branch Lines of Great Britain*, he would attend as well, buying a single ticket for himself as best he could and sitting somewhere on his own, away from Mother, Sheila and me and our educated friends.

It was this getting of tickets that so often made the situation terribly plain. Mother, followed by Sheila and me, was an admirer of both Kenneth Grahame and A. A. Milne, so when *Toad of Toad Hall* came on in London just before Christmas one year, she decided that the three of us would go up to see it. This may sound extravagant, though in fact financially it was not, as we paid nothing for the railway journey, but from another point of view it may well have seemed exaggerated to spend ten hours of one day in travelling in order to see *Toad of Toad Hall*. Certainly our schoolfriends' mothers thought so when our boasting got back to them. Father came up with us – he was essential in railway journeys for protection and the carrying of whatever luggage there might be – but did not attend the play. I do not know how he spent the afternoon.

I do not know either how he spent his evenings while we were all in Torquay, if he cooked for himself or how he managed. I suppose Mother must have made some arrangements, but my impression was that he was just dumped. I am sure that there was a certain resentment on his side and a certain guilt on Mother's: he would relate much oftener than was necessary how one night he had suffered such severe twinges of indigestion that he had been driven to taking a pinch of soda, which he had heard was beneficial, only to find out later that it had been the wrong sort of soda, not powdery bicarbonate but the shiny hard sort that went in with the cabbage to keep it green while it was boiling, and Mother in her turn told the story with much more bravado and laughter than was necessary, remarking that that was why he had been such a good colour recently.

My own feelings of frustration and annoyance at being uprooted and borne off left me no energy to think of his plight. He must have been very lonely. What I now imagine is that he played the gramophone every evening. I think this idea is based on a single memory of coming home one night from some expedition with Mother and Sheila, up the dark back garden path, to see the gaslight floating out of the dining-room window apparently bearing with it the tinny strains of one of his much-loved, often-played records. Uncle Ted, in one of his carpentering spells, had made us a gramophone, a handsome light-wood cabinet with a great deal of beading, and we had amassed quite a collection of records over the years. (Mother often persuaded Sheila and me to ask for a gramophone record as a birthday or Christmas present; it was almost as good as a book.) Father's favourites were the 1812 *Overture*, Schubert's *Unfinished Symphony* and the Overture to *Tannhäuser*, and I imagine him winding up the creaking machine and playing them, over and over again in the lonely house, till we came home at the end of the school holiday.

Mother's compulsive need to keep dashing to Torquay was one thing; her habit of excluding Father from company while we were at home, though obviously connected with it, was another. There was no straightforward reason for it: he was a good-looking, respectable, well-mannered and well-spoken man, not a person of whom on the face of it she needed to be ashamed. Socially his family was above hers, and, with his local background, he had more prestige in Exmouth than she had.

He had left school at the age of fourteen, but he set great store by education and was proud of his skill in some of its minor manifestations: he had beautiful handwriting – individual, easy and sophisticated – and was most particular about spelling: it upset him to see ACCOMODATION in a landlady's window. He was by no means a philistine: he had the greatest respect for culture in general and a veneration for literature, especially the poetry of Milton. He had never read widely or deeply, it is true, but the respect was there, and it took the form of wide-ranging quotation. We had a series of *Gems from the Poets* in the bookcase in the front room, which he often dipped into and used, but his chief quotations were from Dickens and W. S. Gilbert, and he spoke them with such complete and loving appropriation that for many years I thought they were his own words. To this day I can hardly persuade myself that he was not the first to say 'Quiet calm deliberation disentangles every knot', though it was in no way his own style of talking.

He never read trashy novels as my mother did, but he was irritatingly dependent on the newspaper – we took the *Daily Mail* – and not only recited its news and views without the slightest attempt at personal judgement or interpretation, but also blindly accepted its pronouncements on matters that he could have checked from his own observation. A columnist once told the readers, for example, that they could be sure to recognise a new type of aeroplane even when they could not see it, as its engine made a noise that the writer rendered in print as 'yow-zer'.

For weeks Father identified the remotest drone as the 'yow-zer' of the new plane.

He was a gullible man, a sucker for bargain offers, free gifts and unique opportunities. He had no idea what the world was really like: his happy fantasies about the rape of young girls by designing monsters offering drugged cigarettes gave him no inkling of how coldly terrible life could be. He was physically clumsy, always dropping things or tripping, so that I was horrified to watch him jumping on to the running-board of a train after it had started (this often happened); I was sure he would miss his footing and fall underneath, but, strangely, he never did. Everybody said he was tactless, and so he was: I have never known anyone harp so remorselessly on a subject that everyone else was longing to drop. He had a series of jokes, too, dreadful old chestnuts that he told repeatedly to the same people at what never seemed to be the right moment. But his tactlessness was only a symptom of his failure to recognise that people might be saying other than they meant or thinking something without saying it at all. This made him blind and deaf to the polite fictions of society. I remember one evening at the Paignton Assembly when a Brother who was rather more worldly than the others – he was the one who owned the hotel near the sea-front – had got up an informal sing-song, of hymns, naturally, and Brethren from the local Assemblies were invited to come forward and perform. Father had sung one solo, and so had everybody else who had a voice at all, and the proceedings were clearly drawing to a close. Brother Wilkinson got up and asked, in unmistakably dissuasive tones, if any Brother had another solo he would like to offer. Father had several; he liked singing, and this was a good opportunity, so he stepped up again, at which Brother Wilkinson said dismissively that after all he was afraid there was no time left. Father blushed purple and went back to his seat. I must have been purple, too, with embarrassment, with rage at Brother Wilkinson, with rage at Father and with pity for Father.

He also failed to see that people were often as simple and straightforward as they appeared to be. He could imagine meaningful looks and significant coughs when those who were supposed to be giving them just happened to be looking or coughing. His terrifying assumption that people were feeling warmly welcoming towards him when they were not, alternated with his other assumption: that they were against him when they were not. Once when he was praying at the St Marychurch Gospel Hall, Brother Curtis had a fit of coughing which I feel convinced was quite genuine – certainly he nearly choked trying to suppress it – but Father believed for ever after that it was directed at him, though there was nothing in the least pointed in his prayer, and he had always been on cordial terms with Brother Curtis.

He would not realise that the twentieth century was, by and large, run on commercial and professional lines. He fancied he had a flair for advertising and was always sketching out illustrated captions which he sent to the makers of the product concerned, hoping soon to see his idea realised on the biggest hoardings of the Exeter Road railway arches. As soon as I discovered the fact myself, I explained to him that big firms employed advertising agencies, but he took absolutely no notice. His suggestions were nearly always based on some aspect of his much-loved railways. One I remember depicted an ox caught between the level-crossing gates, thus blocking the line to approaching trains; it bore the caption 'A Bovril sandwich is a great stay.'

He loved my mother devotedly and was proud of her. He was always wishing he could give her extra comfort and luxuries, such as a fur coat, though in fact he had given her greater comfort than she was born to; the

Bradham Lane house had a bathroom, for example, which was more than her parents' house had, or that of either of her sisters when they were first married, and gaslight as opposed to lamplight, and she had more to spend on food than any of them. But he was a weak character, and, as the years went by, increasingly dependent on her, which was, I suppose, what sometimes made him turn on her, not with firmness or real self-assertion, but with petulance and even spite. I remember one Sunday teatime when we were sitting by the fire in the front room, relaxing between Sunday School and Gospel Meeting; my mother was settled very peacefully on the sofa and said to him, coaxingly rather than commandingly, 'Oh, John, do go and make the tea.' To her obvious surprise and certainly to ours, he replied quite nastily, 'Why should I?' I suppose she had been commanding for so long that she could not with impunity go back to coaxing.

A second incident was more serious. It took place about a year before her death. We were having tea – it must have been a Sunday again – and Mother was saying something about feeling tired and unwell, and Father retorted most unsympathetically, 'Go on, Queen, you're as strong as a horse.' Mother, terrifyingly, burst into tears. Sheila and I glared at Father reproachfully. It was about this time that I had a recurrent dream: Mother was lying on the railway lines of a station, having apparently fallen off the platform. A train was approaching but she could not move. It hit her and she flew into pieces. Father, who was standing on the platform watching, laughed heartily.

As far back as I can remember Mother had made a great show of being exhausted. It was a small house, she was at home all day, the shops were near, and when we were at school there cannot have been a great deal to do, certainly no more than many women today would fit in with a full-time job. The obvious explanation is that she was bored, but there must have been more to it than that. Later on, when we were at the Grammar School, she did take up teaching again, supply teaching in the Exmouth schools, and was a great success. She was popular with the staff, most of whom she knew already. They thought she was rather a card; she made one of the junior teachers, who was about to be married, laugh in prayers when they came to the bit which said, 'Bless all who are engaged in this school.' She was popular with the children too; compositions were crammed with remarks like, 'My teacher is that kind Miss Beer.' The authorities liked her work; one H.M.I. was really impressed by the tactful way in which she coped with a demanding child who yelled, 'Miss, Miss,' at every question, hopping down the aisle with anguished upraised hand. But in spite of the new interest and her undoubted success, she used the work as a weapon against us all the same, or rather as a method to win our gratitude. She told a friend in our hearing that as she came cycling round the corner into Bradham Lane after a day's teaching half dead with fatigue she would say to herself, '*Now* perhaps those girls will believe I love them.'

Sheila and I retaliated by resentful hints that we were being neglected. A splendid opportunity arose when we caught measles and were really quite ill. Mother had just started on a course of supply teaching when we came out in rashes and was therefore in a quandary, as she felt she ought not to let the school down. She solved the problem by asking Nurse Markby to look after us while she was out. This seemed a most sensible course of action to everybody but Sheila and me. We thought we were more important than supply teaching; after all, we had been trained to think ourselves the centre of the universe, under Mother's hand. So we played Nurse Markby up terribly all day and magnified our symptoms and sufferings to Mother in the evening. In short, we behaved very badly indeed.

To outsiders in general we no doubt seemed unpleasant, unnatural children. We had been brought up to be helpless. Even when we were in our teens we were not trained to help with housework of any kind, except occasional washing-up, or with cooking. We sometimes did the shopping, and that was all. We were not taught any domestic skills and certainly had no inclination to learn any voluntarily. We were cosseted and protected from all conceivable risks and imaginable perils. Once when we were going down to Torquay a few days before Mother, we were not allowed to do even the last stage of the journey, the six miles by quiet branch line from Newton Abbot to Torquay, by ourselves; Father had to come all the way with us, though it meant missing his connection back to Exeter from Newton. We were thirteen and fourteen at the time. We were fed like Christmas geese, and with expensive delicacies, too: tinned fruit for tea was a luxury for people of our class, but Mother nearly always had a plateful of pears set out ready for Sheila and me – never for herself – though she quickly put them in the larder if a neighbour called so as not to be accused of pampering us. To us she emphasised the treat by telling stories about the privations of her own youth: her parents had not always been able to afford meat, and the whole family had often sat down to a dish of runner beans with a small lump of butter in the middle.

We were not left to form relationships for ourselves; our friendships achieved what organic growth they could under Mother's eye and with her constant intervention and stage-management. It was not that we were forbidden to play with rough children; we were barely allowed to play with any children at all. Mr Tucker had a large nursery garden behind the house in Norfolk Terrace, and we greatly enjoyed running or wandering round it with Peggy and Joy. This was permissible, but, if we stayed too long, Mother became very reproachful and sad and accused us of not loving our home any more. Although we would not have altogether changed places with the young Tuckers, we felt envious of their liberty. The fact that there was no staircarpet in their house – as Mother was always telling her sisters – seemed a small disadvantage in comparison, though I was glad we had staircarpet. I never quite knew what to make of the way they spoke to their parents. When Peggy wanted a bath the night before she went away for a holiday and was told there was no hot water, she said that when she got there she would scrape off the grime and send it back in an envelope. Mrs Tucker smiled affectionately, as she did on the occasion when Phoebe, who was older than the rest of us, said that she was longing for the day when she could leave home. Actually we suffered for Phoebe's remark that evening, for my mother had been present when she made it, and when the three of us were alone together Mother burst into tears and said how she dreaded the day when either or both of us would say anything so heartless.

For the last seven years of our life at Exmouth we had a dog, Bill, a mongrel that looked more like a wire-haired terrier with Airedale's feet than anything definable else. I had little feeling for him. Pets are supposed to mean a great deal to children, but he was very much Mother's dog – we have photographs of her with Bill on her knee as though he were a baby – and my chief relationship with him was what I called playing, but what many other people might have called torturing. I had a tiny shirt which my mother had once made as a model for a needlework class in her teaching days, and I used to ease him into this and then let him go, knowing that it would madden him like a straitjacket and send him scudding around on the lino in paroxysms of frustration. I knew the very type of toffee, too, that would clamp his jaws frenziedly together when he had chewed it into malleability.

We were never taught to be kind to animals or to consider their nerves. Orphans and the poor were what counted, though we were not left to be charitable and unselfish; we were forced to go through the motions, even with rage in our hearts. One Christmas it happened that I was given two purses, one very pretty and one nothing like so attractive. Mother at once assured me that I had no need for two purses and that I was going to send one of them to the little girls at the Orphanage. I soon became fairly resigned to sending the orphans the unattractive purse, only to be told I was giving them the pretty one, on the utterly feeble grounds, it seemed to me, that its donor lived a long way away, while we frequently met the donor of the ugly purse. The next Christmas I was given a handsome box of chocolates; before I had finished exclaiming, Mother whipped them out of my hands, brutally undid them and handed them round the Jeffery circle, first of all to my detested grandmother, who helped herself hugely. If my mother was trying to train me to set little store by personal possessions and not just being officious, her action was ill-advised as it had exactly the opposite effect.

I do not remember Father taking part in our moral upbringing at all; his advice was confined to telling us to keep our shoulders back and to sound our aitches, to pay our debts and to save. He was unwaveringly and uncritically proud of both of us, always sure that our entries to competitions would win, that the eccentric photographs we took with our first box-cameras had really captured the spirit of the scene, and that we would both end up as headmistresses. He was particularly proud of me; he thought my poems were wonderful, my painting truly talented and my singing voice as lovely as that of his favourite soprano Isobel Baillie. He even praised my looks, which needed some ingenuity, as I was pale, thin, straight-haired and strong-featured. Sheila was everyone else's ideal of girlish beauty, rosy-cheeked, curly-haired and plump, and my mother and aunts were always raving about her appearance; but every time this happened my father, with unusual courage, would think up something to say on my behalf, for example, that I had a straight nose, or a patrician nose, as he was fond of putting it, as a sort of pun.

Although he prayed that we might be headmistresses, he wanted us to get married too; illogically, as in those days married women had to give up their careers. He was anxious that we should marry well and was convinced that we could have the pick of the land if we chose. He never made these remarks in front of Mother, as it would have given her an opportunity to jeer at men and marriage, but when he was alone with us he often came round to the subject and once, surprisingly, made a comment on the Jefferys which revealed something of his true feelings about them: 'Your mother's people,' he said, 'wouldn't mind if you married dustmen, as long as they were saved.'

Of course, we saw how weak he was and how subservient to Mother, but as long as one parent was strong we felt secure enough. It was only later when, in desperate need, we tried to depend on him, that we realised how incapable he was of assuming any real responsibility, either because he had always been weak or because Mother had sapped what strength he had. For the first decade of our lives he was a perfect father: he was tall and manly-looking, he earned money and provided, he carried us, he carried the suitcases, he made a good job of the garden and he played with us. The Abbott's bus of our childhood gave way to a schoolgirls' game which became an important ritual in our lives: General Knowledge Questions. Every evening when we were in bed Father came into our room for ten minutes or a quarter of an hour and, at our earnest request, asked us a string of questions, about the state of the world, political and geographical, the authorship of books and so on. The one criterion was that there had to be a short factual answer that was either right or wrong, such as India or Alexandre Dumas or Mussolini. We were all very good at this without knowing anything about the Ganges but its location, without ever having read *The Three Musketeers* and without even beginning to understand what Fascism involved. We often made terrible howlers. We were convinced that there was a book called *The Forsyte Saga, I* (on the lines of *I, Claudius*, perhaps, or *Her Privates We*) because we had misread it from the book lists we were always poring over to try and trip each other up. We did not know what a saga was, or a forsyte, our version made an intriguing and rhythmical title and a search after anything like knowledge was not the point of the game.

Mother listened to all this from the front bedroom with both doors open. Sometimes on summer evenings she sat looking out into the lane and the opposite field. More often she went to bed at the same time as Sheila and I did. Father stayed downstairs afterwards for what seemed like ages; whatever he did seemed to involve padding from dining-room to kitchen backwards and forwards endlessly.

As a family we had such limited dealings with the world that our relationships with each other were not likely to be modified by any outside influence. Two events did leave their mark on us, but as one was connected with Torquay relatives and the other with Littleham Gospel Hall, they were not really external. The first happening was the birth of a son, David, to Olly and Jack. This took place in our front bedroom, where Sheila and I had been born; Nurse Goodman would have been in attendance had she been free. Mother had eagerly taken Olly's pregnancy under her wing, and indeed my aunt had been in need of protection, as Grandma Jeffery had seized the opportunity to be more awkward than usual. The actual confinement had been a production of Mother's too: Sheila and I had been banished to Torquay while it took place; Jack had been forbidden to show up till everything was over and so was still in Torquay himself; Father, I felt, was only saved from exile by being indispensable as a runner to and from the Littleham Cross telephone-box.

Mother, as I have said, had always longed for a son, and the baby's turning out to be a boy was a godsend to her. For the rest of her life she so doted over him and – Sheila and I felt – made such a fool of herself where he was concerned that we became very jealous and much more resentful of Mother than before, though he was a sweet baby, and we would have been as fond of him as we pretended to be had there been no emotional complications. If Mother's new infatuation had given us more liberty we might have felt it was worth it, but unfortunately she had enough possessiveness to go round.

The second happening was that Mother fell in love with Brother Restall, soon after he joined the Littleham Assembly. He certainly was attractive. He was Welsh and had an enchanting soft voice. He was tubercular and had nearly died several times, but did not look exactly delicate, merely gentle like his voice. He had rich relations, owners of a big store in Exeter, which added greatly to his glamour in giving him access to a car and to one of largest houses off the Salterton Road. A happy time began for all our family. Sheila and I became very fond of Uncle Donald, as he asked us to call him. It was quite natural that as a youngish bachelor he should be very often at our house, and after a few months he was invited to come to Scotland with us on our annual holiday. He accepted with every appearance of enthusiasm and the holiday was a great success. Mother now started keeping grown-up hours. Instead of going to bed when Sheila and I did, she put us to bed and then stayed up herself with the adults; we could hear them downstairs laughing and talking for hours, a common experience of childhood, I suppose, but one that we seldom had.

Mother's feelings naturally got mixed up with religion. Uncle Donald often spoke in the Morning Meeting, and very soon after his arrival she was declaring that no one could lead her to the throne of grace like Donald Restall. As her love for him grew she became superficially honest about it, frequently exclaiming in a swashbuckling manner, 'If I were fifteen years younger Donald Restall would have been the man for me.' This apparent acknowledgement of the situation was her way, I think, of pretending it did not exist. Whether Father faced it or not I do now know – I imagine not – but his behaviour, even if it were ostrich-like, was precisely what would have been thought of as civilised and intelligent, had it been conscious: he kept up a calm and steady friendship with Donald throughout Mother's infatuation and her inevitable disillusionment.

It happened quite soon and most predictably. Donald fell in love: not with Mother but with a pretty, low-voiced girl who worked as a saleswoman in his rich relations' store in Exeter. He confided in Father and Mother from an early stage and long before he had any grounds for hope, so that poor Mother had to listen to outpourings about how he was not worthy of Muriel, simply not good enough for her, and so on. Hope eventually dawned, however, and Muriel was brought down to Exmouth and introduced. Father, Sheila and I thought she was sweet, and even Mother, though she loathed her on sight and indeed long before that, had difficulty at first in actually picking on any deficiency or misdemeanour. However, an opportunity was provided at the next Morning Meeting, which Muriel attended with Donald, to the lively interest

of all the Sisters: Muriel did not know her Bible. As the
various Saints announced their texts, she found Timothy
and even Deuteronomy, but Ecclesiastes had her hopelessly
beaten, and over went the Bible to Donald, in what we
thought was a sweetly confiding way until we heard
Mother on the subject at dinner. It was a point of honour
among the Brethren to know the Bible, to be able to
recite the names of the books right through, both Old
and New Testaments, and to be capable of finding any
reference at top speed with the minimum of rustling.
Muriel had failed.

As the courtship proceeded normally through engagement to marriage, Mother's temper, which had been
sunny for so many months beforehand, darkened and
flashed. At first we were, as a family, included in the
planning and discussions, and particularly those concerned
with the building of the house higher up in Bradham
Lane which Donald was preparing for his bride, and
that his mother was to share with them. Though it was
not very big it was grand in conception, with a flat
roof and battlements. Sheila and I thought it was magnificent and called it the Castle. As soon as there was a
staircase we wandered all over it, working out where
everything would be. When we got home from one of
these visits I asked Mother where Muriel would sleep,
wording it from the woman's point of view, but meaning
to enquire which of the main bedrooms the married couple
would have. The question was perfectly sensible, therefore, but I am not sure it was innocent; if it *was* malicious,
it got the reception it deserved. Mother lashed out,
'With old Mrs Restall, of course,' so venomously that
even Father said, 'Queen,' in feeble remonstrance.

As the wedding drew near we saw less and less of
Donald and Muriel. For one thing the rich relations
(whom Mother despised, incidentally, because they
could not spell and signed their letters with Mr or Mrs

in front of their name) had taken up Muriel. For another it was dawning on Donald that Mother did not like Muriel, and he naturally wanted to protect his fiancée from any coldness or hauteur. I am sure he did not guess the reason for Mother's dislike, and he was too happy and busy to look into it. After the wedding Mother, Sheila and I saw them only at the Gospel Hall, but Father, whose unawareness had caused him to behave so cleverly, often called at the Castle and stayed for hours.

For Mother life not only settled down again after this, but seemed positively to be improving. There were some very good signs: she wrote to the University College of the South West at Exeter to find out about extra-mural classes in French: she made enquiries about a house for sale behind Phear Park. Quite apart from giving her new objects of interest, both these courses would have tied her decisively to Exmouth. But it was too late.

CHAPTER ELEVEN

A Wonderful Result

I LOVED the Grammar School as much as I had loved the Council School. I did just as well there, too, except for a setback in the first term when I came fourth in the class. Mother was furious with me about this, and it was with great surprise that I heard her telling someone in Bradham Lane that it was simply to be expected with sensitive children that in a new environment they should be distracted by all that was novel and stimulating and therefore do less well in their school work. Her tone implied that it was a credit to them. I am not sure which was her real view, but she was not called on to apologise to the neighbours ever again, as I was soon back in my stride, winning prizes at every opportunity.

As a matter of fact there was not a great deal that *was* novel about the Grammar School. The continuity from the Council School, with regard to educational methods, friends, activities and home attitudes, was absolute. The buildings, of course, were different, much grander. The central part of the school was a beautiful, spacious country house; it had formerly been the Grange, and its personality as a private dwelling was still so dominant that the whole Grammar School was more often than not referred to as the Grange by the townspeople. Some darkly creosoted huts and bicycle-sheds were clustered round it, and across from its main entrance stood the recently built gymnasium which was the pride of all, with its confident motto-frieze MENS SANA IN CORPORE SANO. In the rambling grounds there were various half-hidden tennis-courts and a big open playing-field, in the middle of which seagulls used to settle if it was left quiet for even two minutes.

I had worked very hard to get to the Grammar School, but, although it was a great satisfaction to be there at last, the place did not seem a higher sphere in any snobbish sense. My classmates were mostly the same ones I had crammed alongside at the Council School, and we were all pleased to be there together. The children I had not known before came from outlying districts, not from any nobler background. Neither were the accents, manners or attitudes of the staff more noticeably middle-class than those of our previous teachers. Mother, it is true, talked from time to time about 'good names', detecting from this evidence birth and breeding in a boy called Perrott and a master called Bamfield. I believe they *were* both fairly distinguished Devon names, but we all referred to Mr Bamfield as Daddy Bampus from first to last and had no particular occasion to look up to Perrott.

Two of the hallmarks of the new education were homework and hockey. Games were a shock after the shambling Country Dancing and the drill which were the only physical activities there had been space for at the Council School, but homework seemed perfectly normal. To spend the evening in study was no great change for children unaccustomed to gadding and trained to serious reading. Sheila and I worked at the table in the dining-room while Mother sat in the corner, knitting and watching and time-keeping. I never protested openly at this constant surveillance, but every so often I was at some pains to defeat it on the quiet. Once I pretended to study the prescribed chapter in the Geography book with my eyes unfocused so that I could not see a word, turning the pages at careful intervals and simulating tremendous concentration; I was praised for my application and allowed to leave the table. This was an isolated gesture, however; for the most part I did my homework meticulously, especially compositions, which I worked at with near-hysterical zeal for hours.

Home still dominated our school lives. We were still forbidden to join in outside activities, such as Girl Guides, and my transient wish to be a Guide was not compulsive enough to beat down Mother's resistance on this point. We were still not allowed out with our friends except for odd hours in nearby territory. This became a bone of contention when the newly opened swimming-baths on the sea-front grew so popular that hardly an afternoon seemed to end without someone's saying, 'Come down the baths tonight,' and our having to be evasive. Mother still cultivated the staff. There was no Parent–Teacher Association any more than there had been at the Council School, but Mother, as before, set up an unacknowledged one of her own. Her friendship with Miss Fleming soon gave her a foot in the camp.

We continued being friendly with the Tuckers and walking to and from school with them, but we acquired other friends. Miss Fleming had two boarders, Kathleen Evans and Mollie Lane; they were farmers' daughters and came from Dunkeswell, a village much too remote for them to live in while attending school. They were in my class, and I liked them both, especially Kathleen, with whom for a while I achieved the exclusive kind of friendship that books about girls had taught me to expect. Even had I not liked them, however, I imagine the friendship would have been forced on me by Mother, who saw in them, as Miss Fleming's boarders, interesting potential and cultivated their acquaintance from the start.

Mother organised this part of our life like every other. Kathleen, Mollie and the Tuckers were invited to our house, and we acted charades, with Mother, and sometimes Father, as audience. Mother was an excellent listener and spectator: she was appreciative and intelligent and laughed in the right places. Father could be a terrible trial, as he took it all very moralistically. Once when Peggy Tucker had given a skilful impression of a Frenchwoman complete with French exclamations and suitable accent and gestures, he drew me aside afterwards and asked me heavily if I knew what 'Mon Dieu' meant, which I said I did, but he went on to tell me that it meant 'My God' and wondered how we could take the name of God in vain like that in a charade. I tried very hard to explain that though of course it meant 'My God', it didn't really mean 'My God', but he hammered relentlessly on and on till I could have screamed. That evening, instead of siding with Mother purely for strategic reasons, I thought I had a glimpse of what she had to put up with and felt sympathy.

Sometimes Mother got up competitions for us, with an outside judge – usually Nell Down – and prizes and refreshments. We might have to write a poem or paint a picture, but whatever it was we entered for the contest anonymously and in fact Sheila and I seldom won. It was all most enjoyable, though, with real suspense and excitement. Mother was wonderful at anything like that; she had such vitality. I realise it must have been bad for Sheila and me never to run wild, never to be free from supervision and organisation, but a great deal of gaiety and drama and company came to us from Mother's management, and on the whole I liked having my development stunted in this way, though obviously I did not consider the situation in these terms.

Such moments of rebellion as I had were dumb: I had no words for them even in my own mind, and my feelings were in any case mixed. One evening, after I had been studying in school the poem that began:

> What was he doing, the Great God Pan,
> Down in the reeds by the river?

I was entertaining my friends in the dining-room with the natural suppositions raised by this question. Strangely, I must have forgotten that the dining-room door was open and that Mother was sitting in the front room looking out into the lane and listening. (I have an odd surrealistic vision of her doing this, remembering her in a state of visible conflict, as if her eyes were going one way and her ears another.) The girls were screaming with laughter as I set forth my speculations as to what the Great God Pan was really doing down in the reeds by the river – very innocent by the way: he was going to the lavatory – when I heard Mother calling me into the front room. I got a stern telling off for vulgarity, but at least it was just, as I *was* being vulgar – Father had seen blasphemy where none existed – and in a way it was comforting to feel there was someone who would stop me going too far. I never had this sense of security with Father.

Exmouth Grammar School was technically co-educational, but in practice it amounted to nothing much more than that boys and girls were taught under the same roof. I was never in a mixed class at all, though Sheila was. There seemed to be no principle behind it: segregation and desegregation followed each other haphazardly, presumably at somebody's whim. It just so happened that as I went up through the school, my form was I, II or IIIG as opposed to I, II or IIIB. Certainly the school was not run on co-educational lines from the point of view of educational theory or practical organisation. A very few of the pupils had a boy-friend or a girl-friend at the school, but these few were generally regarded as unhealthily precocious or even common. Most of us just avoided the opposite sex, apart from the one occasion when we were thrown together and directed to mix, that is, the school party, and this was always the scene of acute embarrassment and boorishness on both sides. At my first school party, when I was eleven, the ice was destined to be broken by a game where scrambled names of towns were pinned on to us and we had to guess each other's; one boy pushed off every enquiring girl by growling 'Go away. Mine's Cardiff.' And when we came to Sir Roger de Coverley, with one line of boys and another of girls, the unwillingness of nearly everyone to take the hands of his or her partner at the top led to milling chaos.

I tended to think of boys of my own age as smelly, rough, ignorant and big-booted, and nothing shook me in this opinion till after I had left Exmouth Grammar School at the age of fourteen. The older boys seemed different, however; I can remember their names in a long list which I can never have really heard, as it is neither alphabetical nor in order of scholastic or athletic merit: Hitt, Bulled, Marshall, Parsons, Berry, Tait, Laurie, Knowles, Tootell, Pullin. They were all heroes, distant ones, not necessarily doing anything heroic like winning the high-jump or a scholarship to Oxford, but walking along the corridor or exchanging sophisticated jokes; they always seemed to be cheerful. The essence of their activities and status was somehow caught on a winter afternoon about half-past four, when the school orchestra was practising in the gym for the Christmas Party. It was a small orchestra, and by no means all the older boys were members of it, but nevertheless, as it was confined to seniors, it seemed to represent their quality of initiation and light-hearted accomplishment. It was magical to go past in the dusk when the rest of the school had fallen quiet and the seagulls were back on the playing-field and hear the boys belting away inside. When they had practised seriously for long enough they always allowed themselves the treat of playing a hit of the time, which they lammed out with real spirit:

> The bravest man was Captain Brown
> And he played his ukelele as the ship went down.

The jaundiced view of sex which we must have imbibed from a lifetime of Mother's comments and hints was at no stage amplified or corrected by any teaching on the subject. Mother herself left us to pick up what information we could as best we might, and there was no school subject which included or led into such material at the right moment; by the time we had got to pods in Botany we were old enough to giggle at them as being a caricature of humans. It was school, however, which had provided all the answers: how babies were born was discussed among ourselves with a fair degree of accuracy (the Tuckers were authorities here, as Mrs Tucker had a baby when Peggy and Joy were over ten) and other branches of the subject were filled in by the dirty jokes which some of the girls used to tell in the shrubbery. I did not understand all these jokes at the time, though I knew enough about their structure to realise when to laugh, but over the years their import dawned and provided a coherent body of knowledge. Some of the stories were really filthy, in an unappetising, unfunny sort of way, but others were mild enough, like, for example, the sad, sick story, couched in terms of the Great War over a decade after the Armistice, which ran as follows: a lady (the characters in these stories were always referred to as ladies) got married, but on the honeymoon nothing happened, so her mother advised her to buy a really tempting nightdress; when still nothing happened she lifted up the hem one night saying wistfully, 'Shot silk, 1934', to which her husband replied, even more wistfully, lifting up the hem of his nightshirt, 'Shot off, 1914.'

It was at the Grammar School that I realised that some people have sex appeal and others do not. Mollie Lane was the central piece of evidence that led me to this conclusion. She was not very pretty – photographs show her as probably the plainest member of the Hockey First Eleven – nor brilliant, though conversable and quite intelligent, but every time one walked round any corner of the school, inside or out, there seemed to be the flounce of a gym tunic and the withdrawing of a blazer sleeve, as Mollie broke away from some encounter. And when we all – Miss Fleming's boarders, the Tuckers and Sheila and I – went for pre-breakfast runs to train for the Sports (a practice frowned on by Mother, but permitted from time to time) a pounding figure in shorts would be certain to come round some leafy turning and start pounding along beside Mollie. Her ability to win devotion was her downfall, though I am sure only very temporarily, in my last year at the Grammar School. She and the rest of us had been playing our usual beach game of jumping off the sea-wall and Mollie had run a splinter into her foot which turned septic so that she had to go into hospital for a few days. At the first visiting hour Miss Fleming dutifully arrived, only to find a visitor there before her, a sixth-form boy, sitting on the bed. Mollie was in dreadful disgrace; I had left Exmouth before she was received back into favour, if she ever was.

Sheila and I attracted no such attentions, but then neither did any of our friends. Perhaps, in view of Mother's certain reaction to such a situation, it was fortunate we did not. Her attitude, however, was only an exaggerated version of that adopted by Miss Fleming and in a mild way by Mrs Tucker and Mrs Martin. Mother thought there was something innately undesirable about sex, which the others, with the possible exception of Miss Fleming, did not, but they would all have agreed in open discussion that it was for later on, when School Certificate was safely behind us; sex was a time-waster, an enemy to study and therefore to ultimate success in the world. If we children did not see it quite like this, we saw the strength of both the argument and of those voicing it, and were happy enough with our girl-friends and our schooling and did not particularly envy Mollie.

We dressed and looked like little girls and on the whole felt like little girls. Once a note was thrown on to my desk by a passing boy which said, 'Dear Pat, I love your sister Sheila very much.' I showed it to Sheila, but she did absolutely nothing about it and neither did the boy, and I was merely left wondering what to make of it: did he really expect me to act as go-between or was he twitting me on my lack of looks?

At the Grammar School I began to suffer from my name, both parts of it. At the Council School I had never thought that Beer was funny, and it is not easy to see why at this stage I was overcome with shame when it was called out or mentioned or, worse still, when a teacher new to me took over some lesson and I had to state it aloud myself. Beer is a common name in Devon, and I cannot in fact remember anyone there ever laughing at it. In any case, there were funnier names in the school: one boy was called Tripe. I really hated being called Pat, and in this case the trouble had begun at the Council School, where I had begged hard to be called Patricia and no one had taken the slightest notice. The abbreviation irritated me out of all proportion to its mild degree of ugliness; I suppose it was the crude familiarity of those who did the lopping without as much as a by-your-leave that caused me such furious annoyance. By the time I arrived at the Grammar School, however, I was almost resigned to the fact that people were going to do it, whatever I wished and said, and my requests in the first form to be called Patricia were swept aside without much resistance on my part. If I had been the sort of child who attracted dashing nicknames, if I had had red hair or an uncontrollable temper and been called Ginger Beer, for example, I would not have minded so much, but I was not the type.

I was neither popular nor unpopular at school. At one stage I was the victim of a little mild bullying from a girl called Beatie Tozer whose mother kept a pub in the Exeter Road. It lay on the Sunday morning route to the Gospel Hall, and before we moved to the Littleham Assembly my own mother had tended to sweep past it, which might have annoyed Beatie and her mother had they been looking out, but I think Beatie's animosity was due simply to her resentment of my priggishness and intellectual pretensions and perhaps to her perception of the fact that some of Mother's feelings about people who kept pubs had rubbed off on to me. Whatever the cause, she set about her campaign quite skilfully. Once we were having a long piece of work given back which had been marked out of twenty. Before the books were returned Miss Skinner discussed the work and singled me out for praise. Then as the books were being handed round, Miss Skinner asked me to give out some other piece of apparatus, which I did, arriving back at my desk just as the marks were being called in and just as she got to my name, second or third on the list. 'You've got nineteen,' said Beatie helpfully, as I moved to pick up my book. By this time Miss Skinner was waiting and I was opening my mouth to give in this mark when some instinct made me glance at the book first; the mark was fourteen. It would have been a real coup for Beatie if it had come off.

On the whole, though, I was quite well liked, in spite of my pretensions in general and my specific boasting about such matters as our holidays in Scotland and our trips to London. Faith Ratcliffe was the real sufferer in this field; Mr Ratcliffe was a prosperous builder, and if ever there was a school collection for anything he always provided Faith with ten shillings for it, an enormous sum compared with the sixpences and shillings the rest of us had been given to bring, and the school magazine always contained long boring lists of books he had donated to the library. Mother never let us in for anything like that. I was not exactly popular: I was no leader;

I had no charm or magnetism to make me one; I was grotesque in the gym and on the games field; but I could talk readily and hit off a good remark often enough to be accepted by schoolgirls as something of a wit. I was not the sort of person to be elected as Form Captain; I once was, but only because I told everyone that if they elected me I would not try to stop them talking between lessons, which was the main task of the Form Captain. Of course, once I was elected I did try to, but there was so little satisfaction in the office that I never practised politics again.

I liked all the staff except Miss Osborne and felt comfortably certain that all the staff except Miss Osborne liked me. She was the gym mistress (Black Nag we called her after one of her own Country Dances), and my utter ineptitude at her subject was quite enough to antagonise her, but I think there must have been more to it than that, as according to one of the girls, she said I irritated her so much she felt like jumping on me. She certainly acted as though she felt like jumping on me, but it seems odd that she actually said so to a pupil, though she did have close favourites (as gym mistresses tended to do more than most teachers) to whom she often spoke indiscreetly. It came as a surprise to me that I was no good at games and gym. I had been quite adequate in all that had been required of me at the Council School and, outside school, really good at activities like walking and swimming that I could do in my own way and in my own time, but now, faced by apparatus of every kind – things to hit and to hit with, ropes to climb, horses to jump on to, bars to dangle from and turn somersaults over – I became helpless, clumsy, frightened and obstinate. I was thin and beginning to be tall, I apparently had no muscles to leap or support myself with, I hated heights and I loathed hurting myself, not so much because of the pain as because of the damage. The curved sticks and frozen ground of hockey, the wood, leather and hemp of gym kept me sore and dented and resentful for four years. I could see no good coming of it, either, or understand what it was supposed to be training people for or to be. Though I had to admit that the girls who were good at games and gym were among the prettiest and the nicest, there was always the example of Miss Osborne herself whom a lifetime of such pursuits had not saved from being physically graceless and a bad loser.

Another new experience, but of a similar kind, was to find myself hopeless at an academic subject. Again, nothing had happened at the Council School to prepare me for this failure: I had been at the top of the class for Arithmetic as for everything else. Now, however, with disconcerting suddenness, I became quite unable to cope with it, and even less with Algebra and Geometry, which popped up like djinns at this stage. It can hardly have been the fault of the teaching; obviously the methods of those days were not as enlightened as they have since become, but they were no worse than those employed in other subjects, and they were not so inept as to hinder anyone but me. I was unequivocally at the bottom of the class, with the less gifted and the downright stupid soaring right above me, term after term, year after year. No one, not even Mother, urged me to try harder, it was so clear that anyone as competitive as myself would be good at anything if she possibly could. It was certainly not the fault of the teacher, Mr Civil. He got wonderful School Certificate results out of everybody but me. And finally, it was not the fault of my attitude to him, as I loved him dearly, not with the fuddling sort of devotion that robs people of their wits, but with the enthusiasm that tries to please and to excel in anything that interests the beloved. He was magnificent and different. On Armistice Day he would always put half-a-crown into the poppy tin and take only a penny poppy from the tray. The first

time I saw him do this, my value-for-money mentality
received a jolt from which it did not recover for years.
I cannot point to any other specific thing which marked
him out, but I still think of him as somehow free and
ranging, an impression that a visual memory of him
supports: loping across the playing-field four times a day
to and from his house at the far corner of the grounds. He
was fond of me and, when I was eleven, spent a great
deal of time sitting beside me in my desk with his arm
around me, working through my sums and laughing
with real delight as he came to each mindless mistake.
When I left school he wrote me a letter, wishing me luck
and saying he would always remember me with pleasure
for my unwavering cheerfulness and arithmetical inac-
curacies. This I found saddening, not because of the
second point – after all, if one has to have a weakness,
I suppose it might just as well be an endearing one –
but because of the first point. Much as I admired cheer-
fulness in others and would actively have wished to be
cheerful in testing circumstances myself, the idea of
unwavering cheerfulness – the fixed idiot grin of in-
sensitivity – put me off, especially when I considered
how in this particular case it had masked so much
bewilderment and even despair at failure. It suggested,
horribly, a part I might have to play whether I liked it
or not, the grinning good sport.

At all other subjects I excelled. In saying that there
was complete continuity between the teaching methods
of the Council School and those of the Grammar School,
I mean that this is what it boiled down to; the staff did
try, repeatedly, to get us to look at life, to observe,
experiment and deduce, but we were all very recalcitrant,
finding it easier and safer to learn something out of a book,
as we had always done. I was fond of Botany as I could
draw and colour neatly and got great pleasure out of
doing the circular diagrams of flowers which showed

their construction, and I liked the glamour of the lab, but I could not get used to writing notes in anything but the imperative and neither could anyone else. It seemed natural to all of us to say 'Take a buttercup' and quite artificial to say 'We took a buttercup' (the wording which Miss Morgan insisted on), which made it sound like a compulsive experiment made in a spirit of free enquiry, with no idea of what the outcome was to be. And we found it impossible to obey her other instruction, which was not to look in the textbook to see how many petals the buttercup had before actually taking it, though in this we felt we were being realistic, as the petals were missing, unrecognisable or stuck together so often that we should have had to dissect more buttercups than there was time for to be sure of what a quick, surreptitious glance at the textbook told us in a second, and we presumed Miss Morgan did not wish us to learn the wrong fact.

Mr Earp, who taught Geography, from time to time made similar efforts to get our noses out of the textbooks, but as he did not relate the subject consistently to our own experience and as there was no practical or outdoor work to shake us up, he had no more success than Miss Morgan. I myself did pretty well on a system of reflexes and verbal connections: if he said 'Dewsbury' I said 'shoddy', though I had no idea what shoddy was nor much of a notion where Dewsbury was. This procedure usually got me praise and good marks, but every so often the absurdity of it all seemed to strike him, as, for example, when we were doing Salisbury Plain: knowing I had frequently been to London, and was the only child in the class who had, he asked me what colour the soil of the Plain was. I was completely at a loss and rather affronted to be asked something before we had studied the relevant chapter. So he sat on the table and swung his legs saying, 'Blue? Green? Mauve?' and every impossible colour he could mention with each swing. We all thought this was very funny, and I described the incident at home as an example of his wit. Mother crossly pointed out that I had seen the soil of Salisbury Plain dozens of times and wearily wondered what the point of these educational trips to London could be.

Mr Walker ran the Scientific Society, which was very popular, and he came up against the same problem. The meetings always followed the same pattern: a series of three or four short talks by pupils. I can remember Mr Walker urging us again and again to speak from our experience, to describe, for example, the contents of one of the rock-pools at Orcombe Point or a visit to the Withycombe brickworks, or to speak about some hobby, but nobody ever did as he said. We were all keen to speak; he had no difficulty in filling up the programme. But we got our material exclusively from encyclopaedias and travel books, and came eagerly forward with talks on *The Far East*, *Man through the Ages*, *Astronomy*, and *The Charm of the Cotswolds*. I gave one on *Volcanoes*, illustrating it with a startling cross-section of a volcano out of the *Children's Encyclopaedia*, which curled up in the fierce heat of the lantern and was never the same again.

These were secure and happy years, and I remember the staff mildly and with affection and in a composite way. They were benevolent, and did not on the whole develop and display their personalities at our expense. They were not colourless but among them were no angular eccentrics, not even Mr Hughes, the Headmaster who also taught History, though he came nearest to it with the power to terrify which his office and his commanding presence gave him, and the unmistakable footfall, which one of the senior boys could imitate so well. I was really fond of Miss Fleming, who taught French, and was a very nice woman indeed, and I liked Miss

Morgan, Miss Timms, Miss Skinner and Miss Rafter; there was no reason not to.

Occasionally a member of staff stepped forward from this genial background and did something startling of a personal nature. Miss Morgan had a heart-attack and was away for a term. Miss Skinner got caught cycling down the path by Withycombe Church where it said, at both ends, NO CYCLING, and was taken to court. The *Exmouth Chronicle* reported that 'the young lady said naïvely that she hoped to get by on the quick'; we savoured this bizarre statement with its surprising vocabulary – 'young lady', 'naïvely' – for weeks. Mr Walker and Miss Rafter became engaged. The news burst upon us one morning in class when a girl who had just heard it from her parents came in late and began to whisper it round the form under cover of a lesson. The message was getting along nicely until it reached someone who said, 'They're not!' right out loud. Fortunately the teacher in charge let us have our laugh. There was considerable speculation during the next few months about how many children they would have. I was severely told off at home for mentioning this aspect of the subject at all, but I was able to express myself at school with the parody:

> What is love, 'tis not hereafter,
> For Charlie married Kitty Rafter.
> What's to come is still unsure.

The school gave them a mahogany standard lamp; the staff gave them a Devon pewter tea-service and a cut-glass bowl; they retreated into the background again and lived happily ever after.

The years went by, marked not so much by the seasons as by Sports Day, Prize Day, examinations and the appearance of the school magazine. At Prize Giving I always shone, from the day I came down the steps with my maroon leather copy of *Jane Eyre* with its inscription in Miss Morgan's handwriting; she always did the prize labels. I was an inveterate prizewinner and I liked the every-man-for-himself atmosphere much better than the house loyalties of Sports Day. The school had houses in the same spirit that we had as a school song an adaptation of *Forty Years On*. We were Athenians, Trojans, Spartans and Corinthians. Sheila and I were Athenians; siblings had to be in the same house, the authorities seeming to envisage terrible fratricidal war otherwise. I was glad to be an Athenian as the other houses had unfortunate associations: Spartans courted hardship, 'Corinthians' was a book in the New Testament, Trojans struck a slogging unglamorous note. I never contributed anything to the success of the Athenians, but I enjoyed the day, with aesthetic pleasure, brought on by many sights and sounds: the newly-cut grass, the tight rattle of the bean-bags, the coloured sashes (blue for Athenians, yellow for Trojans, red for Spartans, green for Corinthians), the sound of someone's small brother piping, 'They're highering the rope,' or of a housemistress snapping, 'May the best man win,' the sight of Mr Heath time-keeping and Mr Civil firing the starting-gun, and the gleaming of the massed cups and trophies, so different from the books I was used to holding out my hand for, the cheering and the ostentatious calling out of nicknames as the heroes and heroines went forward.

At home there was little to mark out the passage of these school years, for their pattern was cumulative rather than cyclical. Mother identified herself more and more with our educational progress, to the extent of getting cross if we mentioned that we were not looking forward to some particular lesson when she felt that she herself would have enjoyed it and done well. Father stepped up his boasting about our prowess to the men in the office who took to retorting, 'In a few years' time they'll only be getting married,' to which Father replied darkly and to his own complete satisfaction, 'Knowledge is power.' We became increasingly tied to Mother's apron-strings. At one point she allowed us to spend a weekend at Dunkeswell on the Evanses' farm, the first time we had ever been away from home and relatives. Unfortunately we caught the wrong bus back and got stranded at Ottery St Mary, whence we were rescued by Mother in a state of hysteria. We were never let loose again; next time we went to Dunkeswell she went too and had a wonderful time queening it over Farmer Evans on the subject of education. She asked him if Kathleen would be staying on after School Certificate, and to her delight he said, 'But is there any more for her to learn?'

Mother chose to laugh at this, but from the way in which she herself treated School Certificate anyone might well have supposed that there was no goal beyond it. Sheila and I took the examination at the same time; she was fifteen, and I was fourteen. I had caught her up, because of some administrative reorganisation and a burst of theorising about when School Certificate should ideally be taken. This brought difficulties, not so much where Sheila and I were concerned, though the conflict between a wish to protect and a wish to dissociate made both of us uneasy, but between Mr Heath and me. His daughter Allison was now in the same form as myself, and so he had to put us both first, as a tie, in English. I could plainly see all the embarrassments he would incur in putting either of us absolutely first, but his compromise made me as impertinent as I dared to be and less attentive to him than before.

I remember revising for the examinations better than I remember taking them. In one way these were festive days. From Easter onwards Mother opened up the front room, otherwise used only on Sundays, every evening.

It was a light room, looking out into the lane and the cornfield, and contained our best lino and our best furniture: the rexine three-piece suite and the piano which no one now played except Mother. (Sheila and I had shown no aptitude at all, not even after years of lessons.) Here we worked, night after night, pleased and encouraged by the gala nature of our surroundings and panicking only occasionally: I sometimes had a vision of there being some easier, more physical way of mastering the contents of all the books we brought home, a primitive vision of opening up my head and packing them inside. Mother promised us Jantzen bathing-dresses if we did well. She got a catalogue from Thomas Tucker's, and we pored over it and made our choice long beforehand; mine was to be a bright orange model called Lido.

Although these days were mostly exciting and pleasant, there was an air of melancholy in them. The summer had only just begun, but there was already something autumnal in the atmosphere, an end-of-epoch feeling. There seemed no grave reason for this. A war was coming, but we were isolated in so many ways that for us it was not a conscious fear. No one we knew was ill; we could not have guessed that death was drawing in so close. It was perhaps nothing more serious than the sad undersong of great effort with perhaps a realisation that there was more to Farmer Evans's remark than Mother could laugh off: from now on we might become rather lonely in pursuit of all our aspirations.

The examinations came; day after day we took them, discussed them expansively for an hour, then settled down again to more revision. I did so badly in the Arithmetic paper that I came home in a state of collapse, which moved Mother to words she had never used to me before: 'Never mind dear, you did your best,' but the next paper was one I could do and I was confidently off again, to the end of my eleven subjects.

When the results came out in August I felt like Cardinal Wolsey who graduated at the age of fourteen. I cite Mr Hughes as reported in the following term's issue of *Exmothiensis*; he was speaking at the first Prize Day I did not attend: 'The Headmaster also referred to the Honours Certificate with three distinctions and four merits in School Certificate, together with Exemption from London Matriculation, gained by Patricia Beer and said it was a wonderful result not easily equalled in any school.' When I first heard the news I wished that even for five minutes I could believe that the Saints who fell asleep in Jesus really did know everything, because by this time Mother was dead.

CHAPTER TWELVE

Death

SHE had had a lump in her side for some years. She never told us about this, but she used to discuss it so loudly with Olly when we were all out walking that she must have wanted us to know. Her allusions to the lump got progressively relaxed and optimistic, as it was popularly held that a lump could not be cancer if it had stayed much the same for two years. She had not been to the doctor about it.

One Saturday afternoon in July we were on the beach. At this period in our lives the beach hardly ever meant Straight Point, or even the Tuckers' hut, but Miss Fleming's hut. It was not on the beach itself, but set back on the other side of the promenade; it had a number and not a facetious name.

There had been a storm; rolls of very smelly seaweed had been washed up and lay in long tiers from the Pier to Orcombe Point. In the aftermath of the storm, the estuary and the bay looked restless and uneasy and as though the water had lost weight. The sky was greyer than the sea. But it was warm enough and possible to bathe, and we had just returned to the hut to dress when Mother got up and said she had a bad pain and would go home. This was quite without precedent, but she looked normal and spoke firmly, and the resulting discussion seemed to last only a minute. Miss Fleming suggested ways and means, but Mother walked resolutely off and I doubt whether either of us offered, even unconvincingly, to go with her.

We did not hurry away from the beach, but cycled home, rather apprehensively, at our usual time, to find her in bed. She stayed in bed all through Sunday while we moodily and resentfully tried to look after ourselves. Sheila and I carried things upstairs, I suppose, from time to time, but Father now went more freely in and out of the bedroom than we did. After years of being turned out because one of us felt ill or could not sleep or had had a nightmare, or when Torquay relatives came to stay, he had now resumed his original right to be there. Mother was in pain and kept being sick.

On Monday she was no better, and it was clear that the doctor would have to be called. Nurse Markby was asked to be there to let him in; there was no question of our staying home from school. He came in the afternoon, and, when we got home at half-past four, Mother called us upstairs to tell us cheerfully that it was gastritis or possibly some upset caused by the smell of the seaweed on Saturday. She begged us not to mention this last suggestion to Miss Fleming when she enquired, as it could seem to be blaming her hospitality. She had obviously put on a great show of its being nothing much to the doctor, and we heard later that he had not examined her, but had stood over by the window, chatting his way to a diagnosis. The vitality of the effort she had made left her long before nightfall.

Every year we had a calendar, with tear-off texts, headed APPLES OF GOLD with 'in baskets of silver' underneath in smaller print. On Tuesday this calendar started talking about illness: 'They that are whole have no need of the physician, but they that are sick.' Mark 2:17. To someone as trained to reliance on the Lord's Word as I was, this prescience was not startling, but it was nevertheless impressive.

The news had spread by now, and visitors began to arrive, that is, neighbours; we saw nothing of the Brethren

all this week. Mrs Tucker was kind; she came herself
and sent Eileen. Nurse Markby was often in and out;
her face was too grim to look merely anxious, but she
looked grimmer every day. Sheila and I did not often go
into the bedroom. Mother was so sore she did not want
us near her. She seemed afraid we might fall on top of her.

On Wednesday evening, when she was no better,
Father went up to Littleham Cross to telephone to Torquay. He got Olly, by the usual method of asking someone from the Coaches to run across the road to fetch her,
and begged her to come. She had been expecting people
on the Thursday, but soon decided she could put them off.
There was a painful scene when Father came home and
reported the conversation, as he dwelt more on her first
and momentary reluctance to come than on her promise
to do so, which made Mother cry and say she would
have done it gladly for Olly. I was furious at his tactlessness, but he was master now. That night the noises from
the bedroom were joined by the bizarre and frightening
hiss of a soda-water syphon. It was a novelty in our
house, but Mother craved for something fizzy.

On Thursday Olly arrived with David, which cheered
Mother up; Olly described her rapturous greeting of him.
That evening there did seem to be an improvement.
The text that morning had been, 'I have heard thy prayer,
I have seen thy tears: behold I will heal thee.' 2 Kings
20:5. I had hardly dared to believe it all day, not that I
mistrusted God's power to heal or his benevolent intentions, but it seemed so very pointed and specific. But now
I could, and I got away on my own and, in a storm of
emotion, begged God to forgive me for my doubts and
thanked him again and again for his goodness and
omniscience.

On Friday morning she did not seem so well. The
calendar had disconcertingly withdrawn from the subject
of sickness altogether. We went off to school as usual.

School Certificate was now over, and we were doing nothing more taxing than general knowledge quizzes and reading or drawing in the grounds. We came home to dinner, and as we turned into Bradham Lane on our bikes we saw the back of an ambulance going up the lane and over the top of the hill. We knew who was in it, or rather the ambulance seemed to *be* Mother, disappearing round the corner. She never came back.

The doctor had called again that morning, with a colleague, and for the first time since the onset of her illness he had examined her. They saw, I imagine at a glance, that she had a rupture and said she must be taken to hospital at once. Olly told us how Nurse Markby, overcome, had kept repeating, 'I knew you were ruptured, dear.' It did not occur to any of us that with this knowledge she should have said something. Her position was the same as ours: nurses did not tell doctors what to think and neither did patients, at least not poor patients in Devon in the thirties.

They operated that afternoon. No one at the Exmouth Cottage Hospital was qualified to do it, apparently, for a specialist came down from Exeter, which made us feel we were getting the best. Reports that night were what were usually issued after operations: 'As comfortable as can be expected.' We imagined that this would be quite comfortable, with our faith in Mother's powers of rallying.

On Saturday afternoon we went to visit her. Father picked some flowers from the back garden, rather mean-looking ones, I thought, and lacking in a sense of occasion. He wrapped them up perfunctorily in a limp piece of brown paper. We got out our bikes and half-pushed, half-rode them up to Littleham Cross. The Cottage Hospital was just off the Salterton Road, quite a way down, within quarter of a mile of the sea. It was a steep descent and as we got up speed the paper kept blowing back from the flowers. Father righted it irritably every so often and some petals came off.

I suppose I had expected to find Mother in command of things, weak, of course, but strong underneath it, ill but fighting bravely and successfully. When we reached her bed, half-way down the ward, I saw that she was powerless through and through, with a finality of illness and failure that appalled me. She was too ill to pretend or to put on a show of any kind, but could still feel despair at the poorness of her performance, as she considered it. In a voice that was not her own at all, or at least we had never heard it, she kept telling us of a scene that she must have rehearsed in her mind before the operation: she had planned that she would be very cheerful when we came to see her so that we would go away completely reassured. Not one of us was of the calibre to console her or to help her in any way at all. We just hung about in feeble misery, almost seeming to agree with her self-reproach, till the end of the visiting hour.

Outside again, we were overwhelmed. Father said he wished he had a hundred pounds so that he could have taken her to the Pencarwick, and I think we all felt that money would have helped. The hospital was surrounded by the large double-fronted Victorian villas that had always seemed so much beyond our sphere. Father returned home then, and Sheila and I went down to Miss Fleming's hut where it had all started exactly a week before. Miss Fleming was very kind when she saw our state and explained that people always looked terrible after operations and thought it was a pity we had gone to the hospital that day.

That evening Father went to see the doctor. It was already the sacred weekend when one did not disturb doctors, but anxiety had made us all bold. He came back greatly relieved. The doctor had drawn a number of diagrams to show exactly what the operation had effected and had demonstrated that the condition of the patient was likely to be rather alarming for a little while, making it seem almost like a good sign. It all sounded most convincing, and we went to bed in good heart.

In the middle of the night I was woken not so much by the knock on the front door as by the confusion it caused, candlelight, shadows, people in night-clothes and the dog getting in the way. Sheila and I gathered from the conversation in the hall that the doctor had called for Father to take him to the hospital as Mother was much worse, and Father soon came into our room to tell us this. 'We must trust in the Lord,' he said, and hurried out. He really meant it, and to Sheila and me for that moment he seemed a sublime figure.

Jack, who had arrived that afternoon from Torquay, went with him, and we got into bed with Olly, now installed in Mother's very place in the front bedroom. Hours passed. The dog walked about all the time in the downstairs room. 'Hark at Bill,' Sheila whispered to me when the terrible padding had become almost laughable. We knew, of course, that dogs are restless in a house when someone is dying.

At last footsteps sprang up at the top of the hill, suddenly as they always did, and came down the lane. They were hurrying, almost running, and sounded thunderous in the quiet dark. It was Jack, we could tell. He came up the front steps, up the stairs, and into the bedroom. 'There's no hope,' he said loudly. I burst into noisy crying. Sheila was silent. Olly patted me automatically. She was silent too; I think she realised what it was all going to involve.

That morning Sheila and I saw Mother for the last time. She had been moved to the corner bed and the screens were round it. Her knees were drawn right up, and she had a big bandage round her right upper arm which we could not fit in with the nature of her illness. In a way she seemed more in command that she had been the day before. She knew she was dying. Father had told her in the night, explaining in his own way, whatever that was – I cannot even guess at it – that the operation had been too long delayed, that peritonitis had set in and that nothing could be done. She had replied, 'So I haven't got a sporting chance?' It had not been a question but a last cry of protest. She had accepted the fact by now.

Sheila and I stood at the end of the bed, stiffly side by side, crying. A very young nurse looked in and said, 'Now you mustn't get upset, Mrs Beer.' (The fact that they knew and used her name, which I would not have expected, seemed sinister rather than reassuring.) Heaven knows how many idiotic remarks they had made to her in the course of the night. She felt the full absurdity of this one; she looked quite desperate. But she did not blame the nurse. She only said, 'I do wish they were a bit older.' On the surface she meant the hospital staff, but it could have applied to us. If we had been older, we could have made her see a doctor years before, or at least insisted on proper treatment and a second opinion in the week of her illness, or, if things had still come to this pass, have been easier to leave.

I cannot remember word for word anything else she said. I know she mentioned Heaven and our hopes of meeting there with an almost matter-of-fact confidence to which we sobbed a conventional agreement. Her mind was clear; it was only later in the day, after we had gone, that it became clouded, and she told Father that she would meet us in front of the hospital, as though we were going for a walk or down to the beach.

When we went, Father stayed. He was with her till she died. After a lifetime of relatives and children, husband and wife were alone together at last, though what that now meant I do not know. From a few words Father let slip years after I think it meant a great deal. But perhaps it was nothing new, merely something we children had never understood.

All that day Sheila and I sat in the front room, where we had worked so hard for School Certificate, looking out into the lane. The usual Sunday tide of Morning Meeting, Sunday School and Gospel Meeting had receded and left us stranded for the first time. It was a fine afternoon and a beautiful peaceful evening with the church bells sounding very clear. People we knew went by on Sunday walks, Mrs Martin, Mrs Ratcliffe. They knew nothing of what had happened since Friday, merely assuming that Mother was recovering from gastritis. Mrs Martin saw us and waved, with a gesture and mouthing which seemed to mean she would call next day.

It was beginning to get dark when Father came quietly down the lane. We stood up and turned to face him as he came into the front room. 'Your Mum's gone,' he said.

I remember very little of the next few weeks. Nothing happened, and there was a great deal of talk. The strongest person in our community had died, and we were incapable of proper discussion. Decisions seemed to be taken, but they were not real decisions stemming from the talk. We drifted, talking all the time.

Sheila and I in fact said little. Our opinion was not asked about anything, though most of it concerned us closely. We were not left out through unkindness; on the contrary, people were trying to spare us. We were still babies, apparently, coddled children, for whom others must decide what was best. Mother's death, instead of quickly making us older, made us, in our own eyes as well as everybody else's, even younger. It was decided that we were not to go to the funeral; it would be too upsetting for us.

We should have gone to the funeral. We should have stayed with Mother while she was dying. When we last saw her she was thinking and talking and even planning, if one can use that word for the anticipation of a reunion in Heaven, and no imagination could supply us with the final stages of her approach to death. We should have seen her in her coffin, if only because she had thought it right for us to see a great many people dead in theirs. She should not have been deprived in all these ways, and neither should we. She was robbed of her due, and we were forced into a helplessness and inexperience that made it impossible for real grief to begin. I have said it was all done through kindness, and I am sure that as far as conscious design went this was so, but I wonder if, underneath, there was not a wish to shut us out from the rites, a reaction against our total monopolisation of Mother while she was alive, or perhaps a way of taming us for the future.

There was no discussion about where Mother was to be buried. Unquestionably it had to be Torquay. Father kept insisting that she should be wearing her wedding ring, though nobody contradicted this. I remember absolutely nothing about the day of the funeral, neither the setting out and return of my father, aunt and uncle, nor any description of the event at all. It must have been soon afterwards that they started talking about the tombstone. Mother herself had always admired granite and actually asked that she might have it. Everyone knew this, but gradually she was given white marble, to match her father's and her mother's, and indeed the three graves were later combined into a plot with a spare space, which has not been needed to this day.

There was quite a wrangle about what was to be put on the stone. 'Harriet' or 'Queen' was the first argument. My father wanted her real name, he said. He also wanted her surname, his name after all, to appear on the top line. He moved his right hand as he spoke, seeming to trace it out. No one appeared to be arguing him down, but as the inscription stands she seems more the daughter of John William and Emily Jeffery than the wife of A. W. Beer of Exmouth. There had to be a text, so that passers-by might be struck and perhaps even be saved. My grandfather, because of the suddenness of his death, had 'Be ye therefore ready also.' My grandmother's was the less pointed 'Whose faith follow', though in fact her death had been just as unexpected as his. For my mother they chose, after a long evening with the Concordance, 'Looking unto Jesus.'

In these weeks relationships changed. Up to this time Sheila and I, under a superficial appearance of amity, had been deeply divided by the normal rivalries of childhood and united only occasionally by a conspiracy or a joke. We now formed, almost from one day to the next, an equally deep alliance, which was to last when the emergency was over, if it ever was. The brief authority that Father had assumed during the days of Mother's illness now left him. This change, too, was permanent: never again, as far as I saw, did he exercise any authority at all or take on any responsibility. In the next few years it worried him profoundly if we asked his advice about anything and we learnt not to. He welcomed our brash and ill-founded assertions of confidence, the result of this rejection; they made him feel he could rely on us, which, in fact, from the time of Mother's funeral he tried to do: for company, for emotional satisfaction and for moral support.

Our religious beliefs did not fail us. There was no reason why they should; our training in reliance on the Lord's Will had prepared us for just such a catastrophe as this. They seemed rather marginal, though. Talks about tombstones and black clothes were more to the point and, in all these, Mother's known will was set aside and her imagined wishes clung to like the Gospel.

For example, she had always declared that she hoped no one would go into mourning for her when she died; it had been one of her themes. Now Sheila and I were fitted out with white frocks and black accessories: hard shiny straw hats, black patent belts and shoes; a treacherous compromise.

Over everything now lowered the most grievous discussion of all: about how and where we were going to live. The plan which from the first seemed most acceptable because most firmly assumed was that the three of us should go to live with Olly and Jack in Torquay, jointly buying a new house, as theirs would be too small. Although Mother had never suggested this, either when she was speaking theoretically, as about the mourning, or when she knew she was dying, the plan was taken as having her seal and signature.

When the news of this possibility got around the town, several people who normally minded their own business were goaded, most understandably, into giving advice. Mrs Jones, of the Exmouth Assembly, wrote Sheila a sensible letter saying that in her opinion Sheila should leave school and make a home for her father. Another Sister asked why Father did not get a housekeeper. It obviously seemed outrageous to everyone outside the family that a woman should be expected to disrupt her own home life, for the third time in ten years too, for two girls who only had a few more years of school and a man who would marry again, neither could anyone agree with the family that a girl of fifteen and a girl of fourteen were completely incapable of shifting for themselves.

One result of the rumours was a suggestion which would have solved the problem, a suggestion which, ironically, I am convinced that Mother herself would have liked. Miss Fleming offered to have us as boarders so that we need not change schools and the Bradham Lane house could be kept on. Our holidays could be spent in Torquay as they always had been. This was such a rational proposal that it was entertained for nearly a week. How it was finally turned down I do not know. Father seemed now to be completely without will or wish. He ricocheted from one adviser to another, repeating everything when he came home with no comment or opinion of his own at all.

So we left Exmouth for ever. The journey to Torquay was as desolate as my mother's must have been when she first came to Exmouth, and it was by the same route too. Instead of going up round Exeter because of the privilege tickets, we took the Starcross ferry, as Olly and Jack had no such concession. The circumstances of a family other than our own were beginning to dominate. A sharp wind, which blew our black hats off, was coming across the estuary as we walked over the damp boards of the landing-stage towards a side of the river that I have never liked.

THE DEVON LIBRARY

Following the warm welcome which has greeted *The Cornish Library* we have felt emboldened to cross the Tamar and explore the literary heritage of its neighbour, Devon. Both counties have outstanding and varied scenic beauty. Both have a powerful maritime tradition and each has a strongly marked local character. There the similarities might seem to cease. But Devon has a literature every bit as robust and distinguished as the Cornish. *The Devon Library* will seek to do justice to this and to present the best of Devonian fiction and non-fiction in attractive paperback editions.

Titles in print or shortly to be published:

A Devon Anthology	*Jack Simmons*
Widecombe Fair	*Eden Phillpotts*
Devon	*S. Baring-Gould*
Mrs. Beer's House	*Patricia Beer*
The Initials in the Heart	*Laurence Whistler*
Diary of a Provincial Lady	*E. M. Delafield*
Father and Son	*Edmund Gosse*
The Thief of Virtue	*Eden Phillpotts*
Dewer Rides	*L. A. G. Strong*
Crossing's Dartmoor Worker	*W. A. J. Crossing*
Lorna Doone	*R. D. Blackmore*
The Old Stag	*Henry Williamson*
Westward Ho!	*Charles Kingsley*
On the Moor of a Night	*Jan Stewer*
Devon Short Stories	Ed. *Wendy Monk*
The Hound of the Baskervilles	*Arthur Conan Doyle*

All the books in *The Devon Library* are numbered to encourage collectors. If you would like more information, or you would care to suggest other books that you think should appear in the series, please write to me at the following address: Anthony Mott, The Devon Library, 50 Stile Hall Gardens, London W4 3BU.

THE DEVON LIBRARY
NUMBER ONE

A Devon Anthology

Devon has always been set apart from up-country England. With Cornwall it was 'anciently one province', and yet it is as different from that county as from the rest of England. Devon has excited strikingly varied feelings, vividly expressed by many writers.

Charles Kingsley and Gerard Manley Hopkins praised its beauties. Coleridge recalled with nostalgia the bells of Ottery St Mary, where he was born. But Herrick loathed 'dull Devonshire' (though he left some touching epitaphs on Devonians) and Keats thought it a 'slipshod' county of cowards – though he liked the idea of romping with Rantipole Betty of Dawlish. Francis Kilvert draws an appetising picture of the girls wading on the beach at Seaton and Fanny Burney a vigorous one of the tough fisherwomen of Teignmouth. Devon, too, was the cradle of the Forsytes, as it was of their creator.

Professor Simmons has ranged widely and deeply through the literature of his county, and his composite picture is a true likeness. It is also the perfect sampler for other titles in *The Devon Library*. Here, illuminating the unique character of their county, are the people of Devon: their speech, proverbs and customs, their literature and their history – from Roman times to the Plymouth air-raids, from Drake and Raleigh to the Lynmouth floods.

THE DEVON LIBRARY
NUMBER TWO

Widecombe Fair

Eden Phillpotts knew Devon, and the Devon character, as well as anyone who came to write about the county. Above all he knew, and loved, Dartmoor. The *Dartmoor Cycle* of novels has come to be remembered and admired above all his other work.

Of the Dartmoor novels none was more popular in its day than *Widecombe Fair*. From its pages came a wildly successful play, *The Farmer's Wife*, and two films. There was something about the author's joyous celebration of the Devon character which caught and held the public imagination.

The story of the farmer in search of a wife is only one of several comedies and tragedies of village life here skilfully woven into a satisfying whole. And throughout the book individual personalities emerge, some good some bad, some delightful others absurd, each shot through with the authentic breath of Devon.

L.A.G. Strong, himself a novelist of Devon, wrote of *Widecombe Fair* 'The whole book is mellow and warm as the sunlight of early October in the coombes and hollows of the moor. This is how the people of Devon spoke, round about the start of the twentieth century, accent for accent, rhythm for rhythm, caught and set down with the skill and faith of an artist in words who knew and loved them.'

THE DEVON LIBRARY
NUMBER THREE

Devon

First published in 1899 the Reverend Sabine Baring-Gould's *Devon* was one of a two-volume set, *A Book of the West,* the second of which dealt with Cornwall. Baring-Gould was a popular and prolific writer of novels, biographies, and what might be called discursive guide books, of which this was an outstanding example.

Vigorously written, like all his works, it contains a quite extraordinary amount of information on the landscape, the people, the history, the customs and folklore, the crafts and industries of Devon; before the internal combustion engine came to change utterly the life and character of the countryside.

There is nothing which escapes Baring-Gould's rampaging curiosity: no ancient song or verse unrecorded, no village superstition ignored, no curious legend unexcavated. Consequently much of what is inherited local knowledge today owes its continued provenence to him. He was not always loyal to the facts – he loved a good story far too much to reject it because the evidence might weigh against the truth of it – but he was a heaven-sent serendipitist.

Devon is not only informative and unfailingly entertaining. It is a remarkable tribute to the literary squarson of Lew Trenchard, who loved the county and pricelessly recorded its character and history, before much of it disappeared for ever.

THE CORNISH LIBRARY

'Well-chosen works from a literary heritage which is as rich as clotted cream.'
The Times

The aim of *The Cornish Library* is to present, in attractive paperback editions, some of the best and most lasting books on Cornwall and the Cornish, both fiction and non-fiction.

Titles in print, or shortly to be published:

Up From the Lizard	*J. C. Trewin*
A Cornish Childhood	*A. L. Rowse*
Freedom of the Parish	*Geoffrey Grigson*
School House in the Wind	*Anne Treneer*
Rambles Beyond Railways	*Wilkie Collins*
A Pair of Blue Eyes	*Thomas Hardy*
The Owls' House	*Crosbie Garstin*
Twenty Years at St. Hilary	*Bernard Walke*
Troy Town	*Arthur Quiller-Couch*
The Ship of Stars	*Arthur Quiller-Couch*
Hands to Dance and Skylark	*Charles Causley*
High Noon	*Crosbie Garstin*
A Cornishman at Oxford	*A. L. Rowse*
China Court	*Rumer Godden*
Wilding Graft	*Jack Clemo*
The West Wind	*Crosbie Garstin*
Love in the Sun	*Leo Walmsley*
Lugworm: Island Hopping	*Ken Duxbury*
The Splendid Spur	*Arthur Quiller-Couch*
Hawker of Morwenstow	*Piers Brendon*
The Cathedral	*Hugh Walpole*
The Stone Peninsula	*James Turner*
Cornish Years	*Anne Treneer*
The Devil and the Floral Dance	*D. M. Thomas*
Deep Down	*R. M. Ballantyne*
Corporal Sam and Other Stories	*Arthur Quiller-Couch*
The Cornish Miner	*A. K. Hamilton-Jenkin*
Happy Button	*Anne Treneer*
A Short History of Cornwall	*E. V. Thompson*

All the books in *The Cornish Library* are numbered to encourage collectors. If you would like more information, or you would care to suggest other books that you think should appear in the series, please write to me at the following address: Anthony Mott, The Cornish Library, 50 Stile Hall Gardens, London W4 3BU.